Carol J. Adams

NEITHER MAN NOR BEAST

Feminism and the Defense of Animals

■ ■ ■

CONTINUUM · NEW YORK

1995
The Continuum Publishing Company
370 Lexington Avenue, New York, NY 10017

Printed in the United States of America

Library of Congress Cataloging-in-Publication Data

Adams, Carol J.
    Neither man nor beast : feminism and the defense of animals /
Carol J. Adams.
        p.   cm.
    Includes bibliographical references and index.
    ISBN 0-8264-0670-X
    ISBN 0-8264-0803-6 (pbk.)
    1. Animal welfare.   2. Animal rights.   3. Feminist theory.
    4. Vegetarianism—Social aspects.   5. Women's rights.   I. Title.
    HV4708.A248   1994
    179'.3—dc20   94-21360
                                                                      CIP

Acknowledgments will be found on page 258, which constitutes
an extension of the copyright page.

for my parents
Muriel Kathryn Stang Adams
and Lee Towne Adams
gifted teachers
of many topics, one lesson

And then, occasionally, when [Blue, the horse] came up for apples, or I took apples to him, he looked at me. It was a look so piercing, so full of grief, a look so *human,* I almost laughed (I felt too sad to cry) to think there are people who do not know that animals suffer. People like me who have forgotten, and daily forget, all that animals try to tell us. "Everything you do to us will happen to you; we are your teachers, as you are ours. We are one lesson" is essentially it, I think. There are those who never once have even considered animals' rights: those who have been taught that animals actually want to be used and abused by us, as small children "love" to be frightened, or women "love" to be mutilated and raped. . . . They are the great-grandchildren of those who honestly thought, because someone taught them this: "Women can't think," and "niggers can't faint." But most disturbing of all, in Blue's large brown eyes was a new look, more painful than the look of despair: the look of disgust with human beings, with life; the look of hatred. And it was odd what the look of hatred did. It gave him, for the first time, the look of a beast. And what that meant was that he had put up a barrier within to protect himself from further violence; all the apples in the world wouldn't change that fact.

And so Blue remained, a beautiful part of our landscape, very peaceful to look at from the window, white against the grass. Once a friend came to visit and said, looking out on the soothing view: "And it *would* have to be a *white* horse; the very image of freedom." And I thought, yes, the animals are forced to become for us merely "images" of what they once so beautifully expressed. And we are used to drinking milk from containers showing "contented" cows, whose real lives we want to hear nothing about, eating eggs and drumsticks from "happy" hens, and munching hamburgers advertised by bulls of integrity who seem to command their fate.

As we talked of freedom and justice one day for all, we sat down to steaks. I am eating misery, I thought, as I took the first bite. And spit it out.

—Alice Walker, "Am I Blue?" 1986

Contents

8 ▪ *Contents*

Illustrations

Women come to represent the extreme of man's fears for himself and his freedom. Since humanity is defined against animality, women threatened this self-conception to the extent that they were counted as members of the human species. Woman's apparent inability to escape her physiological "animal" nature establishes her as an omnipresent challenge to a conception of the human being as transcending animality. In this regard, Sophocles' quip, "a modest silence is a woman's crown," cited approvingly by Aristotle, and Thucydides' remark in the Periclean funeral oration, that woman's greatest glory is to be "least talked of among men," each takes on an interesting hue. For speechlessness on the one hand and invisibility or absence in human discourse on the other are the traits not of persons but of animals. . . .

It was precisely the sharpness of the Athenian conception of manhood that bore with it a necessary degradation and oppression of women, a denial of the status of "human" to women. To the extent that women were viewed as part of the human species, they would recall to men the species' animal or "natural" aspect. Alternatively, women could be denied fully human status and remain the somewhat less threatening repository of the "lower elements" of existence. Seen in this context, Aristotle's infamous characterization of women as "deformed males" bears significance as more than incidental misogyny. Aristotle does not merely posit the general inferiority of women but describes them as "incomplete beings," their thinking as "inconclusive," and the female state in general as a condition of "deformity and weakness." Women are also depicted as "matter" in need of the "form" only men can supply. Women are therefore not merely lesser humans than men but less-than-human, malformed, and ill-equipped for the human project, creatures in a gray area between beast and man.

—Wendy Brown, *Manhood and Politics*

Preface

Consider the image on the cover: A cow shaped as a slim, human female body.[1] Unlike beasts—conventionally defined as quadrupeds—this animal has successfully become bipedal. Thus, this image is neither man nor beast. Nor, interestingly, is she of any specific race. Combining human femaleness with cow femaleness while underemphasizing the udders or breasts glorifies the anorexic, human female body. It also imposes a sexualized element onto our picturing of cows. This image accompanied an article in the *New York Times* on a low-fat, low-cholesterol ground "beef." *Beef*, of course, can come from cows or steers.[2]

The emphasis on differences between humans and animals not only reinforces fierce boundaries about what constitutes humanness, but particularly what constitutes manhood. That which traditionally defined humans from animals—qualities such as reason and rationality—has been used as well to differentiate men from women. It is not surprising, therefore, to find images that combine those already equated in patriarchal culture.

We have inherited a Western philosophic tradition that posits women as closer to animals and as maintaining the animal functions for the species (e.g., reproductive and child-rearing functions). Historically, as the epigraph to this preface illustrates, women were positioned in between man and the other animals, so that women, and especially women of color, were traditionally viewed in Western culture as neither man nor beast. The initial feminist response to this positioning between man and beast—found for instance in Mary Wollstonecraft and continuing today in liberal feminism—is to say "we are not animals, we are humans." But this position assimilates the malestream culture's contempt for animals within feminist theory.[3] The human/animal boundary is left secure, while women are moved from one side of it to the other. An alternative feminist position asserts that we are not man, since man is not and never can be generic, and we are not beasts, since beast exists largely as metaphor for human behavior, as self-judgment. Rather than resituating any of the players from one side to the other, this position calls the human/animal dualism into question.

The concept of beast exists to be self-referential, as a comment on humankind. Animals actually are neither man nor beast—neither mere caricatures of their own lives, nor stupid—but, like human beings, animals with social needs and interests. Feminists, too, are neither man nor beast. Feminists who defend animals challenge human beings to stop considering animals as beasts. Feminists and profeminist men also challenge persons born with penises to stop thinking of themselves as "man,"[4] not only because being a man is tied into identities about what "real men" do and don't do (real men don't eat quiche, real men hunt— this we know from the homophobic insults that hunters hurl at animal defenders), but because "man" (read: white man) can exist as a concept and a sexual identity only through negation ("not woman, not beast, not colored," i.e., "not the other").

Defenders of animals often elicit charges that we can either be for animals (beasts) or humanity (which remains man-identified). But this charge results from dualistic thinking that presupposes that our interests and needs are in opposition. This dualistic thinking is part of the problem: at some point humans no longer saw ourselves as animals. It results from a patriarchal framing of the discussion. The progressive feminist response is to eliminate such reactionary dualisms.

The goal of feminist defenses of animals is that humanity will shed its Euro-American malestream orientation, will shed its urge to demarcate some "ultimate" differences between us and the other animals, will reject a vertical hierarchy of humans above animals. Jane Tompkins observes that "to see animals differently would require human beings to see themselves differently also."[5] But upon what theoretical ground should feminists who defend animals stake such envisioning of animals and humans? On the one hand, malestream animal rights and liberation theory appears to place itself squarely within an Enlightenment epistemology of autonomous subjects, a liberal paradigm riddled with the contradictions of concepts of freedom that included enslaved humans. On the other hand, just when feminist grand narratives presuming a unitary "subject," a universal "woman," or "one lesson" (or that there is *any*, much less *one*, lesson!) come tumbling down, some of us appear to be urging yet another grand narrative—"animals." Such an anachronism seems to marginalize our theoretical contributions. However, the tumbling away of a unitary subject opens up space for discussing other-than-human subjects.[6] As the destablized human subject opens up the space to acknowledge animal subjects, our notions of humanity could also be shorn of gender, race, and species preoccupations.

Feminist defenses of animals insist that we must acknowledge and accept accountability for what we do to others' bodies. Concerned about the language of animal *rights,* we are searching for alternative ways of framing the issues that the exploitation of animals raise. We reject a cultural construction of some bodies as so completely and solely matter that their bodies become immaterial, unimportant. Animals' bodies do matter. Feminist defenses of animals offer liberation from a conditioned mind frame that devitalizes other beings. We insist that our inactions as well as our actions have consequences. We affirm that we all share the same universe in which we are a community of subjects—no matter how fragmented the notion of subject—not a collection of otherized objects. In this way, we respond with integrity, respecting bodies. We anticipate that from such envisioning all of us will emerge conceptually as neither man nor beast. Through these positions, we honor connections and we refuse complicity with body-denying policies and actions. These responses offer points of connection in solidarity with those who challenge other social oppressions.

I did not know when I decided to become a vegetarian in 1974 that I was beginning the process of becoming a theorist on the situation of animals in contemporary culture. My primary commitment—then and now—has been the feminist movement, a lightning rod that grounds my work and my thought. In addition, antiracist analysis and activism have been, to me, embedded as a part of this feminism.

Since the mid-seventies I have been associated with the movement to stop violence against women, and with litigation and activism against institutionalized white supremacy. On the one hand I trained to be an advocate for rape victims; started a hotline for battered women; became involved at the state and national level addressing problems women face when abused by their human male partners. On the other hand, I joined a local branch of the NAACP, challenged racist housing policies, worked to increase black home ownership, oversaw testing (defined by Derrick Bell as "an effective, but too little utilized, technique to ferret out bias in the sale and rental of housing"[7]), and coordinated a challenge to the license renewal of a racist and sexist radio station, the only community-based challenge from the Reagan era that was successful. Throughout this time of confronting both intimate and institutionalized forms of violence, I noticed the times when forms of violence intersect: Where sexual violence, racist violence, *and* violence against animals were expressed in one act or a sequence of acts that announce the connections between these outwardly disparate forms of violence. Thus I found myself arguing for and attempting to create antiracist feminist theory that includes animals. In this, *Neither Man nor Beast* presumes the radical shift in perspective my first book, *The Sexual Politics of Meat* proposed, in which I attempt to place an antiracist feminist analysis in the service of interpreting the exploitation of animals, especially those who are consumed by people.

I take these as my givens:

- First, oppression is a reality. Privilege is the state of being for those who benefit from oppression. Race- and sex-hate crimes are ways that oppression is maintained and perpetuated.
- Second, just as gender and race are constructs, so too is species. They are categories of social construction that have been postulated as essentially natural.
- Third, environmental exploitation takes place through social domination of the bodies of some people by other people. The legacy of colonialism is that elite Euro-Americans have institutionalized oppressive systems that control non-dominant white people and people of color as well as exploiting the natural resources of the land upon which they live. Owners and decision-makers maintain high profits for the few by passing on the costs to the many in the form of low wages, high prices, bad working conditions, and toxic side effects. Many of us are seeking new structures that do not uphold the exploitation of people or the earth and its other creatures.
- Last, feminism does not solely address relationships between women and men, but is an analytic tool that helps expose the social construction of reality. For instance, feminism identifies how gender becomes a marker of the oppression of animals too, as when rodeos feature a competition that involves putting lace underpants on a calf.

Toward the end of *The Sexual Politics of Meat* I quoted from feminist philosopher Sandra Lee Bartky who observed, "Feminists are no more aware of different things than other people; they are aware of the same things differently. Feminist consciousness, it might be ventured, turns a 'fact' into a 'contradiction.'"[8] For the past five years, a central aspect of my task as a feminist theorist has been to turn the "fact" of animals' status as exploitable into a contradiction. To do this, I have drawn upon feminist theory, philosophy, and theology. This book represents the results of this process. The title *Neither Man nor Beast* captures some of the contradictions that an antiracist feminism seeks to expose.

Issues I raise in the following pages are not meant to be a systematic laying out of a grand theory, but rather are suggestive of the issues that need to be addressed. They emerge out of concrete experience and address survival issues of women and animals, rather than arising from a philosophical a priori. The building of the book reflects the contigencies and necessities out of which feminist theory arises. Specific instances and occasions offered an opportunity to reflect further on certain aspects of a feminist defense of animals. Each of the chapters therefore is a discrete analysis of a specific issue, yet together the chapters build toward a conceptual and philosophical framework for discussing animals, women, and domination. My goal is to equip us to recognize what we humans do to the other animals, especially through the institution of corpse eating, while also helping us understand why it is difficult to take a critical stance.

My starting point is not that of animal-rights theory, which seeks to extend to animals moral considerations based on their interests, sentience, and similarity with humans. Although my writing is *informed* by this argument, I recognize many other issues besides that of animals' subordination as problematic. I am not patching animals onto an undisturbed notion of human rights, but am examining the place of animals in the fabric of feminist ethics—a starting point that already presumes that exploitation entails more than the exploitation of animals. This clarification is necessary to insure that this book is cleary situated in the reader's mind in an a priori problematic of human-nature relations.

My emphasis here is on *ideology*. An ideology that ontologizes animals as usable precedes the issues associated with animal-rights discourse and feminist theory. My attempt is to expose this ideology, not through what some see as the animal-rights strategy of ethical extensionism from humans to some nonhumans, but by exploring the result of a human-animal dualism that is embedded within a racist patriarchy. This dualism has precipitated both animal defense as well as the suspicions of it.

Once one begins to make the theoretical, theological, philosophical, and inherently political claim "neither man nor beast" in response to sexist, racist, and speciesist beliefs, a raft of objections to resituating animals erupts: "What about hunting?" "Don't plants have life too?" "What about the (human) fetus?" "What about carnivorous animals?" "What about feminism's commitment to pluralism?" "What about Genesis 1 where God gives man dominion over the earth?" In the following pages I provide answers to these questions; the framework I offer in which to place discussions about animals arises from my understanding of feminism. I conclude by using this feminist philosophical framework to critique Christian humanocentric theology. This inclusion of theological issues is necessary because of the coercive nature of God-talk in reinforcing the human/animal dualism in this christianized culture.

Feminist theory explores a range of concerns using a range of theoretical approaches. Issues of representations of women, reproductive rights, sexual violence, racist violence and white supremacy, environmental exploitation, the relationship between knowledge, power and value, the imaging of God, are issues that intersect with the defense of animals. Responding to specific questions that presented themselves about these feminist concerns, the chapters in this book grew organically. They are based on social justice issues—in this my methodology and theory reinforce each other. They presume the integrity of those who have been made neither man nor beast in a white supremacist patriarchy—women, people of color, nondominant men, and animals. They protest inequities and injustice. They envision possibilities.

In approaching the same things differently, a profound dissonance occurs. Of course, exposing contradictions by its very nature produces dissonance: that is one of the tasks of feminism in defending animals. Traveling around the country, I have often been asked what I thought of Julia Child's comment about vegetarians, *viz.* that we have a "hang-up" with food. But, incorporating contradictions into my response, I counter, we do not have a hang-up with food, we have a "hang-up" with what some people *call* food. Whose bodies matter? In debates about corpse eating, most people have a tendency to identify with the consumer rather than the consumed.

In the many discussions about animal experimentation that animal defense has prompted, a basic feminist insight has been ignored: feminist philosophy has turned the "fact" of scientific objectivity into a contradiction. Before we can debate the efficacy of "animal models" we must ask: "*Whose* science are we talking about?" Just as we more readily identify with the consumer rather than the consumed in corpse eating, so with science we identify with the *knower,* not the *known.*

Similarly, much Western debate on the environment and treatment of animals includes a discussion of Genesis 1. It appears that even atheists believe they have a God-given right to eat animals. But as a feminist theologian, I step back and say, "Whose God?" Again, I find that the process of identification is usually with the (male) Creator, and not (his) Creation or creatures.

In *The Sexual Politics of Meat* I developed the concept of the absent referent to identify the process by which the animal used for corpse eating disappears both literally and figuratively. Animals in name and body are made absent as animals in order that flesh can exist. If animals are alive they cannot be meat. Thus a dead body replaces the live animal and animals become absent referents. Without animals there would be no corpse eating, yet they are absent from the act of eating flesh because they have been transformed into food. Animals are also made absent through language that renames dead bodies before consumers participate in eating them. The absent referent permits us to forget about the animal as an independent entity. The roast on the plate is disembodied from the pig who she once was.

Turning a fact into a contradiction often involves restoring the absent referent, so that we reclaim the consumed, the known, the creation. That is the project of this book: identifying the terrain occupied by those who as "animals" are neither man nor beast, and the interlocking system of oppression that defines them as such and places them there. As part of the process of restoring the absent referent I will intercede with [*sic*]s when animals are referred to as "its" and presume the personhood of animals. Each animal possesses a unique individuality, sentience, and completeness of self in one's self and not through others, and should exist as such for human beings, not as tools or as food.[9]

When I became a vegetarian, I did not knowingly set out to become a theorist about animals. But this is where my feminist consciousness has taken me. One aspect of animal oppression is that benefiting from their oppression is made easy for us all, while resisting that oppression is more difficult. Vegetarians for instance cannot assume that we will be able to be fed at any restaurant we enter, while corpse eaters have their diet federally subsidized through a variety of programs that keep down the cost of producing dead bodies. Privilege is protected. From the position of privilege, responding to injustice appears to have many impediments.

This book arises from and speaks to this privileged experience, rooted in my instance in the United States. It is this privilege of consuming animals with impunity that deeply concerns me, our habits of consumption that I challenge. At times I use feminist insights about violence against women to identify patterns in the treatment of animals. My presumption here is that systems of violence are interlocking, thus insights from one elucidate experiences of another. For instance, this is the framework for "The Feminist Traffic in Animals" and "The Arrogant Eye and Animal Experimentation." At times I establish a dialogue between seemingly separate movements, such as in "Abortion Rights and Animal Rights" and "Reflections on a Stripping Chimpanzee." Sometimes I apply basic insights about the structural nature of violence to both issues, such as when I examine institutional violence in "Feeding on Grace," which draws on work I have pursued in understanding sexual violence.[10] In "On Beastliness and the Politics of Solidarity," I draw upon my own experiences challenging white supremacy to explore the way the concept of beastliness has been used against people of color in general and African-Americans in specific. My goal is to place the animal defense movement firmly within movements that challenge the social oppression of humans, to establish points of connections that create solidarity. In "Bringing Peace Home," I articulate an intersectional approach to understanding violence against women and violence against animals.

In earlier years of this wave of feminism, feminist theory erred by speaking about the experiences of women when what it was actually addressing was the experience of white, middle-class women. This book seeks to expand even further the accountability of feminist theory. Women live embedded in a social world that includes the other animals (both dead and alive), representations of the other animals, and attitudes toward the other animals. These inevitably influence women's lives and the way that oppression is experienced and resisted. Recognizing how women are positioned as neither man nor beast allows us to embrace aspects of women's lives often left unexamined by anthropocentric approaches.

When one recognizes that systems of domination are interconnected, one sees that as Alice Walker argues "we are one lesson." Thus, for instance, during the Clarence Thomas hearings, when Anita Hill spoke of her experience of sexual harassment, her reference to Thomas's description of pornographic representations of bestiality begged for interpretation. This aspect of her experience received little or no commentary. Pondering the humiliation she reported feeling at hearing about women having sex with animals, I thought of many instances when women's sexual violation and exploitation were linked with that of animals. I also recalled the specific bestializing discourse applied to African-Americans in the dominant culture.[11] Her humiliation of hearing about bestiality must be set within a framework that recognizes the unique situation of African-American women, positioned as they were by white supremacy between white women and animals: pornographic images exploited that positioning as neither man, white woman, nor beast.

The pages that follow represent a feminist quarrel with the "facts"— the givens—of all animals' lives today, including ours. I am not alone in this. I know of at least one feminist bookstore owner who slips Peter Singer's *Animal Liberation* into book purchases feminists make while wearing fur coats, or another feminist who puts literature about vegetarianism into others' book bags when lunches feature dead chicken sandwiches. They offer opportunities for others to acknowledge the contradictions, to recognize the opportunity for solidarity given to those who are "neither man nor beast." When we acknowledge the contradictions—living beings treated as food, as models, as objects—will we respond by further conceptual distancing that disowns our relationship with other animals? Or will we seize the opportunity to reclaim the consumed, the known, the creation?

Acknowledgments

We are one lesson, but there are many teachers. I am greatly indebted to feminist philosophers Nancy Tuana, Melinda Vadas, and Karen J. Warren for recognizing that my work resonated with feminist philosophy, setting me down the path of feminist philosophy, and being loving and caring guides along the way. They asked the questions that began this book, and have provided attentive readings of much of it. Josephine Donovan and Susanne Kappeler have been important colleagues in the work of bringing feminist theory to the subject of animals' lives. I thank them for their constancy, their insights into the issues, and their suggestions in response to my writings. Thanks to Batya Bauman, Marti Kheel, and Tom and Nancy Regan, consistent supporters and advocates for my work. In addition to these supportive critics, parts of the book have been read and critiqued by Duane Cady, Gary Comstock, Paula Cooey, Theresa Corrigan, Marie Fortune, Greta Gaard, Stephanie Hoppe, Mary Hunt, Ynestra King, Jay McDaniel, Charles Pinches, Marjorie Procter-Smith, Beth Robinson, Ron Scapp, Brian Seitz, Andy Smith, and Teal Willoughby. I thank them for their criticisms and wisdom in response to my work.

Thinking and writing about the place of animals in our anthropocentric culture has been exciting and stimulating because of the thoughtful reflections and valuable support of a growing network of individuals, including Frank Ascione, Carol Barash, Neal Barnard, Jane Caputi, Kathleen Carlin, Jane Cullen, Karen Davis, Dana Forbes, Leigh Nachman Hofheimer, Roberta Kalechofsky, Gus Kaufman, Jr., Steve Kellman, Victor Lewis, Carol Wiley Lorente, Jennifer Manlowe, Cathleen McGuire, Tim Morton, Ingrid Newkirk, Bina Robinson, Martin Rowe, Drorah O'Donnell Setel, Ken Shapiro, Andy Smith, John Stoltenberg, Kim Stallwood, Valerie Stanley, Betsy Swart, Jane Tompkins, and David Wasser. Each offered valuable information and enlightening conversations;

I am greatly in their debt. DeLora Wisemoon and Pam Willhoite, valued associates involved both in the movement against violence against women and Feminists for Animal Rights, continue to be precious Texas connections in this oppositional work. My friends Paula Cooey, Pat Davis, Marie Fortune, Mary Hunt, Jayne Loader, and Marjorie Procter-Smith have offered loving support and criticism. Evander Lomke is an editor who responds with equal doses of grace and understanding critiques. I thank him for the friendship that flourishes in the space that such responses create. Thanks, too, to Bruce Cassiday for his work on the manuscript.

Many individuals who read *The Sexual Politics of Meat* have been moved to send me other examples of the intersections of sexism and speciesism. This book includes some of the images that I have received. I am grateful for the many readers who have provided an ever-expanding gallery of the cultural depictions of woman as meat and animal as sex object, and in specific thank Patricia Barrera, Nancy L. Bischof, Emily Culpepper, Hilary L. Martinson, and Ingrid Newkirk.

Over the years many friends and colleagues have talked with me "of freedom and justice one day for all." They—and this vision—are present with me as I write. I pray that I have honored our hopes in these pages. Failures in insight or execution are my own.

Expanding an analysis such as represented in this book is a process, both with a community of friends and colleagues, and for myself in my understanding of oppression. This book represents where I am now in 1994, but its best hopes are realized as others continue and expand the analysis proposed here.

Special thanks to Mary Hunt for suggesting the title of the book. I appreciate the support of Susan kae Grant, and am pleased to be able to include two photographs from her multidimensional installation, *Vestiges*. Gene Mason conscientiously responds to the exigencies of writing with a computer. The interlibrary loan staff and reference departments of the Richardson and Dallas Public Libraries have continued to provide unflagging and invaluable support. Thanks to Patricia Lamb Feuerstein, a member of Feminists for Animal Rights and a fine indexer, for her work on the index for this book.

I experience the grace of my vegetarianism with Bruce, Doug, and Ben. Thanks to them for living flexibly with life under the cloud of deadlines and especially to Bruce, who offers ongoing commitment to the daily struggles of enacting a vision of inclusion, for providing the feeling of place that grounds my work, and for "dinners of vegetables where love is."

And to my parents, thanks to them for welcoming the many animals who were a part of our lives as I grew up (particularly Cyrano, Jimmy,

Nicky, Peanuts, Pepi, Sally, Mary, Brownie, and Demeter—teachers all) and especially for instructing me at a young age that injustice is something one challenges.

I am working on a book, *The Meat Market,* which will present and analyze a collection of images similar to the ones in this book and on its cover, and the ones that appear in *The Sexual Politics of Meat,* and on its cover. If you come across such images, please send them to me, care of The Continuum Publishing Company, 370 Lexington Avenue, New York, New York 10017–6503.

Part 1

Examining
the Arrogant Eye

The Bible says that all of nature (including woman) exists for man. Man is invited to subdue the earth and have dominion over every living thing on it, all of which is said to exist "to you" "for meat." Woman is created to be man's helper. This captures in myth Western Civilization's primary answer to the philosophical question of man's place in nature: everything that is is resource for man's exploitation. With this world view, men see with arrogant eyes which organize everything seen with reference to themselves and their own interests.

—Marilyn Frye, *The Politics of Reality*

1

Eating Animals

When we talk of eating animals, we are referring to eating nonhuman, rather than human, animals. But then, we rarely talk of eating (dead) animals at all. We talk of eating "meat." And once we begin talking about eating "meat" we are in the realm of cultural production that poses as individual decision.[1] Herein lies the problem. For what "meat" eaters see as "a nagging moralistic tone" in vegetarians (as one philosopher puts it)[2] might actually reflect the response that "meat" eaters bring to any attempt to expose the cultural construction of the eating of animals' corpses. As another philosopher retorts: "There can be no doubt that almost all people in Western countries have a vested interest in maintaining the status quo because they are strongly identified with the taste for meat. . . . The identification promotes a stream of self-supporting arguments."[3] Is the vegetarian voice a judgmental one or is the "meat"-eating listener defensive? Will any discussion that names the raw material—the living animal—and exposes the manner of "meat" production and the accompanying production of "meat's" meaning face a problem of tone and voice? We will see.

For this (supposed) nagging tone, this (perhaps) resistant response, the admitted self-interest of all involved in the debate, is not without effect on the writer and reader of this work. Either one consumes cooked animal flesh (do you?) or one does not (I don't). There is no neutral ground from which to survey this activity and the debates about it.

Complicating this contested terrain is a startling but little-acknowledged fact: most abstainers from flesh know a great deal more about "its" production than do most consumers of dead animals. (Since flesh is from once-living animals, I question whether the word *it* is appropriate to use about them once dead.[4]) Ethical vegetarians know (often by heart): the size of a veal crate (twenty-two inches by fifty-four inches), a hen's cage (four hens in a twelve-by-eighteen-inch cage); the ingenious contraptions for controlling birth mothers' reproductive activities ("rape rack" for inseminating, "iron maiden" for delivery); the amount of top-soil erosion caused by cattle (85 percent); or the amount of all raw materials consumed in this country for livestock foods (one-third).[5] Whereas abstainers generally know a great deal more about the production of flesh than the consumers, discursive power resides in those with the least knowledge. When former President Reagan (who did not know French) met François Mitterand (who knew both English and French) what language do you think they spoke?[6] In the dominant culture, bilingual vegetarians must always speak English. Indeed, because of the discursive control exercised by the dominant flesh advocating culture, it is when vegetarians attempt to speak "French" (that is, reporting on slaughterhouses, factory farms, the threat of *E. coli* from eating dead bodies) that they are accused of having a nagging moralistic tone.

Vegetarians and corpse eaters approach the same phenomenon—the consumption of dead animals—and come to opposite opinions: is it "meat" or a corpse? life or death? humane slaughter or murder? delicious or repulsive? nutritious or fat-laden? departure from tradition or return to tradition? Corpse eaters see vegetarianism as a fad; vegetarians see eating animals as a larger fad. Corpse eaters see vegetarians as Puritans, legislating others' enjoyments; vegetarians see animal eaters as resisting awareness, indulging in fantasy about where flesh comes from. Corpse eaters generally accept the cultural construction of the farm as benign, friendly, and family-based. Vegetarians see an alternate view: industry-owned, cruel, and factorylike. Corpse eaters ask, "Why did you stop eating animals?" Vegetarians respond with Plutarch, saying, "You ought rather, in my opinion, to have enquired who first began this practice, than who of late times left it off."[7] While vegetarians regard the word *vegetable* with respect (it's life-giving, the purported root of the name vegetarian), flesh-advocating cultures see it as an appropriate term for brain-dead individuals.

The "moralistic" vegetarian and the "vested interest" corpse eater cannot meet on neutral ground to examine their conflict over what appropriately should be consumed by human animals and the facts that inform this debate. Not only is there no disinterested observer to this tradition—i.e., one is implicated either by choice of flesh or resistance to flesh—but there is no impartial semantic or cultural space in which to hold a discussion. We live in a flesh-advocating culture. One version of reality appears to be the only version, and in this claims its own comprehensiveness. Conflicts in meaning are resolved in favor of the dominant culture. Thus, vegetarians face the problem of making their meanings understood within the dominant flesh-advocating culture. As the feminist detective in Lynn Meyer's *Paperback Thriller* remarks early in the novel, "I could tell you now that I'm a vegetarian, but let's just leave it at that. I won't go into the reasons. If you don't understand them, there's not much I can say; and if you do, there's no need for me to say anything."[8]

The battle for interpretation is evident as the dominant culture attempts to redefine even the notion of vegetarianism. Can one eat a dead fish or a dead chicken and be a vegetarian? Yes, according to the American Society for the Prevention of Cruelty to Animals, who coined the words *pesco-vegetarian* and *pollo-vegetarian*.[9] The dominant culture eviscerates the critique of its diet by absorbing it, implying that dead cows, rather than any animal's corpse, is the problem. In the face of "vegetarians" who eat dead chicken and fish, people who don't eat anything with eyes (except potatoes) must search for other terms. As I argued in *The Sexual Politics of Meat*, what is literally transpiring in the widening of the *meaning* of vegetarianism is the weakening of the *concept* of vegetarianism by including within it some living creatures who were killed to become food.

The Case of the False Mass Term

In the use of the term *meat* we have a clue to the cultural hegemony achieved for the eating of animals. We also witness the production of meaning and the actual production of (what some see as) food. The term *meat* represents what Willard Quine calls a "mass term."[10]

Mass terms refer to things like water or colors; no matter how much you have of it, or what type of container it is in, water is still water. You can add a bucket of water to a pool of water without changing it at all. Objects referred to by mass terms have no individuality, no uniqueness, no specificity, no particularity.

When we turn an animal into "meat," someone who has a very particular, situated life, a unique being, is converted into something that has no distinctiveness, no uniqueness, no individuality. When you add five pounds of hamburger to a plate of hamburger, it is more of the same thing, nothing is changed. But if you have a living cow in front of you, and you kill that cow, and butcher that cow, and grind up her corpse, you have not added a mass term to a mass term and ended up with more of the same.[11]

Because of the reign of *meat* as a mass term, it is not often while eating a corpse that one thinks: "I am now interacting with an animal." We do not see our own personal "meat" eating as contact with animals (in the lifetime of an average animal eater that would be 984 chickens, 37 turkeys, 29 pigs, 12 cattle, 2 lambs, 1 calf, and more than 1,000 fish) because it has been renamed as contact with food. But what is on the plate in front of us is *not* devoid of specificity. It is the dead flesh of what was once a living, feeling being. The crucial point here is that we make some*one* who is a unique being and therefore not the appropriate referent of a mass term into some*thing* that is the appropriate referent of a mass term. We do so by removing any associations that might make it difficult to accept the activity of rendering a unique individual into a consumable thing. Not wanting to be aware of this activity, we accept this disassociation, this distancing device of the mass term *meat*.

Mass terms also function when a specific term is being used ambiguously such as *chicken, lamb, turkey*.[12] In accepting their presentation in Saran Wrap packages as mass entities and calling this "chicken," the individuality of each chicken is lost; thus does the dominant culture acquiesce to gathering eighty thousand living chickens together in one warehouse. Just as the dominant language denies them individuality, the institutions created to hold them while alive deny them the opportunity to make the expressive gestures that characterize and give meaning to their individual lives. Pigs cannot root; chickens cannot peck, calves cannot nurse. These activities do not fit into the profit requirements. "The meat industry is a high-volume, low-profit-margin business, and it is structured to raise, fatten, slaughter, and merchandise its product as quickly and cheaply as possible."[13]

In essence we are to view the living animal as though already dead, already a mass term (this may explain the existence of the redundant term *dead meat:* through warehousing of animals we now have *living meat*). We are encouraged to "Forget the pig [or a cow, a chicken, etc.] is an animal."[14] Instead we are to see them as machines or crops. A recent example of erasure of animals can be found in the United States Department of Agriculture's description of cows, pigs, and chickens as "grain-consuming animal units."[15] As Colman McCarthy points out, this makes people "animal-consuming human units."[16]

Using *meat* as a mass term implies its own comprehensiveness though it only transmits a partial reality. It *appears* to represent the sole meaning; rather, it actually represents one of many competing meanings. Not only does it require all to speak English, it implies that there is no other language, such as French, in which to converse. The conflict in interpretation that besets the vegetarian-corpse eater debate occurs in part because of the false comprehensiveness accorded to the flesh-advocating perspective. The term *meat eater* appears neutral, but it is instead evasive. The terms corpse eater or flesh eater (or the Greek-derived *creophagist*) may feel judgmental, but they are, in fact, accurate. And as we are helpfully reminded by the 1881 quotation from the *Saturday Review* that the *Oxford English Dictionary* uses to illustrate its definition of *creophagous:* "The average kreophagist is by no means convinced that kreophagy is the perfect way in diet."[17]

Although *meat* is accepted as a mass term, it is not one. Production of *meat* can occur only with individuals (seven to nine billion of them a year). Since mass terms require no modifiers (i.e., we do not have to say *extremely wet* water), appropriate and informative modifiers that might challenge *meat's* neutral associations are omitted—such as *recently butchered, individual cow*-meat. Indeed, an animal's name modifies the word meat *only* when that form of animal flesh is not consumed, i.e., *dogmeat* or *horsemeat,* but not *fishmeat* or *lambmeat.*

In accepting *meat* as a mass term, we assume that it is accurate and adequate. As a result the rendering of animals as consumable bodies is a given rather than a problem. But none of us chooses *meat's* meanings, we either adhere to them or reject them.

In rejecting *meat* as a mass term, renaming occurs. One begins to speak French. We reorient our relationship with the dominant culture in part by reevaluating that culture's language. Where corpse eaters see "complete protein," or "a man's meal" or "what would a meal be without it?" vegetarians see dead bodies, plain and simple. Language about "meat eating" normalizes the eating of dead bodies. As Colman McCarthy observes, "Such words as meat, beef, pork, veal or poultry are the Adolph's Tenderizers of language: They make gruesomeness palatable."[18]

If the dominant language breaks the association between dead bodies and flesh—gruesomeness replaced by palatability—does that mean that to rejoin them automatically brings about a vegetarian consciousness? Not necessarily. But what is curious about the dominant discourse is that it goes to such lengths to maintain the disassociations. Steve Kellman points out how "sanitized, cosmetized viands lull us into forgetting their bloody origins."[19] The absence of awareness of the origins, and the energy that is used to maintain disassociations, suggests that a rigid separation between the appetitive and awareness must be maintained for much corpse eating to continue. As the hero of "Get a Life," a recent television comedy show, observed: "There are certain questions that should go unanswered, like where does meat come from?" The appetitive (especially as it desires flesh) is a drive we do not necessarily deal with, or want to deal with, on a cognitive level. The common response when the issue of corpse eating is brought up over a meal confirms this: "Let's not talk about it, it will ruin my dinner."

As a result, the cultural concepts and presentations by which we know "meat" rely on fantasy, rather than reality. Charlie the Tuna begs to be caught and eaten; an animated hot dog desires nothing more than to be an Oscar Meyer wiener. When lamb chops are discontinued from the menu of hotels because Shari Lewis and "Lamb Chop" are visiting, the unreality of these associations become clear. Or when a newspaper's headline announces that reindeer-meat sausages have received USDA approval for interstate shipping by proclaiming "On Dasher, on Dancer, on toast"—the unreality is promoted. After all, Dasher, Dancer and Lamb Chop represent fantasies, not flesh-and-blood animals.

This fantasy is encouraged by flesh promoters. "My chickens live in a house that's just chicken heaven," according to Frank Perdue—all 25,000 of them in each darkened "house." The 1985 "Beef Gives Strength" promotional campaign was pulled when the New York State attorney general's office called it "deceptive."[20] One hundred and fifty years ago, Henry David Thoreau exposed the homeopathic fantasy in the belief that flesh gave strength as he walked alongside a man plowing a field with an ox. Despite the fact that he relied on the strength of a vegetarian animal, the farmer protested that he needed flesh for strength.

The Sexual Politics of Meat

Perpetuating the fantasy minimizes awareness, appealing instead directly to the appetite: "Somehow, nothing satisfies like beef."[21] And the appetite being appealed to is constructed as man's. Masculinity appears to require both satisfaction *and* beef. In a *New York Times* story about the opening of a new men's store, we learn: "In keeping with the masculine spirit of the evening, the hors d'oeuvres were beefy. Roast beef on toast. Chunk chicken in pastry shells. Salmon and saucisson. None of that asparagus and cucumber fluff here."[22] A chain of French restaurants in the Dallas-Fort Worth area added rotisserie (dead) chicken "to satisfy the hunger of male patrons for something meaty."[23]

When an advertisement claims that "meat" is "real food for real people" the implications are obvious. We want to be included; we want to be real people; and so we are absorbed into the dominant viewpoint. To resist the eating of animals causes one to be excluded from the culturally constructed "we," and to announce one's difference. If I do not see "meat" as a real food, than I am not a real person. The subtext here is, "If I am not real, I am not a man." Inevitably, cultural images of "meat" appeal to human male-identified appetitive desires. Thus, Gretchen Polhemus was hired by the Nebraska Beef Board because her presence "adds a unique and attractive element that embodies 'The New Beauty of Beef.'"[24] The association between attractive human female bodies and delectable, attractive flesh appeals to the appetitive desires as they have been constructed in the dominant culture in which we interpret images from a stance of male identification and human-centeredness. Thus, animals who are available for corpse eating are represented in one menu as doing the cancan. (See Figure 1.) In such an image, as with the one on the cover, bi-pedal animals become neither man nor beast, but are rendered as consumable feminine entertainment.

Or consider a kitchen tool called the "Turkey Hooker." (See Figure 2.) Designed to be used to move a cooked turkey corpse from the cooking pan to the serving plate, it hooks into the gaping hole that was once the neck. Accompanying an image that shows the "turkey hooker" in use, is a fantasy image of a turkey in high-heeled shoes, one wing placed seductively, invitingly, behind her head, hints of breasts showing. In large print, we are told: "AN EASY PICK UP FROM PAN TO PLATTER."[25] In late 1993, a Fort Worth restaurant promised its patrons a "Hillary dinner": two big thighs, two small breasts, and a left wing. Charging that a Harvard private club, Pi Eta, promoted violence against women in its literature, two hundred students picketed it in 1984 (the same year that Harvard University cut its ties with men's clubs). Prompting the protest was a letter that had been sent to club members that referred to women as "pigs" and "promised those club members who attended the club's parties 'a bevy of slobbering bovines fresh for the slaughter.'"[26]

An article about "How to Kill a Chicken" describes the look of dead chickens after their blood stops flowing, and they are scalded so that someone can remove their feathers:

> skinny, absurdly skinny, a characteristic withheld from the patrons of supermarkets, where the chickens are sold sans feet, their necks jammed inside the body cavity and their scrawny carcasses squeezed into spurious plumpness by tight fitting paper tubs tightened even further by tough plastic wrappers. Miller's back room employs no such cosmetics, and for the [dead] chicken lover the result is an appalling and funny overdose of truth, sort of like a centerfold feature showing the Playmate of the Month undergoing a gynecological exam.[27]

"Vanitas: Flesh Dress for an Albino Anorectic" by Jana Sterbak was displayed on a mannequin in a Montreal gallery in the early 1990s. It would remain undisturbed until the fifty pounds of salted flank steak decomposed, then another $260 worth of fresh flesh would be added.[28]

In the construction of these images, the consumer is presumed to be a human male who consumes both images of female beauty and large hunks of dead animals. Many ironies are contained within this camouflage of reality by fantasy: the fat-laden flesh portrayed by an anorectic female body (as on the cover); the butchered, fragmented, bleeding flesh of dead animals presented as beautiful; male animal flesh (such as beef) paraded as female flesh; the equation of prostitution and corpse eating;

Figure 1: The Cancan

Figure 2: The Turkey Hooker

the pornographic imaging of animals and women. We should not be surprised that Meat is the name of a sex club in Manhattan.

When "meat" is claimed as "real food for real people" the message is that vegetarians are unreal people, "they" but not "we," "sissies" or "fruits" but not "he-men" or Iron Johns.

The Trojan Horse of the Nutrition Community

The coercive nature of a "meat"-advocating culture is further evidenced by the traditional nutritional approach to corpse eating. The framing of the question of eating dead animals as a question of nutrition regularizes corpse eating. Although it is one of many discourses available, the concept of the Four Basic Food Groups—"the Trojan Horse of the nutrition community"[29]—has been the nutritional discourse assigned to us for debating the eating of animals.

Until 1956, there was no idea of the "Basic Four Food Groups" (milk, "meat," vegetable-fruit, and bread-cereal). Before that, flesh and dairy industries spent millions of dollars in advertisements that advised us to "eat more meat" and "drink more milk." The "Basic Seven" had been introduced during World War II; this had supplanted the "Twelve Food Groups" used as a guideline during the 1930s. According to the American Meat Institute, the years from 1938 to 1956 saw a declining rate of corpse consumption. While the introduction of the four basic food groups is often cast as an important nutritional device created to aid people, it is clear that the dairy and flesh industries were alarmed by the instability of their market. Working closely with the government United States Department of Agriculture (USDA), they reduced the number of food groups while allotting greater space to their specific products.

The four basic food groups are a literal representation of how a question of production and promotion becomes a nutritional consideration. The reason for the four basic food groups, we are told, is to insure that we are getting our recommended daily amounts of protein, calcium, vitamins, and iron. The Basic Four Food poster that inculcated generations from 1956 until recently indicated that flesh and dairy products were an excellent source of these items. It made this claim because it measured these products from a *producer's* point of view (nutrients per *weight* ratio) rather than a *consumer's* point of view (nutrients per *calories* ratio). Examining this choice of measurement, it appears curiously unhelpful to consumers—"people do not eat until a certain weight of food has been consumed but rather until Caloric requirements are satisfied"[30]—while extremely favorable for producers: foods high in fat like flesh fare better when measured by weight rather than calorie. Turkey flesh can be claimed to be 96 percent fat free when measured by weight, although 28.6 percent of the calorie content is fat.

Although there is no recommended daily allowance for weight in the diet, foods are interpreted according to weight in these charts to hide a consumer's concern—concern about fat and calories. "Fat is lighter (specific gravity .913-.945) than water, the chief constituent of fruits and vegetables, so fatty foods will show up well in a nutrient/weight sort; but since fat is high in Calories these foods do poorly in a nutrient/ Calorie sort."[31] As a result, "if foods are sorted and preferenced by nutrient/Calorie rather than nutrient/weight ratios, animal foods lose their clout and the whole 'Basic Four' concept evaporates." It evaporates because excessive intake of protein and fat, fostered by the traditional basic four food groups, poses a greater health risk than the obtaining of calcium, protein, and iron from vegetables, grains, and fruits. The typical Western corpse indulger's diet is high in animal fat and protein, while lacking in fiber. This diet is associated with increased risk of cancer, heart disease, obesity, diabetes, and osteoporosis.[32] In fact, some vegetable foods protect against diseases such as atherosclerosis and cancer, while high-fat foods increase risk for these diseases.

In April 1991 the Physician's Committee for Responsible Medicine (PCRM) introduced a new four-food groups of whole grains, vegetables, legumes, fruits. (See Figure 3.) This proposal from a group that might generally be marginalized by the dominant discourse garnered quite a bit of media attention.[33] But soon its radical evisceration of a flesh diet seemed unimportant, because—perhaps to confuse matters—lower-echelon USDA staff members unveiled a new representation of the four basic food groups.[34] No longer contained within a wheel that imparted 50 percent of its space to dairy and "meat," the four basic food groups were to be illustrated through a New Age pyramid, with flesh and dairy products toward the apex, though now inhabiting less space. This diminishment in space, even though counteracted by the placement of flesh and dairy in hierarchically superior locations, was not acceptable to the beef and dairy industries. In encapsulating their space, the pyramid appeared to shrink their nutritional importance as well. Protesting this to the USDA—the pyramid was "confusing," it "stigmatized" their products, both by the reduction of size, and by their placement next to that of fats and sweets—the flesh and dairy industries succeeded in having the new image withdrawn. As one newspaper reported, "Industry Beefs, USDA cowed."[35]

Just as the traditional nutritional measurement of flesh by weight instead of calories ignored its serious health implications, so constructing the argument about eating animals in solely nutritional terms—no matter what the shape—ignores the context for the nutritional debate. The

THE NEW FOUR FOOD GROUPS

FOR OPTIMAL NUTRITION

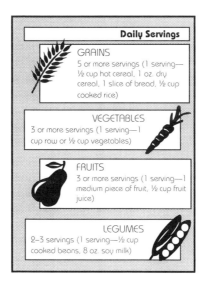

Daily Servings

GRAINS
5 or more servings (1 serving—½ cup hot cereal, 1 oz. dry cereal, 1 slice of bread, ½ cup cooked rice)

VEGETABLES
3 or more servings (1 serving—1 cup raw or ½ cup vegetables)

FRUITS
3 or more servings (1 serving—1 medium piece of fruit, ½ cup fruit juice)

LEGUMES
2–3 servings (1 serving—½ cup cooked beans, 8 oz. soy milk)

Figure 3: The New Four Food Groups

Figure 4: The USDA

dead animal industry and the dairy industry together are the second largest industry in the United States. Through the USDA's four basic food groups we have government sponsorship of an animal-based food diet. Instead of being seen as industry-sponsored propaganda, it can be viewed neutrally as government-sponsored education, lifting cultural promotion to an even greater coercive dimension. (See Figure 4.) The four food groups might be called not the Queen's English, but the government's English.

After a series of consumer surveys, costing $855,000, showed that the pyramid was not confusing, it survived and was reintroduced to the public in 1992. However, while realigning them from circle to pyramid, it does not destabilize the concept of the four basic food groups. In fact, it continues to reinforce the idea that dairy products—what I call feminized protein[36]—are essential to a diet. When analyzed as an industry rather than a food product, the dairy and egg industry cannot be so

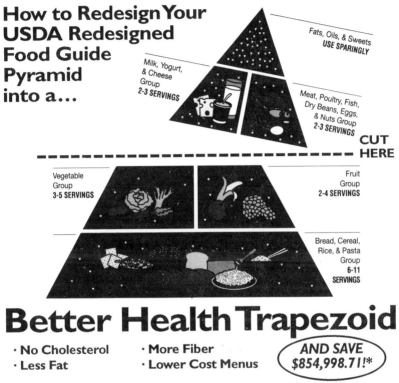

How to Redesign Your USDA Redesigned Food Guide Pyramid into a...

Fats, Oils, & Sweets
USE SPARINGLY

Milk, Yogurt, & Cheese Group
2-3 SERVINGS

Meat, Poultry, Fish, Dry Beans, Eggs, & Nuts Group
2-3 SERVINGS

CUT HERE

Vegetable Group
3-5 SERVINGS

Fruit Group
2-4 SERVINGS

Bread, Cereal, Rice, & Pasta Group
6-11 SERVINGS

Better Health Trapezoid

· **No Cholesterol**   · **More Fiber**   *AND SAVE $854,998.71!*
· **Less Fat**   · **Lower Cost Menus**

*Based on a cost comparison of the USDA's redesign ($855,000) and a pair of safety scissors ($1.29).

Figure 5: Better Health Trapezoid

easily separated from corpse production: it supplies *veal* calves, chickens for soup and stock, exhausted cows for *burgers* and other *meat*. Remember, too, that milk is produced in surplus in the United States, and having a government image and concept that assures a market for its product is a great boon. PCRM responded by destabilizing the pyramid, and proposing in its place a trapezoid. (See Figure 5.)

During the 1993 *E. coli* scare, in which at least two children died as a result of undercooked meat, and many more became sick, the focus of debate was not "why do we continue to eat dead bodies?" but "how should dead bodies be cooked so that we do not die from them?" Vegetarians around the country listened with ears that heard repeated evidence for the need to abandon the eating of flesh. Corpse eaters listened with anxiety for assurance that they could continue to eat flesh. Not surprisingly, the dominant culture determined the focus of the debate, all kept respectfully within the confines of government English. New labels to appear on all dead flesh will warn of the need to cook dead bodies completely before consuming them. If the labels were in vegetarian "French" they might say:

> Warning: This is a dead body, recently executed. The decaying process has already begun. You do not need to eat dead animals to stay healthy. Reduce your risk of getting six out of ten diseases that cripple and kill Americans: Boycott this product and choose vegetarianism.

*   *   *

If the words favored for insulting others are any sign, the animals whom humans consume do not figure grandly in any hierarchy of value: you cow, eating like a pig, chicken-brained, chicken-hearted, turkey, and so forth. Feminist Karen Davis, founder of United Poultry Concerns, suggests that "in coming days we may marvel at the strange phenomenon of constituting ourselves by the intimate act of eating beings we despise."[37] But can the dominant discourse allow for such marveling, such introspection, when it comes to eating animals?

In a sense, vegetarians are no more biased than corpse eaters about their choice of food; the former, however, do not benefit as do the latter from having their biases actually approved of by the dominant culture through the coercive effects of a government-sponsored corpse diet. As a result, in this culture, it requires less energy, less knowledge, less concern, less awareness, to continue eating animals than to stop. Yet it may be that the unexamined meal is not worth eating.

2

The Arrogant Eye
and Animal Experimentation

What distinguishes man from woman is his access to representation, to cultural symbolization, the power of naming, in
which he uses women, along with all the other silent animals,
as symbols, as objects for representation.

—Susanne Kappeler

Animal defenders address the attitudes of a patriarchal culture toward the other animals; the people whose conduct they discuss are people who are constituting themselves as subjects in a culture suffused with
human male cultural symbolization. Feminist critiques of science and of
representation illuminate the issue of animal experimentation. Animal
experimentation is part of a patriarchal culture in which science, like
masculinity is "tough, rigorous, rational, impersonal, competitive, and
unemotional."[1]

John Berger first argued in "Why Look at Animals?" that we have
transformed animals into spectacles, and so restricted our interactions
with animals that they have disappeared from our lives as independent
beings, diminished to representations of human fantasies regarding what
is exotic, wild, or sentimental. In "Why Look at Women?" Susanne
Kappeler shows how in this respect women are interchangeable with the
other animals. Her insights into the way in which the dominant subjectivity in patriarchal culture—men's—is constructed through objectifying
others provide a framework for exploring the feminist implications of
the oppression of other animals. In particular, the rituals associated with
the vivisection of the other animals and animal experimentation reveal
a fundamental way in which twentieth-century patriarchal culture looks

at animals. Within patriarchal culture, constituting oneself as a subject involves having an object who is looked at. By its reliance on the object status of the other animals, nonhuman animal experimentation provides one means for achieving subjectivity as it is constructed within a racist patriarchy.

Problem 1
The Arrogant Eye: The Human Male Gaze

In a world ordered by sexual imbalance, pleasure in looking has been split between active/[human] male and passive/[human] female. The determining [human] male gaze projects its phantasy onto the [human] female figure which is styled accordingly. In their traditional exhibitionist role women are simultaneously looked at and displayed, with their appearance coded for strong visual and erotic impact so that they can be said to connote *to-be-looked-at-ness*.

—Laura Mulvey[2]

The history of representation is the history of the [human] male gender representing itself to itself—the power of naming is men's. Representation is not so much the means of representing an object through imitation (matching contents) as a means of self-representation through authorship: the expression of subjectivity. Culture, as we know it, is patriarchy's self-image.

—Susanne Kappeler[3]

In patriarchal culture, gaze is an essential aspect of subjectivity—the act of looking is an aspect of being self-identified, active, assertive, knowing who one is. We are a visually oriented species, but the ways in which we look are socially constructed. One is not assertive in the dominant culture, which so values assertiveness, without being assertive over; one knows who one is by defining oneself against others. "Subjectivity as envisaged in patriarchal culture is attainable but through oppression and objectification: subject status equals supremacy over an other, not intersubjectivity. Only then does it produce the feeling of pleasure, the feeling of life. How can the subject be sure that he is high if no one is low, how can he know he is free if no one is bound?" writes Kappeler.[4] This formula allows for no reciprocity, no "intersubjectivity" as Kappeler calls it. Being a subject requires an object; while our species is capable of a great range of behavior, the cultural relationship paradigmatic in the West is one of subject to object. This paradigmatic relationship is typified by what can be called the human male gaze, arising as it does within a patriarchal culture, and exemplified as it is by the way men look at women. In this paradigmatic gaze, it is what the object does for the gazer and what the gazer does with the object that is important; the object's own intrinsic subjectivity is irrelevant in this relationship.

A primary means of making a subject into an object—of objectifying a being—is through depictions, representations. Representation enables conceptualizations in which the subject-object dichotomy recurs: looking at representations provides the gazer with pleasure while simultaneously reinforcing the distance between subject and object as unbridgeable. We learn within a patriarchal culture that the subject feels himself *to be* by the response he perceives in himself to looking at objects arranged for his viewing. This "arrogant eye" is an aspect of what constitutes human male subjects against human female objects, and contributes also to constituting scientific subjects over the other animals. Because both men and women assimilate patriarchal culture, the human male gaze is exhibited by both when looking at other animals. The practice of animal experimentation is both enabled and reinforced by the unquestioned, culturally established *to-be-looked-at-ness* of animals.

Problem 2:
Animal Experimentation

> The [human] male gender's project of constituting [human] male subjectivity is a serious business that has nothing to do with fictional and playful fantasy. It is the means by which the [human] male subject convinces himself that he is real. . . . He feels the more real, the less real the Other, the less of a subject the Other, the less alive the Other. And the reality he creates for himself through his cultural self-representation is the Authorized Version of reality, the dominant reality for all of us.
>
> —Susanne Kappeler[5]

We cannot know how the other animals subjectively experience looking, and we seldom make the inquiry: particularly in animal experiments the environment is constructed so that the only look is that of subject to object, and the object's look is contained, restricted, eliminated. It is remarkable how many experiments fetishize the animals' eyes in a way that guarantees that the animals will be injured or blinded and thus physically unable to return the experimenter's look. The long-established

Draize test, often used in testing cosmetics and chemical products, involves dripping solutions of these products into rabbits' eyes. A former animal-care trainee at the Gillette testing laboratory in Rockville, Maryland, described what she witnessed one day: "I was walking through the eye room and saw one technician grab a rabbit who had pus draining out of his swollen eye. He forced the eye open to examine it under bright light. I've heard rabbits scream before, but never like that."[6] In the name, "eye room," the arrogant eye achieves an eponymous existence. And perhaps it is because of the importance of sight to us that the Draize test has become so effectively a rallying point for animal defenders.

Consider Helen, a female monkey, whose visual cortext was removed. Helen can scan her surrounding but she is unable to identify what she sees. The title of her experimenter's report on this situation, "Seeing and Nothingness,"[7]—an obvious reference to Sartre's *Being and Nothingness*—makes clear the ontological nature of the human male gaze: Seeing is Being. I see an object, therefore I am a subject. The patriarchal subject is turning subjects into nonseeing objects, thus robbing them of the notion of subjectivity and being.

But as Susanne Kappeler observes the important feature is not blindness per se, but the subject's attempt to turn the "object" into "a nonseeing one—i.e., to rob them of *his* notion of subjectivity and being. But of course, whether blinded or with averted gaze, the animal or the woman still remains a subject"—in reality.[8]

Besides imputing an ontological crisis that accompanies a disabled gaze—not seeing is not being—"Seeing and Nothingness" hauntingly, and no doubt inadvertently, indicts the animal experimentation it enacts. Once her visual cortex was destroyed, Helen was dependent on interaction with others to help her relearn what it was she saw. After making this fact clear, the experimenter, Nicholas Humphrey, reports that because he had to finish his thesis, "she was left to her own devices for about ten months—such devices, that is, as she could manage in a small cage."[9] When Humphrey describes her later opportunity to walk in the open air, he calls it "the experience of three-dimensional space,"[10] conceding that life in a cage is not fully real. Helen's object status is confirmed not only by the impunity with which she can be deprived of sight but also by the restriction to a less-than-real life in a cage.

Kappeler argues: "Viewing and self-expression are themselves actions in the world, actions performed by the culture's legitimated subjects. In the structure of representation, the act of perception, of viewing and of self-expression, is predominant and overlays the represented action of a (potentially) represented agent."[11] The way most people learn about animal experimentation—scientist to scientist, animal supporters to their constituency—is through representations and reports. The denial of access of most lay people to scientific laboratories reinforces the dependence on representations and reports, visual and verbal texts, to communicate the details of the encounter between the arrogant human eye and the other animals. Photographs and videotapes are ineluctably a part of much experimentation these days, reinforcing the subject-object dichotomy enacted by the experimenters themselves. A particularly notorious example comes from the videotapes stolen in 1984 from Dr. Thomas Gennarelli's Head Injury Clinical Research Center at the University of Pennsylvania—a laboratory widely considered as one of the best in the country. (We do not know how extreme this example is because most videotapes of animal experiments are as closely guarded as the laboratories themselves.) The following dialogue is described by a reporter for the *Philadelphia Daily News*:

> The tapes show injured monkeys tied to wooden baby highchairs, drooling from the mouths, arms and legs flapping uncontrollably. Researchers twist their heads from one side to the other and clap hands to see if they respond. In one scene, a dark-haired woman supports a monkey while its [*sic*] arms and legs dangle.
> "She's on TV holding her monkey," a male off-camera voice jokes. "Say cheese."
> Again a male voice says, "Better hope the anti–vivisectionists don't get a hold of this," while a woman tries to get a monkey to move its [*sic*] arms. Another voice says, "He has the punk look." The monkey, which has been shaved from the middle of the chest to the top of the head, has electrodes taped all over its [*sic*] body, and has a red scar in the middle of its [*sic*] head, extending from the back of the skull to its [*sic*] forehead.
> "Show his part to the camera," a man says.[12]

Note the composition of this representation: the human being filmed with the animal is female; confirming the cultural role of the human male gaze that looks at women and animals. "Say cheese," she is told, for she is posing as well. As with photographic representations of women in which they are silenced objects who stimulate banal discussion between men, the voices in this portion of the videotape are men's; the woman, like the monkey, is silenced, and she follows orders given by an off-camera male director. Through such representations women's and animals' object status intersects.

When Kappeler discusses how representations enable the viewer of them to feel real, she posits that "he feels the more real, the less real the Other, the less of a subject the Other, the less alive the Other."[13] What she describes is the situation of animals in scientific experimentation as well as their fates.

The Less Real the Other

Animals are defined as not having feelings, not suffering. Because they do not write or talk to us in languages we understand or admit as language, we presume to know their intellectual capacity: they don't have any. Yet, if animals weren't like humans nothing that applies to humans could be gained by studying them. This is the crux of the problem in justifying animal experimentation. (And note that Mighty Mouse, Mickey Mouse, the Church Mice, and Templeton the Rat notwithstanding, according to the United States Department of Agriculture's interpretation of the federal Animal Welfare Act, mice and rats are not even "animals." Neither are birds!)[14]

The Less of a Subject the Other

The animal experimented upon cannot be a subject, an actor, only an object called the "subject" of the experiment. The animal does not have interests, does not have legal rights. The animals are called "models," "tools," ("suckers" in the Gennarelli tapes), "it."

The Less Alive the Other

The modus operandi of many experiments is to measure what is fatal. The LD50 test, an acronym for Lethal Dose 50 percent, announces in its unabbreviated title that it must seek the death of animals. The LD50 test involves calculating the lethal dose of a substance "as the amount that would kill half the group of animals to which it is administered."[15] Many experiments involve long phases of slow dying before death or euthanasia intervenes. This is a time period during experimentation that could be called precisely the *less-alive* period. The less-alive period is an important time for observation by experimenters. Peter Singer summarizes one report that demonstrates how the less-alive period is observed:

> Anthony Hopkins of the Institute of Neurology, London, poisoned twelve adult and three infant baboons by injecting them with lead in varying doses for periods up to one year. Because earlier experiments on cats had shown that absorption of lead is more complete through the lungs, the doses were injected directly into the trachea, or windpipe, of each baboon, which was then held in an upright position so that the poison could "trickle" into its [sic] lungs. Before death oc-

curred, loss of weight was "striking," five of the twelve adults losing 40 percent or more of their initial weight. Eight baboons had convulsive fits, thirty-four convulsive fits being observed, although "it is likely that others occurred when no observer was present."

In one baboon, seizures began with "twitching around the right eye, spreading to the rest of the right side of the face. During the next fifteen seconds the right arm became involved, and then seizures became generalized." Seizures were "occasionally preceded by a cry" and were sometimes "precipitated by a sudden movement of the animal as it [*sic*] tried to avoid transfer from one cage to another or whilst reaching up to take a banana." Other symptoms included bloody diarrhea, pneumonia, inflamed and bloody intestines, and liver degeneration. One baboon became so weak it [*sic*] could not stand up, and its [*sic*] left finger could not grasp orange segments. For three weeks before it [*sic*] died this baboon was partially blind; "it [*sic*] groped for proffered fruit and on occasions appeared not to see it." [Again, damage to vision that eliminates reciprocating gaze.] Five of the baboons died in seizures; seven were found dead in their cages; the remaining three were "sacrificed."[16]

Singer reports other examples of experiments calculated to make animals less alive including ones that "'terminally deprived' 256 young rats of food and water."[17] This less-alive period terminates with the animals' deaths, one way or another—if the animals do not die in the course of the experiment, they are put to death.

Problem 3:
The Dominant Reality

Among the whole gamut of coercive structures in patriarchal capitalism, the scenario of vision, the representational structure imposed on them, isolates a partial "content," framing part of a phenomenon, so as to exclude possibilities of analysing the larger network of structures in which it is embedded.
—Susanne Kappeler[18]

The use of animals in experiments is all "for the benefit of mankind. If you don't use animals, you don't do research."
—Henry Foster,
founder of the Charles River Breeding Laboratory[19]

The dominant reality is this: the belief in the necessity of animal experimentation is strongly entrenched. Though some may be saddened by the information that animals are experimented upon, they optimistically have faith that the experimenters are not inflicting cruel suffering, or at least not unnecessarily. Information about animal injuries is filtered against the belief that human deaths may be the consequence if these experiments do not occur and the knowledge they could yield is not obtained. Scientists can be irresponsible toward animal rights because they are focused on a "higher" right, the rights of humans to survive. These rights are positioned as being in opposition.

Essentially animal experimentation is to "scientific knowledge" what pornography is to literary culture, and each is protected by this relationship. Kappeler argues that pornography exists on a continuum with all of patriarchal culture, that it may enact the values of this culture more explicitly, but that all of patriarchal culture conceptualizes women and uses representations in ways akin to pornography. Challengers to the legitimacy of animal experimentation are often accused of being anti-science, neo-Luddites who oppose modern advances in science, advances claimed to have been due to animal experimentation. The questionable nature of the activity within the circumscribed inner sphere—something being done to the animal, something being done to a (usually naked) woman—cannot be questioned because of its relationship to the unquestioned verities of the (human male) culture that encloses them. Where the principle of freedom of speech and the quest for artistic expression protects pornography, the need for scientific truth and progress protects animal experimentation.

While alternatives to animal experimentation exist, (simulators, computer models, cell cultures, living human tissue testing, or clinical and epidemiological studies), animal experimenters have not been asked by those in authority (funding agencies and federal law) to try an alternative and prove it has failed. Certainly, the substitute would not so well confirm the status of animals as objects.

Pornographers say we are just giving the public what they want. Animal researchers say we are just giving the public what they need. Yet what their research focuses on often is "protection" from something we are doing to ourselves or remedying the results of what we have done. Because some human beings smoke, rats and mice must get cancer. It is common knowledge now that next to smoking, animal oppression through the eating of flesh and dairy products is linked to many of the major forms of diseases (heart attacks, certain forms of cancer) that appear in industrialized culture. Experiments continue on what causes cancer while the consumption of these cancer-producing agents also continues; the focus is kept narrowly on the supposed need for scientific experimentation that protects us (making us objects as well) excluding any question of the dominant reality that causes both our object status and our need for protection. The Authorized Version of reality disempowers both consumers and animals.

Problem 4:
Strangers and Other Victims

Under his aesthetic gaze any woman, known or unknown, turns into the "stranger," that object of no interest except for its capacity to stimulate the subject's feeling of life.
—Susanne Kappeler[20]

Animals must be kept as "strangers" to permit experimentation. We could rephrase Kappeler to say, "Under his scientific gaze, any animal, known or unknown, turns into the 'stranger,' *the material,* that object of no interest except for its capacity to be a medium for the subject's sense of knowledge." Strangers are less likely to arouse emotional attachment; strangers already exist within a framework of distancing. They are marginalized beings. The outcry over dogs and cats used for experimentation may be explained because they are defined as pets, not as strangers. The drive for legislation against getting animals from pounds for experiments arises to protect these pets. According to Andrew Rowan, the humane shelters view the forced surrender of cats and dogs to animal experimenters as threatening their cornerstone: "namely, a suffering-free sanctuary for animals."[21]

The Charles River Breeding Laboratory provides "micropigs," "macropigs," and "minipigs" and expects that the increased use of pigs instead of dogs will decrease the outcry against animal experimentation since "everybody eats them"—i.e., pigs have already been rendered strangers through our consumption of their kind.

Animals must be strangers to confirm the myth of scientific objectivity. As Kappeler writes of literature, "The claim to universality stems from the fact of the disinterestedness with which the subject regards the represented object."[22] The other animals, like women, are points of exchange between two or more subjects. According to Kappeler, pornography occurs when the pornographer speaks to another subject, the consumer of the photographic material, about a woman who is an object, a point of exchange between them. Animal experimentation similarly involves one scientist speaking to another scientist about the animal, their point of exchange.

Problem 5:
The Combining of Categories

Pornography connects the centrality of visual objectification to both [human] male sexual arousal and [human] male models of knowledge and verification, objectivity with objectification.

—Catharine MacKinnon[23]

Frequently pornography employs language that celebrates the combining of the categories of "women" and "animals." Besides pornography that explicitly documents women with animals, either as supposedly willing sexual partners, or the use of animals to establish the appropriate animalized environment, we hear of "beaver hunters" who bag a woman, the existence of *Playboar* with photographs of a variety of sexualized pig poses, and the "woman-breaking" tradition of late nineteenth-century pornography that was built on horse-breaking images. In her analysis of this type of pornography, Coral Lansbury finds parallels with the then-current medical treatment of women:

> Women are subdued and held by straps so they can be mounted and flogged more easily, and they always end as grateful victims, trained to enjoy the whip and the straps, proud to provide pleasure for their masters. There is an uneasy similarity between the devices made to hold women for sexual pleasure and those tables and chairs, replete with stirrups and straps, which made women ready for the surgeon's knife.[24]

In protesting the vivisection of the other animals, nineteenth-century women revolted "against a world of [human] male sexual authority." Further, Lansbury argues, "continually animals were seen as surrogates for women who read their own misery into vivisector's victims."[25] The antivivisection movement of the late nineteenth century was predominantly composed of women who saw themselves as the referent in vivisectionists' activities.

The rage these women felt toward vivisection of other animals might have been because they were separated by a vast psychological distance from medical doctors' activities; they were viewed as holding childlike opinions about animals; they were seen as being close kin to the animals themselves; they saw symbols of their own suffering in animal victims. The absent referent in the vivisection of other animals was for these women hardly absent—they saw themselves similarly positioned. As Alice Park wrote with alarm to the *Vegetarian Magazine:* "A physician who will deliberately vivisect helpless, harmless, little animals will just as deliberately vivisect women or any human being he can find to experiment on." Concerned by the increasing role "the medical trust" was exercising in the United States, she encouraged women to "drop all worry about the ballot for a few weeks and get out your 'hatchet' to smash all fond hopes these AMA physicians have to eventually rule our nation."[26]

The permeability of categories remains for us today: we frequently read of studies determining that a high proportion of gynecological surgeries performed in the United States are unnecessary. Cesarean deliveries have skyrocketed for women. Andrea Dworkin, in *Pornography: Men Possessing Women,* and Gena Corea, in *The Mother Machine,* argue the patriarchal source of the epidemic of cesarean section in the United States. Interestingly, cesarean deliveries have become, as well, the standard way to "produce" the most commonly used laboratory animals. The Charles River Breeding Laboratory emphasizes that their animals are "Cesarean-Derived," assuring animal experimenters that they are thereby receiving "pure" strains.

Problem 6:
Knowledge

> In characterizing scientific and objective thought as masculine, the very activity by which the knower can acquire knowledge is also genderized. The relation specified between knower and known is one of distance and separation. It is that between a subject and an object radically divided.
>
> —Evelyn Fox Keller[27]

It is clear that the *pursuit* of knowledge in the dominant society is gendered to begin with. The originating structure that determines both the sorts of experiments to be undertaken and the kind of quantifiable knowledge to be gained is a patriarchal one. Animal experimentation rigidly upholds cultural sex-role presumptions. Because pregnancies are undesirable in many experiments, researchers using mice rely on "seventy males for every thirty females."[28] Other experiments look at female animals precisely for their femaleness. Carolyn Merchant reports that in

England in the 1630s William Harvey "dissected large numbers of King Charles' does just after coition with bucks."[29] Modern experimenters can place an order for pregnant animals with the Charles River Breeding Laboratory. Not only is the control of females reified in the act of the experiment itself, but so also are the categories of "maleness" and "femaleness" as the subjects under study. A fixation on femaleness moves smoothly from the realm of representation to the realm of experimentation.

Men's distance from women, from their own parenting ability and their capacity to feel for others, determines experiments such as Harry Harlow's in which baby monkeys are denied maternal care. Harlow has described the restricted environment he constructed to insure the denial of all affection to the baby monkeys. This environment of nonfeeling mirrors the standard for scientific ideas: reason rules and feelings are controlled. Norma Benney caustically noted that these experiments proved "what most women know and certainly every mother knows, namely, that young ones need the love of their mother."[30]

Although other animals can be experimented upon only because they are not human, if they were not like humans nothing would be gained for humans by studying them. But what precisely is gained? How can pain be measured, quantified, interpreted, especially if chronic pain changes an animal's response? Once gained, how is the knowledge applied? Once the dilemma (animals are different from us; animals are like us) is acknowledged, it attaches itself to the rationale of the animal experiments: Animals are different from us so we can . . . , animals are like us so we conclude . . . . The wedge of differentiation between humans and other animals, which can never be precisely located, is both necessary for and undercuts the premise of scientific knowledge.

That the observer cannot but influence the experiment by the very watching reinforces yet again our awareness of how a patriarchal subject constitutes himself. It is a fact that experiments are often repeated or so designed that they produce results that are not even arguably useful. For instance, although the practical shortcomings of the Draize test are widely admitted, some companies, like Gillette, have scarcely modified or curtailed the use of it. Where experimenters' behavior is so obviously ritual rather than purposive, we must consider the question of agency and sadism.

Problem 7:
Agents and Sadism

We are told that animal experimentation is not sadism. But what mental gymnastics are required to consider what in fact happens to other animals without imputing any human, let alone malignant, agency? The argument is made that experimenters are the products of conditioning in which their peers and superiors reinforce the legitimacy of painful experiment on animals. Experimenters do not see themselves as agents of pain, cruelty, etc., because they do not see themselves as agents. Routine and ritual insulate them from their activities. By viewing animals as tools toward their research ends, they render the transitive verb intransitive; they eliminate agency.

Kappeler writes, "Representation foregrounds content . . . and obscures the agent of representation." Science foregrounds knowledge and obscures the role of the scientist, the agent of scientific experimentation. An experiment on an animal is like representation because neither is "really" happening. It is not happening because the agent is not willing it to happen or to be hurtful. Kappeler reminds us to look at the role of the subject: all else arises out of the subject's need to confirm his subjectivity. How else, really, to explain the repetition of experiments? Repetition, Kappeler suggests, is an essential aspect of pornography, of constructing the subject in patriarchy—"there is a plot: the cultural archeplot of power."[31]

Sandra Harding implicates the capitalist and patriarchal structure of science. She sees a division of labor involving a select group of white decision-making men and women who essentially become scientific technicians: "Because the priorities conceptualized by white males often create ambivalences about the social value of particular projects, research priorities may differ from those of their private lives outside science. Who would *choose* a career goal of building bombs, torturing animals, or manufacturing machines that will put one's sisters and brothers out of work?"[32] While the division of labor and the control of power reinforce the structure of white men's control and posit an absence of agency at the technician level, the arrogant eye is not without a role also. Direct observation of animal "torture" by notable scientists and the fact that scientists achieve notability by their *direct* involvement in animal experimentation (viz., Pavlov, Harlow, Seligman) confirms the presence of agency. They need to be able to say "*I* observed 'y' reaction in these animals after we had done 'x' to them." Scientific knowledge depends on "quantifiable" information; in the case of animal experimentation this requires close attention. Enter the gaze of the arrogant eye, both as an action and a rationale. And that human male gaze involves, to some degree, agency: "*I* am watching *it*."

Theresa Corrigan has remarked on the similarity between the conceptual framework suggested here and Mary Daly's description of the sadoritual syndrome in her book, *Gyn/Ecology*. A fascinating case can be made that inevitably a sadoritual syndrome that targets women will also theoretically undergird the intertwined oppression of animals. Many of the components of the sado-ritual syndrome described by Daly are evident in animal experiments as well as other forms of oppressing animals, such as eating flesh and wearing animal skins: absence of agency, obsessive repetition, token torturers, otherwise unacceptable behavior taken as normal, and scholarly legitimation.[33]

Once the formula for knowledge is understood as shaky if not bankrupt ("animals are not like us so we can. . . . , animals are like us so we conclude . . ."), then the two sides to this formula can be disengaged one from the other. The actions of the former do not neatly lead to the conclusions of the latter. In breaking the premise of the cause and effect of the experiment, in stripping animal experiments of the legitimacy they gain as gendered scientific knowledge, in questioning the premise of "animals are like us so we conclude . . . ," then we are free to look specifically at the phrase, "animals are not like us so we can. . . ." This leads to scrutinizing the agency of the experimenters. What exactly are they doing? We do not necessarily have the absence of sadistic violence, we have the refusal to acknowledge agency.

Problem 8:
Consumption

Representations are not just a matter of mirrors, reflections, key-holes. Somebody is making them, and somebody is looking at them, through a complex array of means and conventions.

—Susanne Kappeler[34]

Animal experimenters reify us as consumers, objects who consume, rather than subjects who decide about the ethics of consumption. This concept explains the testing on animals of cosmetics that promote the "feminine" look, as well as experiments to define what our proper food is—flesh? food coloring? with what levels of toxins? In addition, we become consumers of animal experiments: many of us hear about them without noticing that what is exactly being described happened to certain animals. News reports discussing advances in cancer research or AIDS research usually name the animals used—"a study of rats" or "a study of monkeys." We consume the information, congratulating ourselves, if we are healthy, that science proceeds, helping us to protect ourselves from illness.

But it is also because we are consumers that many scientific experiments continue. Because we (some of us) consume flesh and smoke cigarettes we have scientific experiments on animals to discover cures for the resulting cancer; because we (some of us) use cosmetics, cleansers, etc., product testing on animals continues. If we restructured consumption, we would eliminate the need for many animal experiments. But this is not the point, of course. Animal experimentation is not only a means to an end—a way by which we can hope to continue consuming without changing habits of harmful consumption; animal experimentation is both socially and economically an end in itself. How many people earn their living experimenting on animals? How many people earn their living supplying animals to be experimented on? The Charles River Breeding Laboratory (1–800-LAB-RATS) had sales of $45 million in 1983. How many people earn their living supplying food, cages, and transportation for "lab" animals? What percentage of university budgets is raised from grants funding animal experiments?

Problem 9:
What's the Difference?

> Meat is like pornography: before it was someone's fun, it was someone's life.
>
> —Melinda Vadas[35]

Ron Martin, producer of a live sex show in New York, was asked if he does not think that he degrades women for profit. His reply: "I know I do. So does *The New York Times*. I have one girl who felt degraded every time she stepped outside. She came here because she was constantly getting hit up by men anyway, so why not get paid? Is working here any more degrading than walking down the street?"[36] Some pornographers say, What's the difference between us and the *New York Times*? Animal experimenters say, What's the difference between what we are doing and what you are doing? You eat animals, don't you? Aren't you wearing leather? You benefit from what we do, so why shouldn't we experiment on animals? The subject status imputed to our acts as consumers of information, flesh, and other animal products veils the subject status of the experimenters. Animal oppression thus becomes the legitimating force for the continuance of the system. Neither science nor art stand apart from culture: patriarchal culture is deeply implicated in both.

It has been by and large Euro-American middle-class and upper-class men who have created scientific theorems, ethics, and the ground rules for animal experimentation. They have created these out of the perspective by which they approach the world: as subjects surveying an object world. Zuleyma Tang Halpin observes how intersubjectivity radically threatens such an approach:

> Once a scientist begins to feel for his or her research animal, the self versus other duality begins to break down, and it becomes easier for the interrelatedness of subject and object to be acknowledged. Once this happens, it becomes easier to question the paradigm which proclaims power, control, and domination as the ultimate goal of science. Viewed from this perspective, the animal welfare issue poses a major threat to patriarchal science.[37]

Nonhuman animal experimentation is not an isolated case of animal oppression nor is it unrelated to human male dominance.[38] Animal experimentation is inherent in the way men, especially privileged Euro-American men, have made themselves subjects in the world by making others objects. The human male gaze—the arrogant eye of patriarchy—constructs animal experiments.

3

Abortion Rights
and Animal Rights[1]

A woman attempts to enter a building. Others, amassed outside, try to thwart her attempt. They shout at her, physically block her way, frantically call her names, pleading with her to stop, to respect life.

Is she buying a fur coat or getting an abortion?

On the face of it, the similarity of tactics of the antifur and antiabortion movements, and the focus on "woman as culprit and taker of life" connect the defense of animals with the fetal right to life movement.

In a deliberate echoing of the language of abortion rights, the Fur Information Council of America queries: "If fashion isn't about freedom of choice, what is?" (Abortion, of course.) They continue, "Personal choice is not just a fur industry issue. It's everybody's issue." Obviously the subtext here is hardly submerged. Personal choice isn't just "everybody's issue," it's specifically a woman's issue.

The emphasis on "choice" connects the fursellers and furwearers with the prochoice movement.

The general viewpoint of the antiabortion contingent in the United States, that is reproduced by some animal defenders as well, is "how can animal defenders be concerned about animals and not about human babies [as they erroneously call the fetus in the womb]?" A bumper sticker I have seen in various parts of the country queries: "How Come America? We brake for *animals,* we save the *seals,* and protect the *whales* but WE MURDER OUR UNBORN CHILDREN!!" Other bumper stickers say "Save a whale but kill a baby?" and "When you folks come out against abortion, I'll give up my fur coat." Profetal life writer Nat Hentoff proposes that "the pro-choice Left" should "think of the fetus as a baby seal, *in utero.*"[2]

I know this angry viewpoint of antiabortion activists. It has greeted me in radio interviews, letters to the editors, and in the pages of various publications, including the *Village Voice* and *Animals' Agenda*. In Dallas, I wrote to the weekly alternative paper complaining that they had listed an antiabortion group under the category "feminism" and a pro-animal experimentation group under the category "animal rights." The following week, a response appeared: "It is difficult for me to understand how Ms. Adams could be such an avid supporter of animal rights and not support the rights of unborn human animals. Aren't babies just as important as other animals and shouldn't they have as many and more rights?" (Instructive in this matter is the decapitating of an abortion counselor's cat in the midst of other acts of antiabortion terrorism.)[3]

Meanwhile, some feminist writers are concerned about the language of animal defenders because it appears to uphold the claims of antiabortionists: Donna Haraway, for instance, complains that the tones of animal defenders

> resonate with the pro-life/antiabortion question, "Who speaks for the foetus?" The answer is, anybody but the pregnant woman, especially if that anybody is a legal, medical or scientific expert. Or a father. Facing the harvest of Darwinism, we do not need an endless discourse on who speaks for animals, or for nature in general. We have had enough of the language games of fatherhood.[4]

It is time to say clearly what the difference between a human fetus and the other animals is; to enunciate a politics of abortion rights and animal defense that recognizes their logical intersections not their superficial differences, to repudiate the language games of fatherhood.[5] The fetus, as Susanne v. Paczensky, German abortion rights activist, defines it, is "a human being to be created and grown by a woman if she chooses to do so."[6] But the choice has already been made for the other animals—created, grown, and born. A fetus's dependency upon the pregnant woman—since the fetus is internal to and part of the woman—does not obtain for the other animals, once born.

Animal defenders face the challenge of telling the truth about animals' lives, awakening the world to the reality of how animals are treated, rather than the sanitized "down on the farm" image we are culturally spoon-fed and cling to in order to persist in oppressive actions of eating and wearing animals. We are not necessarily speaking for the animals, but making visible that which those who benefit from animals' oppression wish to keep invisible—the way humans treat the other animals. Animals, after all, are not speechless.

Similarly, abortion rights face the challenge that the dominant culture does not want to know the truth about women's lives. Rather motherhood is romanticized.

Here then are some of the philosophical issues that arise when a feminist examines the commonalities of animal defense and abortion rights.

Premise 1
We Must Not Lose Sight of the Individual

Animal defense theory argues that we must consider the individual animals. We must not let the fate of individual animals become deflected by concerns about species, or habitat, or the environment, or determined by what some consider to be humans' needs to eat and experiment upon animals. It is as individuals that animals experience the consequences of their oppression.

Resistance to recognizing the individuality of each animal is reproduced in the arguments of many antiabortionists. We hear about the millions of abortions performed each year. What we do not hear about is the experience and life decisions of each individual woman connected to those statistics. Even if a form of birth control had a 99 percent effective rate, (name one, please—abortion and abstinence are the only forms of birth control that are 100 percent effective), one out of one hundred women will find herself with an unwanted pregnancy. To this individual woman the failure of birth control is staggering. In fact, it is estimated that worldwide each woman experiences two unwanted pregnancies in her lifetime.

It is as individuals that women become pregnant.

The emphasis on the individual animal provides a focus for considering another aspect of the abortion rights issue: we need to recognize the singularity of pregnancy. By this I mean that pregnancy is unreproducible as a moral issue—there is no analogous rights situation to that of a woman who is carrying a fetus within her. Complex attempts to argue from analogous positions have been made. But there are none. There is no preexisting paradigm into which the question of abortion fits, because there is no equivalent to pregnancy.

Terminal animals—animals who exist to become someone's "meat" or "model"—have been stripped of all that makes them individuals, as Barbara Noske observes, they have been de-animalized. We fail to view terminal animals as social creatures. All that remains when we consider animals is the outer shell of "rabbit" or "cow," but not a relational animal. A similar process of decontextualizing the fetus occurs. Whereas animals in most people's imaginations are only body, the fetus has been disembodied, floating as though in space and not at all dependent on a woman's body for sustenance. The fetus can become the sole focus of the concern when the context of women's lives is absent, just as the animal can be the object of human's use when the context of their own lives is stripped away. In both cases, that which is the social part of the context, that which experiences the consequences of decontextualizing—the pregnant woman and the living, breathing rabbit—disappear. They, animals and woman, are the absent referents.

If any "individuality" is referred to by the antiabortion side, it is that of the aborted fetus. The claims of the fetus are often articulated as though they exist in a moral vacuum, detached from any individual woman. This is an example of Cartesian dualism, which those unfamiliar with the arguments of animal defenders need to know is one of the prime sources for the oppression of animals. Cartesian dualism ratifies the human/animal split by claiming that there is a rational/feeling dualism. Cartesian dualism also ratifies the woman/fetus split. Just as we humans are animals, and our rationality cannot exist separate from our embodied and feeling selves, the fetus is not separate from a woman; it is within her. Consider Barbara Ehrenreich's apt description as she discusses the misleading way we are told to visualize the fetus: "as a sort of larval angel, suspended against a neutral background. But no fetus—no living fetus—is suspended anywhere, but anchored to the placenta, housed in the womb, and wrapped in the flesh of a living woman."[7] Or as feminist ethicist Beverly Harrison points out, to impute an "agency of self development" to cells and tissue is deceptive, for it implies that the process of fetal formation is *"not* biologically dependent on the pregnant woman's life system."[8] To separate the fetus from the pregnant woman in discussing the issue of abortion is disingenuous. It is dishonest. It is misogynist. Just as speciesist discourse eliminates the individual animals, the fetishization of the fetus eliminates consideration of the individual woman. This is, of course, their intent.

Premise 2
Self-determination for Women and the Other Animals

Controlling animals and controlling access to abortion is the opposite of self-determination and liberation. Chickens, cows, mice, pigs, *and* women should not be forced to be pregnant against their will. If cows had reproductive freedom, there would be no veal calves and no milk for humans to drink.

Deceptive cultural images deflect us from understanding either animals' or women's right to self-determination. We may tell ourselves that animals want to be our food (like Charlie the Tuna) but this is not so.

Neither is it true that the experience of birth will make an unwilling pregnant woman a mother who will automatically love her baby.

Access to abortion is a fundamental aspect of women's freedom, for these reasons:

- Women's lives are at stake when abortion is criminalized. Abortion is never eliminated, it exists within cultures whatever the law dictates about its legality. For centuries it was a submerged part of women's culture. The question is not will abortions be available but what types of abortion will be available, and for whom?
- Voluntary legal abortion improves women's physical and psychological health.
- The availability of abortion insures that women will more likely reject hazardous forms of contraception such as depo-provera.
- Birth control failure is responsible for over 40 percent of unintended pregnancies.[9]

Premise 3
The "Sentiency" of the Fetus and of Animals Are Not Similar

Is the situation of the fetus legally or morally equivalent to that of animals? Tom Regan, in *The Case for Animal Rights*, discusses this briefly, but focuses his discussion on "the soon-to-be-born." We do not know, or as he says, "it is not *obviously true*" whether the soon-to-be-born have beliefs, desires, and the like. As a result, "the rights view leaves the question central to this debate an open question."[10] Which, of course, it must because at some point we use social criteria to determine what are claimed to be biological facts.

This is how the case was recently made to me:

1. Individuals who behave as if interested in their own well-being and who possess the anatomical structures necessary for perception of and response to environmental stimuli should have their interests respected.
2. Fetal humans [*sic*] develop such behaviors and anatomical structures between five and nine weeks after conception.
3. Fetal humans [*sic*] between five and nine weeks after conception have a prima facie right to respect of interests.

My field work when I was a divinity school student was being an aide at an elite medical school's first trimester abortion clinic. I asked once to see an aborted fetus. It was no longer than an inch. While many nonhuman animals may thrive at this size, no human animals have. Are not social categories being used when it is claimed that this fetus has perception of and response to environmental stimuli akin to any animal? Since social categories obviously reflect the dominant culture, and the dominance of our culture is clearly gender- and species-based, then a series of a priori presumptions has already predetermined what perception means, and how response is measured.

Is a fetus an individual? Does a fetus behave as an individual? What behaviors, precisely, are exhibited by the fetus during the first trimester? A fetus of twelve weeks has muscle reflexes but no developed nerve cell pathways in the brain's cortex that would enable it to experience pain. While I am wary of any claim to "scientific" information, since it is precisely these sorts of claims that are used against antivivisection arguments, I do wish to point out that the American College of Obstetricians and Gynecologists issued a statement on Pain of the Fetus (apparently in part as a response to the deceptively narrated film *The Silent Scream*). The statement, issued February 13, 1984, reads:

> We know of no legitimate scientific information that supports the statement that a fetus experiences pain early in pregnancy.
> We do know that the cerebellum attains its final configuration in the seventh month and that myelinization (or covering) of the spinal cord and the brain begins between the twentieth and fortieth weeks of pregnancy. These, as well as other neurological developments, would have to be in place for the fetus to perceive pain.
> To feel pain, a fetus needs neurotransmitted hormones. In animals, these complex chemicals develop in the last third of gestation. We know of no evidence that humans are different.

As one chairperson of a department of pediatric neurology said: "Pain implies cognition. There is no brain to receive the information."[11] Or as a researcher on the genetic control of brain development states: "An embryo may have fingers, hands, a nose and eyes, even reflex movements, but still no mind. . . . The early embryo, before the development of the mature human brain, has only one quality to distinguish it from all other living things: It has the potential to become a human being."[12]

A fetus, if allowed to develop, may reach the stage at which it has interests; an animal has actual interests.

The speciesism of Homo sapiens is perhaps nowhere more pronounced than in the protestation about the fate of the human conceptus and zygote, while the sentiency of the other animals is declared morally irrelevant because they are not human beings. Some have a definition of meaningful life that is so broad as to encompass a newly fertilized egg, yet so narrow that it does not consider fully-grown animals with well developed nervous systems and social sensibilities. Is it only human beings who should be ends and not means and does human being truly mean zygote? This leads to the next premise:

Premise 4
Our Definition of Personhood Is Culture-Bound

The concept of personhood is not value neutral, so there can be no value-free inquiry into this subject. For centuries, "person" excluded all but Euro-American males, so the idea that by discussing personhood we have entered into some secure ground is itself false. Notions of personhood are dictated by the culture in which persons and others live. Let us be reminded, too, that "it is frequently overlooked or dismissed in the debate about the 'morality' of abortion that the corollary of 'fetal personhood' is forced motherhood."[13]

Will the fetus achieve personhood before women do?

Do pregnant women, the only ones who experience a direct relationship with the fetus, define personhood differently from others, and does this offer a reasonable guide to this discussion? In fact, between 92 and 96 percent of legal abortions in this country occur within the first trimester, and over half occur within the first eight weeks. "These data are significant in understanding popular values about 'fetal life.' They confirm the sense that most women have, in term pregnancies, of developmental differences that correspond to differences, changes, in their relationship/obligation/bond to the fetus."[14]

According to Ruth Macklin, a "low standard" and a "high standard" for personhood exist. If you have a "low standard" then a zygote qualifies for personhood; in this case, though, "scientific development affords a convenient source of objective data used to support antecedently-held views." Macklin suggests that the properties an entity must have in order to satisfy the criteria for personhood are both a potentiality principle and encephalographic activity (which can be used for both the beginning and the end of personhood). This "high standard" for personhood recognizes a neonate or infant beyond a few months or a year.[15] Of interest, this high standard, would be inclusive of animals, too.

Animal defenders extend the notion of personhood to animals. When we watch someone who has a companion animal interact with that animal, we see in that relationship a recognition of that animal's individuality, or, in a sense, that animal's personhood: given a name, touched and caressed, a life that interacts and informs another's. The dominant culture reduces some animals to nonpersonhood status, keeping them in intensive farms, where they are treated as animal machines, while others, what feminists might call the token few, are elevated to personhood status.

Premise 5
The Moral Dilemmas of Abortion Rights and Animal Rights Are Different

The dilemma abortion rights faces is that women are not recognized as competent moral actors. The dilemma animal defenders face is that animals are not recognized as possessing legitimate moral claims upon us.

Women are not recognized as competent moral actors. It is obvious that women have always had abortions; that the women's community developed a variety of ways to end an unwanted pregnancy; that this was not condemned within this women's community, though the men's community throughout the ages has had varied views about the meaning of this.[16] What has been variable about abortion is its legality or criminalization, not its existence. It has always been a woman's choice and always will be one.

After surveying 350 primitive, ancient, and preindustrial societies, George Devereux concluded "there is every indication that abortion is an absolutely universal phenomenon, and that it is impossible even to construct an imaginary social system in which no woman would ever feel at least impelled to abort."[17] From this I deduce the following: women, despite the overwhelming misogyny of moral theory that has posited them as unable to make moral decisions, can and do make moral decisions quite capably. In this regard, they place an unwanted pregnancy within a continuum that remains largely unseen to the outside world's human male moral hegemony. As Beverly Harrison describes it:

> From the standpoint of a woman's experience, a . . . basic . . . moral question operates: "What am I to do about the procreative power that is mine by virtue of being born female?" The question of abortion arises only in this wider human context. . . . A woman's basic constructive line of moral action is responsible life planning in relation to her procreative power. The habit of discussing abortion as if it were a "discrete deed" is a way of formulating the abortion issue as a moral question abstracted out of, and hence irrelevant to, the way it arises in women's lives. . . . The well-being of a woman and the value of her life plan always must be recognized as of intrinsic value in any appeal to intrinsic value in a moral analysis of abortion.[18]

The dilemma of animal defense is the resistance of most people to recognizing that animals have legitimate moral claims upon us. Now I know that this requires us to reopen the question, "Does the fetus have a moral claim upon us?" Or, to put it a different way, "At what point in a pregnancy does a fetus have a moral claim upon those of us who are not its potential mother?" And what do these moral claims mean? At the point at which a pregnancy becomes a civil, political, public *concern* (if there is a legitimate point at which this occurs, the Supreme Court says that it is after the second trimester), does it not also become a civil, political, public *claim?* (By "concern" I mean an issue that is something that the body politic may rightly debate and respond to legislatively; by "claim" I mean a situation that requires a material response by the body politic, rather than an ideological or legal one.) Rather than narrowly focusing on the responsiblity of the potential mother to produce a healthy child and then criminalizing her behavior for failing to honor this responsibility, are we not all responsible for creating a world where all children can be born healthy? For instance, insuring the continued funding of the Women and Infant Children Program (while lobbying for vegetable protein substitutes to heavily relied upon dairy products), funding of prenatal care, child-care provisions, elimination of environmental carcinogens, etc.

A poignant case illustrates what occurs as a result of the narrow definition of moral claims: the US government believes in animal experimentation. Funds are given to make animals drug addicts. Meanwhile, funds are cut for drug detox centers. A pregnant woman is refused admittance at a drug detox center because they have no room as a result of budget cuts. She stays hooked on drugs, and is then charged with endangering the life of of her yet-unborn child.

The lack of social responsibility to the legitimate claims of living beings is appalling and interwoven.

Premise 6
Identification with the Vulnerable
Requires Defining Vulnerability

Some animal defenders and antiabortionists share an intense identification with those they perceive as vulnerable. What determines whether they will identify with the vulnerable, voiceless unprotected fetus instead of the vulnerable, unprotected lab animal, veal calf, or pound animal?

To examine this fully is beyond the scope of this preliminary exploration, but a few issues should be flagged. Andrea Dworkin's *Right-wing Women* makes a compelling case that the reasons women become involved in the antiabortion movement are because they are aware of the immense amount of antiwoman violence in the world, and by situating themselves within the matrix of the traditional family and its values, they are assured of a form of protectionism (or so they think).[19] However, the motivations for men involved in the antiabortion movement are very different. Recent profiles of the men who lead "Operation Rescue"—the group that is using civil disobedience in its attempts to prevent women from entering abortion clinics—revealed that the men see feminists as responsible for their downward mobility, and blame working women for their own economic troubles. They take this extreme hostility into the antiabortion movement, not—as their rhetoric proclaims—to protect the "unborn" but to punish those whom they hold responsible for their social standing. This successfully protects the men from having to develop any economic analysis that might place the blame for their situation elsewhere.[20]

Is there also a dissimilarity in the reasons men versus women become involved in animal defense? Given that the majority of animal defenders are women, does this not in itself say something? Women understand what it means to be deprived of freedom based on biological differences. We know that Western culture has situated women on the boundary of what is fully human, thus women have a very good reason to examine what our culture does to the other animals, while being suspicious of its control of women.

Premise 7
Abortion Rights Contributes to a Nonanthropocentric Ethic

Antiabortionists absolutize each individual fetus. They are deeply anthropocentric in their valorizing of the human fetus. But in a world in which we are attempting to learn how to be in relationship with the rest of nature rather than be triumphantly (though shortsightedly) dominant over nature, the presumption that every fetus should become a human being is glaringly anthropocentric. It ignores the increasing demands upon the environment made by each addition to the developed world. (I say developed world since my focus is on the debate in the United States, and children born in this country consume the world's resources to a much greater degree than children born in other parts of the world.)[21] As John Cobb remarks, "It may be a legitimate criticism . . . to say that the pro-[fetal] life movement has been insensitive to the needs of all forms of life except the human."[22] Rosemary Ruether observes that "the decisions to limit the number of births, both for one's own family and as a part of a global community, is as much a decision for

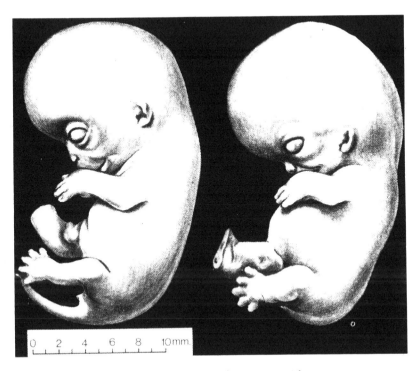

Figure 6: Monkey and Human Embryos

life and for a more adequate distribution of the means of life as is the struggle to end the arms race."[23]

Animal defense relativizes the human species. This is why antiabortionists feel betrayed by it. By relativizing the human species, it also relativizes the human fetus. (See Figure 6 for an example of the relativizing of the human fetus. Note: This example did not arise from within the animal defense movement, but from a feminist examination of the antiabortion movement.) Animal defense and environmental activism are nonanthropocentric. The sacredness of human life is placed within a new paradigm, the sacredness of the earth and its creatures.[24] Given this paradigm shift it becomes more difficult to argue that every human fetus is equally or more important than the earth and its creatures that its birth will impact. This nonanthropocentrism is deeply threatening to antiabortionists and accounts for some of the many instances in which animal defenders are accosted by antiabortionists.

The human/animal dualism undergirds the anthropocentrism of antiabortionists. Eliminate that foundational dualism, and the moral claims of antiabortionists, that human fetal life has an absolute claim upon us, is overthrown. Instead, human fetal life is placed in a new context: legitmate concern for the rest of nature, including its nonhuman creatures.[25]

As I was writing this chapter, I received a note from an animal defender who had just had an abortion. Her letter illustrated this nonanthropocentric commitment as it described her decision-making process when she discovered she was pregnant. She went first to adoption agencies and inquired whether they screened for vegetarians or animal rights activists. She did not want to give birth to someone who would be brought up to oppress animals and exploit the environment. After discovering that there was no possible guarantee that any child she might bear and give up for adoption would not consume or exploit animals, she determined to have an abortion.

One of the best things we can do for the animals is to stop mandatorily filling the world with people, especially in industrialized nations where 22 percent of the world's population consume 70 percent of the world's resources.

Premise 8
A Striking Similarity Exists in the
Medical Profession's Role in Making Abortion Illegal
and in Opposing Antivivisectionism

Some animal defenders say, look at the association between the medical industrial complex and abortion rights.[26] Animal defenders are rightly suspicious of the lobbying efforts of this complex, knowing full well its goal to distort the basic message of those who seek to end the exploitation of animals.[27] But an appeal to animal defenders' legitimate distrust of the medical establishment, by equating medical doctors with abortion rights, distorts feminists' distrust of the medical profession. It also masks the sordid history of the medical profession in criminalizing abortion in the first place. Once we get beyond the rhetoric, what we see is that the AMA's current stance regarding animal experimentation recalls not a proabortion stance, but their antiabortion stance of the early nineteenth century.

Before the middle of the nineteenth century, abortion before "quickening" (when the pregnant woman first felt the fetus move) was an accepted part of the common law of this country. By the end of the century, abortion had been criminalized. This effort was led not by the clergy but by medical professionals. In fact, "American public opinion tolerated the practice of abortion in 1850, and few people outside the medical profession called for its suppression as a social evil."[28] Why did the medical profession act this way? Numerous reasons are offered:

- The growth of irregular practitioners. Medical doctors saw the irregulars offering a service that women wanted, and feared losing their patients. "The best way out of these dilemmas was to persuade state legislators to make abortion a criminal offense."[29]
- An increase in abortions: an estimated one out of three to one out of five pregnancies at this time ended in abortion.
- Nativism and the perception that abortion was being used by married women to limit their families. "Most regular physicians were white, native-born, Protestants of British and North European stock. And so, as they constantly reiterated for twenty years between 1860 and 1880 were most of the women having abortions. The doctors both used and were influenced by blatant nativism. . . . There can be little doubt that Protestants' fears about not keeping up with the reproductive rates of Catholic immigrants played a greater role in the drive for antiabortion laws in nineteenth-century American than Catholic opposition to abortion did."[30]
- Physicians were also very threatened by the change in women's roles. "Regular physicians were among the most defensive groups in the country on the subject of changing traditional sex roles. . . . To many doctors the chief purpose of women was to produce children; anything that interfered with that purpose, or allowed women to 'indulge' themselves in less important activities, threatened marriage, the family, and the future of society itself. Abortion was a supreme example of such an interference for these physicians."[31]

The medical profession, in redefining abortion from an accepted part of the common law, demonstrated the motives and strategies now apparent in the debate about animal experimentation.

They acted through their organization, rather than independently. In fact, through the politics of their antiabortionism they sought to increase the status of medical doctors and to professionalize medicine, as well as to exclude women from obtaining a medical education. Their provivisection commitment also represents an organizational strategy.

They claimed that they had information that no one else had, increasing their status and their control. This politics of knowledge appears in the debate about animal experimentation as well. We are told that medical doctors know something we do not and thus their words should carry more weight than a layperson's. This mystifies knowledge by claiming that only they, "the experts," can truly know the issues: when life begins, for instance, or the knowledge we can get from animal "models."

They used the politics of professionalization to act in their own self-interest. They used the issue of abortion and the claim to special knowledge to establish themselves as *the* medical professionals during a time of laissez-faire government and a proliferation of medical options. Physicians did not actually outlaw abortion in the nineteenth century as much as create "a category of 'justifiable' abortion" and make themselves the custodian of it.[32] The creation of the "therapeutic" abortion exception, a product of the nineteenth century, left in the hands of the medical profession the decision about who could get an abortion. Thus, abortion became "medicalized" in the nineteenth century. Some feminists argue for lay abortion, claiming that the procedure is neither complex nor life-threatening.[33] The Jane collective of Chicago is notable for proving the effectiveness of lay-performed abortion. The growth of the medical industry, including that aspect of it that engages in biomedical research, must be seen not only in relationship to women as consumers, but also to the centuries-long replacement/usurpation of women as healers, midwives and abortionists. When the medical field was *professionalized,* it was also *masculinized.*

Premise 9
Animal Defenders' Antiviolence Stance
Should Align It with Women

Animal defense has been entangled with the false labels of what constitutes violence in the debate about abortion: either we are consistent and thus antiabortion (because abortion is violent) or we are inconsistent and prochoice. I bemoan the shortsightedness of these standards for both consistency and nonviolence. The presumption is that this definition of nonviolence is the acceptable one, and it is applied to a continuum that looks something like this:

violence of war . . .

violence against people . . .

violence against fetuses . . .

violence against animals . . .

But there is another continuum, one that only becomes visible when we take women's lives and experiences seriously. It is the continuum of violence against women:

child sexual abuse . . .
rape, including marital rape . . .
woman-battering . . .[34]
Intercourse and consequent pregnancies are often not a choice in women's lives. When I declare that animals and women ought to have the right to self-determination about when they wish to be pregnant and not be forced into birthing babies against their will, it is argued that animals have no choice, but women enter freely into sexual intercourse. This is simply not true. To ignore that human female animals are abused and coerced is as nearsighted as when humans ignore the fact that non-human animals are abused to benefit the self-interest of people.

Those who wish to open up the discussion of unacceptable violence to forms of violence enacted by people against people (and against potential persons) need to register their concern for the actual, real people whose lives are often ignored when theory is developed—women. The absence of attention to the extensive sexual violence against women and children mystifies this experience by ignoring it. It makes any abortion stance based on a sense of nonviolence hypocritical. It also ignores the violence of enforced pregnancy.

As long as women and animals are ontologized as usable (rapable on the one hand and consumable on the other) both animal defense and abortion rights will be necessary. Both women and animals are ends for themselves, not means for others.

Premise 10
The Argument about Nonbeing Reveals the Subjective Male Stance

The argument of nonbeing goes like this: isn't it better that a cow was brought to life, was allowed to live many years on this earth, and then quickly dispatched, then never to have lived at all? And animal defenders have argued back that one can not experience nonbeing. A cow who never existed does not experience the deprivation of life.

Only those of us who are living can sentimentalize the idea of life without us. Rather than looking forward to the fact that we will not exist in the future because of death, we cast our eyes backwards and think, what if we never existed? We then apply this intensely self-possessed question to ethical issues; and the self possessed with this question is usually the human male subject.

People, but especially men, think that abortion exists as a retroactive comment on their own existence. Thus, whenever abortion is debated, someone stands up and says, "I am glad I was not aborted." This is not the issue. This argument personalizes a state that does not exist—nonbeing—and by appearing to be a rational argument fosters the same reaction when the issue is animal defense.

To conclude, animals have a right to their own lives no matter what we as human beings wish them to do or be for us and a woman needs access to abortion for whatever reasons she chooses not to bear a specific pregnancy. Abortion rights and animal defense make sense together.

4

On Beastliness and a Politics of Solidarity

When animals figure, or can easily be thought of as figuring, in binary oppositions; *they invariably represent the negative term in the opposition:* "the Other, the Beast, the Brute."
—Steve Baker

While juxtaposing and reconciling abortion rights and animal defense is a necessary effort, both movements are actually situated within wider contexts: abortion, within the context of reproductive freedom, and animal defense within the context of challenging all forms of social oppression. Issues related to reproductive freedom indicate the way that social oppression is experienced by women of different races and classes.[1] Situating animal defense within an analysis of social oppression enlarges Alice Walker's recognition that "we are all one lesson."

But a major problem remains: While the reproductive freedom movement clearly arises from and speaks to the experience of women of color, many people of color and some progressive whites eye the animal defense movement with suspicion. The animal defense movement is thought to result from and enact forms of race and class privilege, providing an opportunity for some whites to ignore issues of social oppression. Do white animal defenders put themselves in the place of the animals, thus allowing them not to deal with the privilege they have vis-à-vis other humans? Do white animal defenders identify with animal victims of human privilege because this is a privilege they are willing to foreswear, but not with victims of race and class privilege because these are privileges they wish to maintain? Do white animal defenders betray a lack of empathy if a factory-farmed pig or vivisected monkey can be empathized with but not humans whose faces are at the bottom of society's well?[2] Moreover, because animals' voices cannot be a part of the theorizing of the animal defense movement, has animal defense developed a resistance politics vis-à-vis animals that in relationship to oppressed humans might enact paternalism? Can resistance be translated to solidarity?

Granted animal defense currently is characterized by a "whitened center"—its theorists and national leaders are white, and many are men.[3] All whites are bonded by racism, as bell hooks points out,[4] and it is understandable that when a group of white people come together, the suspicion will arise that it is this whiteness that is the bond that brings people together. But, while predominantly white, the animal defense movement is not a monolithic movement, nor is it necessarily inscribing any "culture of whiteness" in its efforts on behalf of animals.[5] However, anyone not actively resisting racist oppression can be seen as condoning white supremacy. If white animal defenders fail to support challenges to social oppression, the people who will be hurt are those who lack resources. White animal defenders cannot ignore the piece that each is a part of in relationship to others who suffer social oppression.

The Politics of *Otherness*

I have argued that the paradigmatic cultural relationship in the West is one of subject to object. The power differentials that allow some subjects to treat other subjects as objects rotate upon the concept and function of *otherness*. Otherness unites those with power who can declare their similarities to be decisive. Simultaneously, otherness establishes as irrevocable whatever differences have become markers of this otherness (i.e., differences based on sex, race, or species). The process that Zuleyma Tang Halpin observes in scientific objectivity is generalizable to the view of any one in a dominant position in a class-, race-, sex-, and species-stratified culture: "The 'other,' by definition, is the opposite of the 'self,' and therefore comes to be regarded as intrinsically of lesser value."[6] Caroline Whitbeck identifies this as a "self-other *opposition* that underlines much of so-called 'western thought.'"[7]

Concerning the construction of otherness through race, Kimberlé Crenshaw argues: "Racism helps create an illusion of unity through the oppositional force of a symbolic 'other.' The establishment of an 'other' creates a bond, a burgeoning common identity of all non-stigmatized parties—whose identity and interests are defined in opposition to the other." Crenshaw points out that this dynamic of otherness is enthroned within the maintenance and perpetuation of white race consciousness because, "by focusing on a distinct, subordinate 'other,' whites include themselves in the dominant circle—an arena in which most hold no real power, but only their privileged race identity."[8] The designation of otherness empowers by affirming a superficial sameness within one's subgroup.

The Animalizing Discourse of White Racism

If otherness provides entitlement to those who position themselves as the same, the concept of the beast functions to justify perceiving some people as other and disempowering them. The marker of attributed beastliness, of less-than-humanness, exists to constitute whiteness as well as human maleness. One cannot discuss the idea that some people are situated between man and beast without acknowledging the way that white supremacist beliefs depicted people of color in general and Africans and African-Americans in specific: as not (white) man and (almost) beast. Although all people of color have been bestialized, I am going to focus on the experience of African-Americans because that is what I have had personal experience with. While I do see the bestializing racist discourse against African-Americans as representative and instructive, I do not believe nor do I wish to imply that the experiences of all peoples of color are interchangeable.

Euro-American human maleness used the "less-than-human" definitions to demarcate racial as well as sexual differences, to institutionalize racism as well as sexism. Regarding the term "nigger," Toni Morrison observes that it "occupies a territory between man and animal and thus withholds specificity even while marking it."[9]

Delores Williams asserts that the antiblack arguments of the 1800s, in which blacks were classified with monkeys, (though as "'the noblest of the beast creation'"[10]) helped "to mould an American consciousness about the Negro that even today regards black people as beasts, female and male. Therefore, black women (and black men) can be abused and treated like animals rather than like humans."[11] In the prevailing dualistic ontology, equation of any human group with the other animals serves to facilitate the humans' exploitation. As Halpin points out, "Even when groups labeled 'inferior' are not explicitly equated with women, they are often compared to animals, usually in ways designed to make them appear more animal than human (using white males as the prototype of humanity)."[12]

By viewing African-Americans as black beasts, Euro-American men created two pornographic scenarios, one about rapacious black men lusting for white women, and one about lascivious black women available to anyone, man or beast. Both concepts interacted with the notion of white women as pure, virginal and sexless: "Black womanhood was polarized against white womanhood in the structure of the metaphoric system of female sexuality, particularly through the association of black women with overt sexuality and taboo sexual practices."[13] Black men were seen as beasts, sexually threatening white womanhood, a white womanhood defined to aggrandize the sense of white manhood. Black women were seen as sexed, as not able to be violated because they would enjoy anything—including sex with animals. Kimberlé Crenshaw explains how "rape and other sexual abuses were justified by myths that black women were sexually voracious, that they were sexually indiscriminate, and that they readily copulated with animals, most frequently imagined to be apes and monkeys."[14] Indeed, Winthrop Jordan concludes that "The sexual union of apes and Negroes was *always* conceived as involving *female Negroes* and *male apes! Apes* had intercourse with Negro *women.*"[15] Such representations excused as well as invited sexual exploitation by white men.[16] These representations still animate white racism today, from the fact that "men who assault black women are the least likely to receive jail time,"[17] to the continuing strength of the image of the black male rapist of white women (in fact this is statistically the least likely rape situation).

Antiracist Encounters with the Animalizing Discourse

I myself witnessed the way that the "neither man nor beast" figuration that racializes *and* animalizes gender while engendering *and* animalizing race is enacted toward black men and women. In 1977, I became the director of a not-for-profit agency that worked predominantly with welfare recipients, farm workers, and resettled farm workers. I formed an advisory board consisting of representatives from these groups to create some accountability for my work. When, at the first meeting, I asked what concerns existed in the community, the issue that predominated was the need for decent, affordable housing. Simultaneously, a low-income housing project slated to be built in a largely white part of town was turned down by the white city government. I learned that whites had gone door-to-door in the neighborhood where the housing was to be built, asking "Do you want your daughter to be raped by black men?" Here was the archetypal rape scenario for white racists—the specter of the black male rapist that had been used as an excuse for lynching black businessmen and other independent black men earlier in the century— called into service to defeat needed low-income housing. It became the organizing, but rarely acknowledged, mythology in our community.

This scare tactic, of course, did not tell the truth about rapes: the most frequent form of rape is rape by acquaintances—husbands, ex-husbands, lovers, and boyfriends.[18] *Women have the most to fear from men we know.* The racist mythology makes black men the scapegoats of the dominant culture's refusal to acknowledge the fact of women's lack of intraracial safety. And in the force of the mythology of black-on-white rape, the material, emotional, and spiritual needs of rape victims who are women of color are usually neglected. The *fear* of random black-on-white violence triumphs over the *fact* of intraracial woman-abuse and white-on-black rape as a form of racial terrorism:[19] "When Black women were raped by white males, they were being raped not as women generally, but as Black women specifically: Their femaleness made them sexually vulnerable to racist domination, while their Blackness effectively denied them any protection. This white male power was reinforced by a judicial system in which the successful conviction of a white man for raping a Black woman was virtually unthinkable."[20]

Paul Hock's *White Hero, Black Beast* observes that "The threatened assault of the ever erect black buck on the chaste white lady has dominated the mythologies of the American south for more than three centuries."[21] But in fact, these events were unfolding in a small city in upstate New York. My ten years of activism against the white racism of this community and in solidarity with African-American leaders began at this time. Predictably, racist, sexist whites responded to my involvement in this antiracist work with venom. Two examples stand out as I reflect on the way they positioned black men as neither man nor beast. At one of the organizational meetings of whites who were opposed to the housing, white men were heard discussing "Carol Adams and her big black bucks." [*Buck:* "The adult male of some animals, such as the deer, antelope, or rabbit. . . . *Offensive.* Used as a disparaging term for a Native American or Black man." (*The American Heritage Dictionary of the English Language*)]

One of the local radio stations was owned by a man involved with this racist white group. A small-town Howard Stern, his freewheeling talk show included discussions about me. One caller conjectured that the reason I had kept my maiden name upon marrying was because I was married to a black man (white racist logic for why a white woman would disavow her husband's name!). The dilemma I then faced was this: if I said "no I am not married to a black man," this response would be interpreted as perpetuating a form of racism for it would appear that I was disavowing the idea that I might marry a black man. On the other hand, if I reacted by not dealing with it, by not responding to this salacious interest in my life, this nonresponse would allow it to remain a secret. As a secret, it would then feed their speculation about my motives. Either way, their concern was "what kind of man is she attached to?" Their desire was to place me within a male-identified environment, while also looking for a way to discredit me.[22]

White racists could only explain my activism by salaciously sexualizing both my black colleagues and me, seemingly confirming Joel Kovel's observation about racism being inherently sexualized. Citing the charges of rape against black men for touching, approaching, looking at, being imagined to have looked at, talking back to, etc., a white woman, Kovel reports, "A mountain of evidence has accumulated to document the basically sexualized nature of racist psychology."[23] Neither the African-American men nor I could be granted the notion of acting out of motives other than sexual ones. Because of my antiracist work, I could no longer be positioned as an innocent white girl, like those in the white neighborhood who supposedly stood ready targets for the rapacious black man. I was now, not virgin, but whore. But still, I, a white person, was given "possession" (through the possessive "her" in the reference to "her big black bucks") of the African-American men in these white men's fantasies. I, a white woman, was granted greater subjectivity and individuality than the black men being referred to. Completely erased in these white racist discourses were the black women, who were, in fact, the majority of the plaintiffs in the lawsuit. These were forms of our community's unsophisticated "low-tech lynchings." Indeed, George M. Fredrickson argues that "the only way to meet criticisms of the unspeakably revolting practice of lynching was to contend that many Negroes were literally wild beasts, with unconventional sexual passions and criminal natures stamped by heredity."[24] By animalizing blacks, the dehumanizing and destructive violence of lynching could be justified. And just so today, any racism that bestializes its victims enables its own self-justification.

Conceptualizing Freedom—
The Anthropocentric and Racist Way

In a hierarchical social order, being associated with animals functions as a marker of a group's disempowerment and their availability for economic and social exploitation. Winthrop Jordan argues that the Negro-ape association functioned "as a means of expressing the social distance between the Negro and the white man." He cautions, however, that "American colonials no more thought Negroes were beasts than did European scientists and missionaries; if they had *really* thought so they would have sternly punished miscegenation for what it would have been—buggery [i.e., bestiality]."[25] No, what white American culture required was a people whom they could compare with animals, but who were not animals.

A people who are treated like animals but who are not animals, a people of color who were unfree in a country that proclaimed as its central principles freedom and democracy, such marked people offer potent self-referential possibilities for white people. As Toni Morrison asserts, "For in the construction of blackness *and* enslavement could be found not only the not-free but also, with the dramatic polarity created by skin color, the projection of the not-me."[26] Morrison identifies "the parasitical nature of white freedom"[27]: white Americans knew they were free because of the enslaved Africans in their midst. White freedom and black slavery were interdependent. Morrison explains, "The concept of freedom did not emerge in a vacuum. Nothing highlighted freedom—if it did not in fact create it—like slavery."[28] As Alice Walker's epigraph to this book observes about Blue, the horse: "And it *would* have to be a *white* horse; the very image of freedom." Morrison makes this painfully and unavoidably clear.

The debasement of the other animals is so complete that, unlike racially-marked humans, they offer no such conceptual counterweight to notions of freedom. Notions of freedom applied to animals? The idea seems preposterous because many think animals have no consciousness to render such a concept meaningful or applicable to them. (This of course also explains why arguments for "animal rights" and "animal liberation" are so often ridiculed.) The potency of the interdependent nature of freedom and slavery derives from the fact that enslaved *humans* reflect back an enhanced human status to those who are free, an enhancement the species barrier clearly prevents objectified and exploited animals from offering.

It is conventionally said that oppression *dehumanizes,* that it reduces humans to animal status. But oppression cannot dehumanize animals. Animals exist categorically as that which is not human; they are not acknowledged as having human qualities that can then be denied. The presumption of an ontological absence of such human qualities has a priori defined animals as nonhuman.

Resistance against oppression for humans involves recognizing and preserving their "humanity." But, it is a humanity established through a form of negating: just as white Americans knew they were free by the presence of enslaved blacks, so oppressed humans affirm their humanity by proclaiming their distance from the animals whom they are compared to, treated like, but never truly are. A litany of protests erupt from those struggling against oppression, proclamations that assert "we are not beasts, we are humans, not animals!" Given the anthropocentric nature of Western culture's primary conceptualizations, this response is not surprising. As I indicated in the preface, this has been an assertion upon which feminists early staked their appeal for our rights and freedom.

Racist and sexist attitudes expose an elastic, mobile species definition that always advantages elite white males by positioning others as almost beasts. Will antiracist and anti-sexist theory so conclusively accept the inescapable anthropocentricity of the human/animal divide that the result will be a fixed species definition that clearly demarcates *once and for all,* all humans as human beings, thus tacitly but firmly positioning all other animals as "animals"? Consider the synonyms for beast offered by *The American Heritage Dictionary of the English Language* (Third Edition): *"brute, animal, brutish, brutal, beastly, beastial.* These adjectives apply to what is more characteristic of lower animals than of human beings." Will oppositional movements insure that these adjectives always apply only to animals, and thus inscribe as well the hierarchy that positions animals as lower?

Interlocking Systems of Domination

In the preface I argued that an alternative to liberal feminism would be a progressive feminist position that calls the human/animal dualism into question, rather than resituating any of the players from one side of the dualism to the other. But a radical resituating of players actually is called for—it just doesn't rotate upon the human/animal dualism in such a way that it affirms universal differences and absolute otherness. Rather, in and through this resituating, color will lose its character as a barrier, just as "animals" will lose their otherness, and join human animals as a "we" rather than a "they" or a collective of "its." The questions we will need to address in the face of such radical resituating will not be about what constitutes "animalness" and who is an animal. But, given that some people and all animals have been cast as "others," the question will be how to think of ourselves as a "we" without being imperialist or essentialist, without disregarding the particularities of our lives.[29]

Because my goal has been to challenge the values of the dominant culture—and place our individual actions within this challenge—I try to maintain a macroanalysis of culture rather than a microcritique of the individual that could be potentially experienced as an attack. That is why, for instance, in chapter 6, "The Feminist Traffic in Animals," I address the issue of what foods should be served at feminist *conferences.* I believe conversations about issues associated with the defense of animals can occur; I do not think they can be imposed from outside but they grow from a common base of working together on issues that arise from within the community. They must grow organically from the ground where we recognize our common commitments to justice. But white animal defenders will have to relinquish ownership over concepts such as "animals do matter" since they may be changed by different contexts.[30]

Our concern must be with narratives that have meaning within communities, not that are usurped to further a different agenda. The model for such discussions can be found in the recognition that identity is not additive: for instance, one is not a woman ± black ± poor. Kimberlé Crenshaw explains the failure of the additive approach this way: "Because the intersectional experience is greater than the sum of racism and sexism, any analysis that does not take intersectionality into account cannot sufficiently address the particular manner in which black women are subordinated."[31] Patricia Hill Collins argues that

> Additive models of oppression are firmly rooted in the either/or dichotomous thinking of Eurocentric, masculinist thought. . . . Instead of starting with gender and then adding in other variables such as age, sexual orientation, race, social class, and religion, Black feminist thought sees these distinctive systems of oppression as being part of one overarching structure of domination. . . . The significance of seeing race, class, and gender as interlocking systems of oppression is that such an approach fosters a paradigmatic shift of thinking inclusively about other oppressions, such as age, sexual orientation, religion, and ethnicity.[32]

Focusing attention on how oppressions interconnect creates the space for raising the issue of animals. When we recognize that identity is not additive, we begin to concentrate on what bell hooks calls "interlocking systems of domination," a "politic of domination." This latter term refers both to the systems and "to the ideological ground that they share, which is a belief in domination, and belief in notions of superior and inferior, which are components of all of those systems. For me it's like a house, they share the foundation, but the foundation is the ideological beliefs around which notions of domination are constructed."[33] Similarly, feminist theologian and biblical scholar Elisabeth Schüssler Fiorenza does not identify patriarchy as male–female domination, but argues that "one must construe the term in the classical sense, specifically, as a complex pyramidal political structure of dominance and subordination, stratified by gender, race, class, religious and cultural taxonomies, and other historical formations of domination."[34]

Just as identity is not additive but interlocking, so I am not interested as much in analogies between the status of oppressed humans and the status of animals as I am interested in intersections. Analogies on their own can be parasitical. But in intersectional thinking we apprehend the shared ideological beliefs that exist as the foundation of a white supremacist and speciesist patriarchy. For instance, the analysis of racism against African-Americans points both to the specific way attitudes toward animals intersect with human oppression, and grounds the rejection of the additive notion of oppression. But, as the dictionary definition of *buck* revealed an offensive term against both black and Native American men, just so any peoples of color may be—and have been—targets of white supremacy's politics of domination. When white racism uses an animalizing discourse against black people, it demonstrates the way supremacist ideology inscribes intersecting forms of otherness (race and species). The foundation of such ideological practices has undergirded racist treatment of other people of color as well. It is important therefore, always to keep one's perspective on both the methodology of oppression and the configuration of the oppressor. Ecofeminism offers such an approach.

Ecofeminism and Solidarity

Ecofeminism recognizes the maldistribution of wealth and power and its relationship to the abuse of nature. Social domination and the domination of nature are interdependent. Moreover, an ecofeminist approach finds common ground with the environmental activism of people of color who have defined, exposed, and are challenging environmental racism.[35] In describing ecofeminism's focus, Karen J. Warren has identified a "logic of domination" in which differences are deemed to carry meanings of superiority and inferiority and that which is morally superior is morally justified in subordinating that which is not:

> Ecofeminists insist that the sort of logic of domination used to justify the domination of humans by gender, racial, or ethnic, or class status is also used to justify the domination of nature [naturism]. Because eliminating a logic of domination is part of a feminist critique— whether a critique of patriarchy, white supremacist culture, or imperialism—ecofeminists insist that *naturism* is properly viewed as an integral part of any feminist solidarity movement to end sexist oppression and the logic of domination which conceptually grounds it.[36]

The logic of domination undergirds the creation of the other: When others—"not-me's"—are demarcated as "less than" or "lower" because of reified differences, we know to look for some exclusively-defined sameness constituting and empowering the domination of "me's" through negation.

Ecofeminism does not presuppose or posit a unitary voice of women. Its theory-making and activism is global in perspective and authorship. We are not talking about a unity with other women that would erase differences among us, nor enable us to flatten the various experiences that arise from these differences.[37] We are talking about solidarity against an "othering" that motivates and justifies oppression. In recognizing the interlocking systems of oppression and its othering discourse, one sees that, as Alice Walker argues, "we are one lesson." Then our understanding of any individual experience of oppression finds its appropriate framework.

Within systems of oppression we may at times be victims, and at other times beneficiaries, of oppression, if not ourselves oppressors. Euro-Americans who defend animals must acknowledge these multiple identities and precisely how each is a beneficiary of a racist and classist system. So too must men acknowledge how they benefit from patriarchal systems of domination. Within a framework of the interlocking systems of domination, privilege and oppression co-exist. We may ourselves be oppressed by a white supremacist patriarchy and yet also benefit from the oppression of others, especially animals.

Fleshing Out the Connections

Just as there was a material basis motivating the lynchings of black businessmen, so material reasons lie behind the dehumanizing politics of white racism. Desire to control (and justify control) of land and resources often motivates bestializing discourses. Furthermore, the image of beast is connected to performing manual labor. Beasts of burdens, especially mules and oxen, do mindless, heavy labor; the presumption that people of color were most capable of doing manual labor, is one aspect *and* result of the projection of beast upon them. As Patricia Hill Collins comments, "While the sexual and racist dimensions of being treated like an animal are important, the economic foundation underlying this treatment is critical. Animals can be economically exploited, worked, sold, killed, and consumed."[38] Precisely here—in the material production of flesh from animals who are sold, killed, and consumed—can we find the current-day enaction of the effects of a bestializing discourse that designated people of color as manual laborers.

There are approximately fifty-four-thousand nonunionized North American meatpacking workers—almost all of whom are women with a high school education or less, of black, Hispanic, or French-speaking ethnic background. Meatpacking is considered one of the ten worst jobs in the United States, it sounds especially so for women: "Perdue's slaughterhouse workers are mostly poor women who work for approximately $5.50/hour. One North Carolina worker said, 'Most of us treat our pets better . . . than Perdue treats its workers.' She detailed filthy working conditions, sexual harassment and ignored or poorly treated employee injuries."[39]

The flesh packing industry has become increasingly centralized. A few large corporations that are strongly antiunion have driven down industry wages and benefits. Increased technology has permitted an industry-wide speedup, and resulted in some of the most dangerous jobs in America.[40] Meatpacking accounts for the second highest rate of personal injury of any occupation in America.[41] According to the U.S. Department of Labor, "almost one-fourth of the workforce in the poultry industry suffers each year from industrial injuries."[42] Partly because of the frequent injuries, the annual U.S. and Canadian meatpacking plant employee turnover rate is around 60 percent, running as high as 100 percent in poultry plants. Eleanor Kennelly of the United Food and Commerical Workers Union (UFCW), observed that "A meat-packing plant is like nothing you've ever seen or could imagine. It's like a vision of hell."[43] A fire in a chicken processing plant in North Carolina in 1991, resulted in the death of twenty-five workers, most of whom were poor women.

Ninety-five percent of all poultry workers are black women who face carpal tunnel syndrome and other disorders caused by repetitive motion and stress. As "lung gunners," each hour they must scrape the insides of five thousand chickens' cavities and pull out the recently slaughtered chickens' lungs.[44] Most workers who produce dead animals for consumption have not actively chosen these jobs: as African-American activist and writer Beverly Smith observes about the poor black women who work in chicken factories: "Their health was tremendously compromised by what they were doing, but they didn't have control over how they were going to earn a living, or over their work lives. It's not like they decided, 'Well, I'll clean toilets even though I could be a corporate lawyer' or 'I'll go cut up chickens though I could go and be a college professor.'"[45]

The mass term of *meat* accomplishes something else besides euphemizing the process of destruction that enables corpse consumption: it conceals the fact that this process does not happen naturally. Who does the dominant culture employ to effect this destruction? Those most oppressed because of race, sex, and class are those who become the mediators, the transformers of animals into food. Here we can see the interlocking system of domination at work, as it intersects sex, class, race, *and* species oppression. Rosemary Ruether observes that environmental exploitation is not unmediated: "The exploitation of natural resources does not take place in an unmediated way. It takes place through the domination of the bodies of some people by other people."[46]

Defending Animals:
A Progressive, Antiracist Possibility

A progressive, antiracist defense of animals locates itself at the point of intersection of race, class, sex, and species. At this point of intersection, the defense of animals will not be sentimental, but rather it will be filled with sentiment. To be sentimental is to identify, in a limited and limiting way, with the victim and with innocence lost. As I indicated in the last chapter, this plays exactly into a profetal life discourse. It also enacts a controlling patriarchal response that believes in the necessity of avenging anyone under men's protection in a way that recalls white men "avenging" white womanhood by lynching black men.

Sentiment, genuine concern, enacts feminist ethics; it understands what brought about the victimization, and does not ignore our own complex roles within the structures of social oppression. Our goal cannot be to paternalistically advocate for and avenge the "innocent," but to think systematically about the politics of domination. Nor can we attempt to make connections by ripping experience from its history, for instance by claiming that it is a "Holocaust of animals;" this does harm to Holocaust survivors. We must locate our ethic for animals so that it does not hurt people who are oppressed.

My argument about not using animals may be heard as one of ideological purity. But it is not that. The instrumental view of animals that concerns me arises within Western developed culture, in which a discourse of otherness has been used to maintain dominance. My critique is aimed at that dominance. The Cartesian dualism of human/animal, soul/body that inscribes animals as useable is not a legacy of most native peoples. Conversations with native peoples will be different because the ontological positioning of animals in their cultures is different. It is not my goal to condemn the diet of the Inuit, nor weigh in against the fishing rights struggles of native people in North America.[47] Such a stance would not represent the dialogical nature of solidarity, nor would it enact solidarity because it would continue to deflect attention from the oppressive colonial system that has betrayed relationships with native people.

Defense of animals can be embedded in progressive ecofeminist, antiracist work. I envision a rejection of the human/animal dualism as well as a rejection of a dualistic politics that implies we may be for humans or for animals but not for both. Yet, given that oppression works against humans by dehumanizing and animalizing, then attempts at creating a solidarity politics that includes animals runs the risks of appearing to continue that analogy. That is, from a humanocentric perspective of oppressed peoples who have been, if not equated with animals, treated like animals, the introduction of animals to resistance politics suggests that, once again, even in resistance, humans are being equated with animals. But again this is a result of thinking analogically, of seeing oppression as additive, rather than of comprehending the interlocking systems of domination. Patriarchy would suggest we were adding animals on, and through this suggestion keep us from seeing the politics of domination. The arrogant eye resists self-examination.

Part 2

"We Are One Lesson": Transforming Feminist Theory

A small girl and her mother passed a statue depicting a European man who had barehandedly subdued a ferocious lion. The little girl stopped, looked puzzled and asked, "Mama, something's wrong with that statue. Everybody knows that a man can't whip a lion." "But darling," her mother replied, "you must remember that the man made the statue."

—As told by Katie Cannon

[The question is] how to effect a political transformation when the terms of the transformation are given by the very order which a revolutionary practice seeks to change.

—Jacqueline Rose, *Sexuality in the Field of Vision*

5

Ecofeminism and the Eating of Animals

> JEAN: Would you feel raping a woman's all right if it was happening to her and not to you?
> BARBIE: No, I'd feel like it was happening to me.
> JEAN: Well, that's how some of us feel about animals.
> —1976 conversation about feminism and vegetarianism

Ecofeminism identifies a series of dualisms: culture/nature; male/female; self/other; white/nonwhite; rationality/emotion. Some include humans/animals in this series. According to ecofeminist theory, nature has been dominated by culture; female has been dominated by male; people of color have been dominated by white people; emotion has been dominated by rationality; animals . . .

Where are *animals* in ecofeminist theory and practice?

I maintain that contemporary ecofeminist discourse, while potentially adequate to deal with the issue of animals, is now inadequate because it fails to give consistent conceptual place to the domination of animals as a significant aspect of the domination of nature.[1] I will examine seven answers ecofeminists could give for not including animals explicitly in ecofeminist analyses and show how a persistent patriarchal ideology regarding animals as instruments has kept the experience of animals from being fully incorporated within ecofeminism. I will defend these claims by appealing, in part, to interviews I conducted in 1976 of more than seventy vegetarian members of the Cambridge-Boston women's community.[2] These interviews are intended to provide direct testimony to the fact that ecofeminism's theoretical potential, as well as its history, is clearly on the side of animals. They also attest to the importance of first-person narrative in (eco)feminist theory building.

Animals are a part of nature. Ecofeminism posits that the domination of the rest of nature is linked to the domination of women and that both dominations must be eradicated. If animals are a part of nature, then why are they not intrinsically a part of ecofeminist analysis and their freedom from being instruments of humans an integral part of ecofeminist theory? Seven answers suggest themselves. I discuss each in turn.

1. Ecofeminism Explicitly Challenges the Domination of Animals

A strong case can be made for the fact that ecofeminism confronts the issue of animals' exploitation and incorporates it into a larger critique of the maltreatment of the natural world. Consider the "Nature" issue of *Woman of Power: A Magazine of Feminism, Spirituality, and Politics* published in 1988. In it we find articles on animal defense; guidelines for raising children as vegetarians; a feminist critique of the notion of animal "rights" that argues that the best way to help animals is by adopting broad ecofeminist values; an interview with the coordinator of a grassroots animal defense organization; and Alice Walker's moving description of what it means for a human animal to perceive the personhood of a nonhuman animal.[3] In addition to these articles, a resource section lists companies to boycott because they test their products on animals, identifies cruelty-free products, and gives the names and addresses of organizations that are vegetarian, antifur, antivivisection, and multi–issue animal advocacy groups. The resource list implicitly announces that praxis is an important aspect of ecofeminism.

Or consider one of the earliest anthologies on ecofeminism and two of the latest. *Reclaim the Earth: Women Speak Out for Life on Earth,* published in 1983 contains essays that speak to some of the major forms of environmental degradation, such as women's health, chemical plants, the nuclear age and public health, black ghetto ecology, greening the cities, and the Indian tree-hugging movement known as Chipko Andolan. The anthology also includes an essay on the exploitation of animals.[4] A more recent anthology, *Reweaving the World: The Emergence of Ecofeminism* published in 1990, contains an essay proposing that "ritual and religion themselves might have been brought to birth by the necessity of propitiation for the killing of animals,"[5] as well as Marti Kheel's essay that explores the way hunting uses animals as instruments of human male self-definition.[6] This was followed in 1993 by an anthology that placed animals central to ecofeminist theory: Greta Gaard's *Ecofeminism: Women, Animals, Nature*.[7]

Still other signs of ecofeminism's commitment to animals—as beings who ought not to be used as instruments—can be found. Greta Gaard identifies vegetarianism as one of the qualities of ecofeminist praxis, along with antimilitarism, sustainable agriculture, holistic health practices, and maintaining diversity.[8] Ecofeminists carried a banner at the 1990 March for the Animals in Washington, DC. Ecofeminist caucuses within feminist organizations have begun to articulate the issue of animal defense as an essential aspect of their program. The Ecofeminist Task Force of the National Women's Studies Association recommended at the 1990 NWSA meeting that the Coordinating Council adopt a policy that no animal products be served at any future conferences, citing ecological, health, and humane issues. Whether or not all ecofeminists should be vegans is considered one of the current controversies within ecofeminism.[9]

Such ecofeminist attention to praxis involving the well-being of animals ought not to be surprising. Ecofeminism's roots in this country can be traced to feminist-vegetarian communities. Charlene Spretnak identifies three ways the radical feminist communities of the mid-1970s came to ecofeminism: through study of political theory and history, through exposure to nature-based religion, especially Goddess religion, and from environmentalism.[10] A good example of these communities is the Cambridge-Boston women's community. One of the initial ecofeminist texts—Francoise d'Eaubonne's 1974 book *Le féminisme ou la mort*—was introduced that year to scores of feminists who took Mary Daly's feminist ethics class at Boston College. That same year, Sheila Collin's *A Different Heaven and Earth* appeared and was discussed with interest in this community. Collins saw "racism, sexism, class exploitation, and ecological destruction" as "interlocking pillars upon which the structure of patriarchy rests."[11] In 1975, Rosemary Radford Ruether's *New Woman/New Earth* was also greeted with excitement. Ruether linked the ecological crisis with the status of women, arguing that the demands of the women's movement must be united with the ecological movement. The genesis of the two book-length ecofeminist texts that link women and animals can be traced to this community during those years and its association with Daly.[12]

Interviews with members of the Cambridge-Boston women's community reveal a prototypical ecofeminism that locates animals within its analysis. As one feminist said: "Animals and the earth and women have all been objectified and treated in the same way." Another explained she was "beginning to bond with the earth as a sister and with animals as subjects not to be objectified."

At a conceptual level, this feminist-vegetarian connection can be seen as arising within an ecofeminist framework. To apprehend this, consider Karen J. Warren's four minimal conditions of ecofeminism.[13] Appeal to them indicates a vegetarian application articulated by these activist ecofeminists in 1976 and still viable in the 1990s.

Ecofeminism argues that important connections exist between the domination of women and the domination of nature. The women I interviewed perceived animals to be a part of that dominated nature and saw a similarity in the status of women and animals as subject to the authority or control of another, i.e., as subordinate:

> Look at the way women have been treated. We've been completely controlled, raped, not given any credibility, not taken seriously. It's the same thing with animals. We've completely mutilated them, domesticated them. Their cycles, their entire beings are conformed to humans' needs. That's what men have done to women and the earth.

Since ecofeminism is distinguished by whether it arises from socialist feminism, radical feminism, or spiritual feminism, many of the ecofeminists of 1976 identified themselves within these classifications as they extended them to include animals. Socialist feminists linked corpse eating with capitalist forms of production and the classist nature of corpse consumption; spiritual feminists emphasized the association of goddess worship, a belief in a matriarchy, harmony with the environment, and gentleness toward animals; radical feminists associated women's oppression and animals' oppression, and some held the position of nature feminists who valorize women's nature and see women as naturally more sensitive to animals.

The second of Warren's conditions of ecofeminism is that we must understand the connections between the oppression of women and the oppression of nature. To do so we must critique "the sort of thinking which sanctions the oppression,"[14] what Warren identifies as patriarchal thinking allegedly justified by a logic of domination according to which "superiority justifies subordination."[15] The women I interviewed rejected a logic of domination that justifies killing animals: "A truly gynocentric way of being is being in harmony with the earth, and in harmony with your body, and obviously it doesn't include killing animals."

The testimonies of the women I interviewed offer an opportunity to develop a radical feminist epistemology by which the intuitive and experiential provide an important source of information or knowledge that serves to challenge the distortions of patriarchal ideology. Many women discussed trusting their body and learning from their body. They saw vegetarianism as "another extension of looking in and finding out who I really am and what I like." From this a process of identification with animals arose. Identification means that relationships with animals are redefined; they are no longer instruments, means to our ends, but persons who deserve to continue living and toward whom we act respectfully if not out of friendship.[16]

> Feminists realize what it's like to be exploited. Women as sex objects, animals as food. Women turned into patriarchal mothers, cows turned to milk machines. It's the same thing. I think that innately women aren't cannibals. I don't eat flesh for the same reason that I don't eat steel. It's not in my consciousness anymore that it could be eaten. For the same reason that when I'm hungry I don't start chomping on my own hand.

Another described the process of identification this way:

> The objectifying of women, the metaphors of women as pieces of meat, here's this object to be exploited in a way. I resent that. I identify it with ways that especially beef and chickens also are really exploited. The way they stuff them and ruin their bodies all so that they can sell them on the capitalist market. That is disturbing to me in the same way that I feel that I am exploited.

From this process of identification with animals' experiences as instruments arises an ecofeminist argument on behalf of animals: it is not simply that we participate in a value hierarchy in which we place humans over animals and that we must now accede rights to animals, but that we have failed to understand what it means to be a person—the insight that propelled Alice Walker some years later to describe her recognition of an other-than-human animal's personhood. Becoming a vegetarian after recognizing and identifying with the personhood of animals is a common occurrence described by Walker in her essays and by this woman in 1976: "When I thought that this was an animal who lived and walked and met the day, and had water come into his eyes, and could make attachments and had affections and had dislikes, it disgusted me to think of slaughtering that animal and cooking it and eating it." As women described animals, they recognized them as ends in themselves rather than simply as means to others' ends.

The third ecofeminist claim Karen Warren identifies is that feminist theory and practice must include an ecological perspective. Ecofeminism reflects a praxis-based ethics: one's actions reveal one's beliefs. If you believe women are subordinated you will work for our liberation; if you recognize that the rest of nature is dominated you will judge personal behavior according to its potential exploitation of nature. In this regard,

Frances Moore Lappé's powerful book *Diet for a Small Planet* had had a profound effect on numerous feminists I interviewed because it provided an understanding of the environmental costs of eating animals. One stated: "When I was doing my paper on ecology and feminism, the idea of women as earth, that men have exploited the earth just like they've exploited women and by eating meat you are exploiting earth and to be a feminist means not to accept the ethics of exploitation." What she recognizes is that ecofeminists must address the fact that this flesh-advocating culture has successfully separated the *consequences* of eating animals from the *experience* of eating animals.[17]

2. The Environmental Consequences of Eating Animals

One of ecofeminism's attributes is its concern with the consequences of the domination of the earth. It recognizes that the patriarchal philosophy that links women and nature has measurable, negative effects that must be identified and addressed. When we consider the consequences of corpse production—and the way by which each corpse eater is implicated in these consequences—ecofeminism faces the necessity of taking sides: will it choose the ecocide and environmental disaster associated with eating animals or the environmental wisdom of vegetarianism?[18]

The Costs to the Environment of a Flesh Diet

The relationship between corpse eating and environmental disaster is measurable.[19] In fact, advocates for a vegetarian diet have created images that translate the environmental profligacy of corpse production to the level of the individual consumer: the average amount of water required daily to feed a person following a vegan diet is 300 gallons;[20] the average amount of water required daily to feed a person following an ovo-lacto-vegetarian diet is 1,200 gallons; but the average amount of water required daily to feed a person following the standard US corpse-based diet is 4,200 gallons. The same land that can be used to produce flesh for 250 days would provide sustenance for 2,200 days if cultivated with soybeans. Half of all water consumed in the United States is used in the crops fed to livestock, "and increasingly that water is drawn from underground lakes, some of which are not significantly renewed by rainfall."[21]

Animal agriculture is the major industrial polluter in the U.S. Feedlots and slaughterhouses are responsible for more of the country's water pollution than all other industries and households combined. More than 50 percent of water pollution can be linked to wastes from the livestock industry (including manure, eroded soil, and synthetic pesticides and fertilizers). A pound of animal flesh means that one hundred pounds of livestock manure had to be disposed of, often in our waterways. Slaughterhouse waste—fat, carcass waste, fecal matter—is several hundred times more concentrated than raw waste, yet it is dumped into our rivers at the rate of more than two tons an hour. It is estimated that 125 tons of waste are produced every second by animals raised for human consumption; more than half of this waste is not recycled. "American livestock contribute five times more harmful organic waste to water pollution than do people, and twice that of industry."[22] Agricultural crops—more than half of which are harvested to produce livestock feed—are the source of most of the pollutants such as pesticides, nutrients, leachates, and sediment that plague our water resources.

Besides depleting water supplies, corpse production places demands on energy sources: the five hundred calories of food energy from one pound of steak requires twenty thousand calories of fossil fuel. Between forty to sixty percent of the United States' imported oil requirements would be cut if the U. S. population switched to a vegetarian diet.[23]

Millions of acres are deforested to convert land to grazing and croplands to feed farm animals. Then overgrazing or intensive cultivation causes these lands to become desert. Cattle are responsible for 85 percent of topsoil erosion—the loss of the organic soil layer that provides plants with nutrients and moisture. Because of conversion of land to feed animals, wildlife are losing their habitats and are often crushed or wounded during the clearing operations. Beef consumption accounts for about 5 to 10 percent of the human contribution to the greenhouse effect. Among the reasons that water, soil, and air are damaged by corpse production are the hidden aspects of raising animals for food. Before *we* can eat animals, *they* must eat and live and drink water and defecate (and even burp).[24] Producing the crops to feed animals taxes the natural world. Frances Moore Lappé reports that *"the value of raw material consumed to produce food from livestock is greater than the value of all oil, gas, and coal consumed in this country.*... One-third of the value of all* raw materials consumed for all purposes in the United States is consumed in livestock foods."[25] Eighty-seven percent of US agricultural land is used for livestock production (including pasture, rangeland, and cropland).

Uniting Consumption, Maintenance, and Production

Not only is the analysis of consequences an important aspect of ecofeminist thought, but for ecofeminists a failure to consider consequences is one of the results of the dualisms that characterize patriarchal culture: consumption is experienced separately from production, and production is valued over maintenance. By this I mean that as a result of the fetishization of commodities associated with capitalist production, we see consumption as an end in itself, and we do not consider what have been the means to that end: eating (a dead) chicken at a fast-food restaurant is disassociated from the experience of the black women "lung gunners"[26] and the experience of the slaughtered chickens; both groups instead are means to the end of consumption, but because consumption has been disembodied, their oppressions as worker and consumable body are invisible. This disembodied production of a tangible product is viewed as a positive indication of the economy, but maintenance—those actions necessary to sustain the environment—is neither measured nor valued. Currently, maintenance of domestic space or environmental space is not calculated in economic terms—housework is not calculated in the gross national product in the United States, nor are the environmental resources we value.[27] We do not measure the negative environmental effects of raising animals to be our food, such as the costs to topsoil and groundwater. Maintenance of resources is sacrificed to corpse production.

An ethic that links maintenance with production, that refuses to disembody the commodity produced from the costs of such production, would identify the loss of topsoil, water, and the demands on fossil fuels that corpse production requires and factor the costs of maintaining these aspects of the natural world into the end product, the corpse. It would not enforce a split between maintenance and production. The cheapness of a diet based on grain-fed terminal animals exists because it does not include the cost of depleting the environment. Not only does the cost of flesh not include the loss of topsoil, the pollution of water, and other environmental effects, but price supports of the dairy and flesh industries mean that the US government actively prevents the price of eating animals from being reflected in the commodity of flesh. My tax money regrettably subsidizes war, but it also regrettably subsidizes the eating of animals. For instance, the estimated costs of subsidizing the flesh industry with water in California alone is $26 billion annually.[28] If water used by the flesh industry were not subsidized by U.S. taxpayers, "hamburger" would cost thirty-five dollars per pound and "beefsteak" would be eighty-nine dollars.

The hidden costs to the environment of corpse production and the subsidizing of this production by the government maintain the disembodiment of this production process. It also means that environmentally concerned individuals are implicated, even if unknowingly and unwittingly, in this process despite their own disavowals through vegetarianism. Individual tax monies perpetuate the cheapness of animals' bodies as a food source; consequently corpse eaters are not required to confront the reality of corpse production. As much as we bemoan the war industry that is fed with our tax monies, we might also bemoan the support our tax monies give to the the flesh industry that wars upon animals and the environment. Tax monies are used to develop growth hormones like "bovine somatotropin" to increase cows' milk production rather than to help people learn the benefits and tastes of soyfoods such as soymilk—products that are not ecologically destructive.

Maintenance is Productive: The Individual Level

The problem of seeing maintenance as productive occurs on an individual level as well. Activism is judged productive; maintenance as in cooking, especially vegetarian cooking, is usually considered time-consuming. "We don't have time for it—it impedes our activism," protest many feminists in conversations. By not viewing maintenance as productive, the fact that the years of one's activist life may be cut short by reliance on dead animals for food is not addressed. The order we place at the fast-food restaurant or the purchase of flesh at the flesh counter also sends the message that maintaining the environment is not important either. A cycle of destruction continues on both a personal and economic-political level for the same reason, the invisible costs of corpse eating. (See Figure 7, "So, What Will It Be Today?" for an example of making the invisible visible. Note the vegetarian response that accompanies such visibility.)

After conducting the most detailed diet survey in history—the Chinese Health Project—Dr. T. Colin Campbell concluded that we are basically a vegetarian species. This study of the eating habits of 6,500 Chinese revealed that diets dependent on corpse eating and dairy products increase the risk of developing certain diseases. Some of the findings include:

- While the Chinese consume 20 percent more calories than Americans, Americans are 25 percent fatter. The difference is attributed to the source for these calories. The Chinese eat only a third the amount of fat as we do, but twice the amount of starch. In other words the majority of their calories come from complex carbohydrates rather than from flesh foods.
- Overconsumption of protein, especially protein from animal flesh, is linked to chronic disease. United States citizens not only consume more protein than the Chinese (a third more) but 70 percent of that protein comes from flesh foods; only 7 percent of protein for the Chinese is derived from dead animals. Those Chinese who increase their protein intake, especially animal protein intake, have the

Figure 7: So, What Will It Be Today?

highest rates of "diseases of affluence": heart disease, cancer, and diabetes.

- Chinese cholesterol levels are much lower than ours, so that "their high cholesterol is our low," according to Campbell.[29] Animal foods, including dairy products, are implicated in Americans' high cholesterol level. (A diet rich in fat also increases the risk of breast cancer, though many other environmental factors also increase breast-cancer risk.) Jane Brody notes a fivefold to tenfold difference in death rates between countries with high-fat diets and those with low-fat diets such as Japan.[30]
- The Chinese diet contains three times more dietary fiber than the average American diet because of the Chinese reliance on plant foods. Those with the highest fiber intake had the most iron-rich blood.

For women, a diet high in animal fats lowers the age of menstruation—which increases the incidence of cancer of the breast and reproductive organs while also lowering the age of fertility, and thus increasing the numbers of young teenagers who may get pregnant.[31]

The moment when I realized that maintenance must be valued as productive was while I was cooking vegetarian food; thus I was doing what we generally consider to be maintenance. The problem is to escape from maintenance to produce these or any "productive" thoughts. Seeing maintenance as productive is the other side of recognizing the ethical importance of the consequences of our actions.

3. The Invisible Animal Machines

A child's puzzle called "Barn" displays chickens wandering freely, cows looking out the barnyard door, and smiling pigs frolicking in mud. But this is not an accurate depiction of life down on the farm these days. The fissure between image and reality is perpetuated by agribusiness that does not conduct its farming practices in this homespun way. Laws are being passed in various states that prevent the filming of animals who are living in intensive farming situations. (This phrasing is itself representative of the problem of image and reality: "intensive farming situation" usually means imprisonment in windowless buildings.) As Peter Singer points out, television programs about animals focus on animals in the wild rather than animals in the "factory farms"; frequently the only information on these "animal machines" comes from paid advertising. "The average viewer must know more about the lives of cheetahs and sharks than he or she knows about the lives of chickens or veal calves."[32] The majority of animals dominated by humans no longer appear to be a part of nature; they are domesticated, terminal animals who are maintained in intensive farming situations until slaughtered and consumed or laboratory animals such as mice, rats, cats, and dogs. Perhaps as a result, some ecofeminists and most corpse eaters simply do not *see* farm animals at all, and thus cannot see them as a part of nature.

It is instructive, then, to remind ourselves of the lives of individual animals. Consider the case of pigs. A breeding sow is viewed, according to one flesh company manager, as "a valuable piece of machinery whose function is to pump out baby pigs like a sausage machine."[33] Indeed, she does: about one hundred piglets, averaging "2 1/2 litters a year, and 10 litters in a lifetime."[34] Since about 80 million pigs are slaughtered in the United States yearly, this means that at least 3.5 million pig "mother machines" are pregnant twice during any given year. For at least ten months of each year, the pregnant and nursing sow will be restricted in movement, unable to walk around. Though pigs are extremely social beings, sows "are generally kept isolated in individual narrow pens in which they are unable to turn round."[35] She is impregnated forcefully either by physical restraint and mounting by a boar, artificial insemination, being tethered to a "rape rack" for easy access; or through "the surgical transplant of embryos from 'supersows' to ordinary sows."[36]

The now-pregnant sow resides in a delivery crate about two feet by six feet (60 cm x 182 cm).[37] In this narrow steel cage, known as the "iron maiden," "she is able to stand up or lie down but is unable to do much else. Despite this, sows appear to make frustrated attempts at nest-building."[38] Prostaglandin hormone, injected into the sows to induce labor, also "causes an intense increase in motivation to build a nest."[39] After delivering her piglets, "she is commonly strapped to the floor with a leather band, or held down in a lying position by steel bars, to keep her teats continuously exposed."[40]

The newborn piglets are allowed to suckle from their incarcerated mother for anything from a few hours to several weeks: "In the most intensive systems the piglets are generally isolated within hours of birth in small individual cages which are stacked, row upon row, in tiers. . . . At seven to fourteen days, the piglets are moved again to new quarters where they are housed in groups in slightly larger cages."[41] Often farmers clip the pigs' tails shortly after birth to avoid the widespread problem of tailbiting.[42] It is probable that tailbiting results from both a monotonous diet and the pigs' natural tendencies to root and chew on objects in their environment. In essence, "the telos of a hog is the will to root," which is frustrated by their existence in confinement sheds.[43]

> Once onto solid food, the . . . "weaners" are grown on in small groups in pens until they reach slaughtering weight at around six to eight months of age. For ease of cleaning, the pens have concrete or slatted metal floors, and no bedding is provided. . . . Foot deformities and lameness are common in animals raised on hard floors without access to softer bedding areas.[44]

Ninety percent of all pigs are now raised in indoor, near-dark, windowless confinement sheds,[45] a stressful existence that includes being underfed[46] and living in a saunalike atmosphere of high humidity (meant to induce lethargy). Porcine stress syndrome—a form of sudden death likened to human heart attacks—and mycoplasmic pneumonia are common. Once they are the appropriate size and weight, pigs are herded into a crowded livestock truck and transported to the slaughterhouse, where they are killed.

This information on the life cycle of these pigs requires some sort of response from each of us, and the sort of response one has matters on several levels. I respond on an emotional level with horror at what each individual pig is subjected to and sympathize with each pig, whose extreme sociability is evidenced by this animal's increased popularity as pets.[47] On an intellectual level I marvel at the language of automation, factory farming, and high-tech production that provides the vehicle and license for one to fail to see these animals as living, feeling individuals who experience frustration and terror in the face of their treatment. As a lactating mother, I empathize with the sow whose reproductive freedoms have been denied and whose nursing experience seems so wretched. As a consumer and a vegetarian, I visualize this information on the life cycle of sows and piglets when I witness people buying or eating "ham," "bacon," or "sausage."

Intensive factory farming in the United States involves the denial of the beingness of more than seven billion animals yearly. The impersonal names bestowed on them—such as food-producing unit, protein harvester, computerized unit in a factory environment, egg-producing machine, converting machine, biomachine, crop—proclaim that they have been removed from nature. But this is no reason for ecofeminism to fail to reclaim farm animals from this oppressive system. It merely explains one reason some ecofeminists fail to do so.

4. The Social Construction of Edible Bodies and the Cultural Myth of Humans as Predators

Ecofeminism at times evidences a confusion about human nature. Are we predators or are we not? In an attempt to see ourselves as natural beings, some argue that humans are simply predators like some other animals. Vegetarianism is then seen to be unnatural while the carnivorism of other animals is made paradigmatic. Animal defenders are criticized for not understanding that "one species supporting or being supported by another is nature's way of sustaining life."[48] The deeper disanalogies with carnivorous animals remain unexamined because the notion of humans as predators is consonant with the idea that we need to eat flesh. In fact, carnivorism is true for only about 20 percent of nonhuman animals. Can we really generalize from this experience and claim to know precisely what "nature's way" is, or can we extrapolate the role of humans according to this paradigm?

Some feminists have argued that the eating of animals is natural because we do not have the herbivore's double stomach or flat grinders and because chimpanzees eat flesh and regard it as a treat.[49] This argument from anatomy involves selective filtering. In fact, all primates are primarily herbivorous. Though some chimpanzees have been observed eating dead flesh—at the most, six times in a month—some never eat flesh. Dead flesh constitutes less than 4 percent of chimpanzees' diet; many eat insects, and they do not eat dairy products.[50] Does this sound like the diet of human beings?

Chimpanzees, like most carnivorous animals, are apparently far better suited to catching animals than are human beings. We are much slower than they. They have long-projecting canine teeth for tearing hide; all the hominids lost their long-projecting canines 3.5 million years ago, apparently to allow more crushing action consistent with a diet of fruits, leaves, vegetables, nuts, shoots, and legumes. If we do manage to get hold of prey animals we cannot rip into their skin. It is true that chimpanzees act as if flesh were a treat. When humans lived as foragers and when oil was rare, the flesh of dead animals was a good source of calories. It may be that the "treat" aspect of flesh has to do with an ability to recognize dense sources of calories. However, we no longer have that need since our problem is not lack of fat but rather too much fat.

When the argument is made that eating animals is natural, the presumption is that we must continue consuming animals because this is what we require to survive, to survive in a way consonant with living unimpeded by artificial cultural constraints that deprive us of the experience of our real selves, as though some absolute unmediated natural state can be achieved. The paradigm of carnivorous animals provides the reassurance that eating animals is "natural." But how do we know what is natural when it comes to eating, both because of the social construction of reality and the fact that our history indicates a very mixed message about eating animals? Some did; the majority did not, at least to any great degree.

The argument about what is natural—that is, according to one meaning of it, not culturally constructed, not artificial, but something that returns us to our true selves—appears in a different context that always arouses feminists' suspicions. It is often argued that women's subordination to men is natural. This argument attempts to deny social reality by appealing to the "natural." The "natural" predator argument ignores social construction as well. Since we eat corpses in a way quite differently from the other animals—dismembered, not freshly killed, not raw, and with other foods present—what makes it natural?

Flesh is a cultural construct made to seem natural and inevitable. By the time the argument from analogy with carnivorous animals is made, the individual making such an argument has probably consumed animals since before the time she or he could talk. Rationalizations for consuming animals were probably offered when this individual at age four or five was discomforted upon discovering that flesh came from dead animals. The taste of dead flesh preceded the rationalizations, and offered a strong foundation for believing the rationalizations to be true. And baby boomers face the additional problem that as they grew up, flesh and dairy products had been canonized as two of the four basic food groups. Thus individuals have not only experienced the gratification of taste in eating animals but may truly believe what they have been told endlessly since childhood—that dead animals are necessary for human survival. The idea that corpse eating is natural develops in this context. Ideology makes the artifact appear natural, predestined. In fact, the ideology itself disappears behind the facade that this is a "food" issue.

We interact with individual animals daily if we eat them. However, this statement and its implications are repositioned through the structure of the absent referent so that the animal disappears and it is said that we are interacting with a form of food that has been named "meat." The absent referent also enables us to resist efforts to make animals present, perpetuating a means-end hierarchy.

The absent referent results from and reinforces ideological captivity: racist patriarchal ideology establishes the cultural set of human/animal, creates criteria that posit the species difference as important in considering who may be means and who may be ends, and then indoctrinates us into believing that we need to eat animals. Simultaneously, the structure of the absent referent keeps animals absent from our understanding of patriarchal ideology and makes us resistant to having animals made present. This means that we continue to interpret animals from the perspective of human needs and interests: we see them as usable and consumable. Much of feminist discourse participates in this structure when failing to make animals visible.

Ontology recapitulates ideology. In other words, ideology creates what appears to be ontological: if women are ontologized as sexual beings (or rapable, as some feminists argue), animals are ontologized as carriers of flesh. In ontologizing women and animals as objects, the dominant language simultaneously eliminates the fact that someone else is acting as a subject/agent/perpetrator of violence. Sarah Hoagland demonstrates how this works:

"John beat Mary"
becomes
"Mary was beaten by John"
then
"Mary was beaten"
and finally
"women beaten"
and thus
"battered women."[51]
Regarding violence against women and the creation of the term *battered women*, Hoagland observes that "now something *men do to women* has

become instead something that is a part of *women's nature*. And we lose consideration of John entirely."

The notion of the animal's body as edible occurs in a similar way and removes the agency of humans who buy dead animals and consume them:

"Someone kills animals so that I can eat their corpses as meat"
becomes
"Animals are killed to be eaten as meat"
then
"Animals are meat"
and finally
"meat animals"
thus
"meat."

Something people do to animals has become instead something that is a part of animals' nature, and we lose consideration of people's role as eaters of animals entirely. With the mass term of *meat* the agency of the consumer is consummately elided. When ecofeminism acknowledges that animals are absent referents but that we are meant to be predators, it still perpetuates the ontologizing of animals as consumable bodies.

5. Can Hunting Be Reconciled to Ecofeminist Ethics?

Ecofeminism has the potential of situating both animals and vegetarianism within its theory and practice. But should vegetarianism become an inherent aspect of ecofeminism? Are some forms of hunting acceptable ecofeminist alternatives to intensive farming? To answer this question we need to recognize that many ecofeminists (e.g., Warren) see the necessity of refusing to absolutize, a position consistent with a resistance to authoritarianism and power-over. Thus we can find a refusal to condemn categorically all killing. Issues are situated within their specific environments. I will call this emphasis on the specific over the universal a "philosophy of contingency."

An ecofeminist method complements this ecofeminist philosophy of contingency—it is the method of contextualization. It may be entirely appropriate to refuse to say, "All killing is wrong" and point to human examples of instances when killing is acceptable, such as euthanasia, abortion (if abortion is seen as killing), and the struggles of colonized people to overthrow their oppressors. Similarly, it is argued that the way in which an animal is killed to be food affects whether the action of killing and the consumption of the dead animal are acceptable or not. Killing animals in a respectful act of appreciation for their sacrifice, this argument proposes, does not create animals as instruments. Instead, it is argued, this method of killing animals is characterized by relationship and reflects reciprocity between humans and the hunted animals. Essentially, there are no absent referents. I will call this interpretation of the killing of animals the "relational hunt."

The issue of method provides a way to critique the argument for the relational hunt. But first let us acknowledge that the relational hunt's ideological premise involves ontologizing animals as edible. The method may be different—"I kill for myself an animal I wish to eat as meat"— but neither the violence of the act nor the end result, a corpse, is eliminated by this change in actors and method.[52] As I argue in the preceding section, the ontologizing of animals as edible bodies creates them as instruments of human beings; animals' lives are thus subordinated to the human's desire to eat them even though there is, in general, no need to be eating animals. Ecofeminists who wish to respect a philosophy of contingency yet resist the ontologizing of animals could choose the alternative position of saying, "Eating an animal after a successful hunt, like cannibalism in emergency situations, is sometimes necessary, but like cannibalism, is morally repugnant." This acknowledges that eating animal (including human) flesh may occur at rare times, but resists the ontologizing of (some) animals as edible.

Applying the method of contextualization to the ideal of the relational hunt reveals inconsistencies. Because ecofeminist theory is theory in process, I offer these critiques sympathetically.[53] The relational hunt has not yet been fully developed in theory; it remains a rather imprecisely defined issue and is never described as an achievable practice for many— this uncharacteristic imprecision in ecofeminist discourse suggests that the method of contextualization is in some real ways in opposition to the relational hunt, an opposition that is resisted by maintaining the discussion on an anecdotal level. Additionally, it is never pointed out that this is *not* how the majority of people are obtaining their food from dead animals. Though the ecofeminist ethic is a contextualizing one, the context describing how we relate to animals is not provided. Just as environmentalists mystify women's oppression when they fail to address it directly, so ecofeminists mystify peoples' relations with animals when they fail to describe it precisely.

Ecofeminism has not relied on the notion of speciesism to critique current treatment of animals, though its condemnation of naturism, explicitly and implicitly, offers a broadly similar critique. The word *speciesism* has been contaminated in some ecofeminists' eyes by its close association with the movement that resists it, the animal defense movement, which they view as perpetuating patriarchal discourse regarding rights. Animal defense, though, does recognize the right of each individual animal to continue living and this is its virtue. An antinaturist posi-tion does not provide a similar recognition; as a result the individual animal killed in a hunt can be interpreted "to be in relationship." Hunt-ing is not seen as inconsistent with an antinaturist position, though it would be judged so from an antispeciesist position.

An antinaturist position emphasizes relationships, not individuals; the relational hunt is said to be a relationship of reciprocity. But reciprocity involves a mutual or cooperative interchange of favors or privileges. What does the animal who dies receive in this exchange?

The experience of sacrifice? How can the reciprocity of the relational hunt be verified since the other partner is both voiceless in terms of human speech and furthermore rendered voiceless through his or her death? Once the question of the willingness of the silent and silenced partner is raised, so too is the connection between the relational hunt and what I will call the "aggressive hunt." Ostensibly the relational hunt is different from the aggressive hunt, which is seen to aggrandize the hunter's sense of (human male) self rather than valuing any relationship with the hunted animal. Yet we can find in discussions of the relational hunt and the aggressive hunt a common phenomenon: the eliding of responsibility or agency. Consider the aggressive hunters' bible, *Medita-tions on Hunting*.[54] In this book, José Ortega y Gasset writes:

> To the sportsman the death of the game is not what interests him; that is not his purpose. What interests him is everything that he had to do to achieve that death—that is, the hunt. Therefore what was before only a means to an end is now an end in itself. Death is essential because without it there is no authentic hunting: the killing of the animal is the natural end of the hunt and that goal of hunting itself; *not* of the hunter.[55]

The erasure of the subject in this passage is fascinating. In the end the hunter is not really responsible for willing the animal's death, just as the stereotypic batterer is presumed to be unable, at some point, to stop battering; it is said that he loses all agency. In the construction of the aggressive hunt, we are told that the killing takes place not because the hunter wills it but because the hunt itself requires it. This is the batterer model. In the construction of the relational hunt, it is argued that at some point the animal willingly gives up his or her life so that the human being can be sustained. This is the rapist model. In each case the violence is mitigated. In the rapist model, as with uncriminalized marital rape, the presumption is that in entering into the relationship the woman has said one unequivocal yes; so too in the relational hunt it is presupposed that the animal espied by the hunter at some point also said a nonverbal but equally binding unequivocal yes. The relational hunt and the aggressive hunt simply provide alternative means for erasing agency and denying violation.

I have not as yet addressed the fact that the relational hunt is based on ecofeminists' understanding of some Native American hunting practices and beliefs. Andy Smith, a member of Women of All Red Nations, raised the concern that

> interest in Native American hunting to the exclusion of all other aspects of Native culture, is another way of holding to images of Native Americans as savages. This is then further reflected in the misconception that Native people were all hunter types who lived in sparsely populated areas rather than advanced civilizations that were mainly agricultural. This then contributes to the ideology that it was good that natives were "discovered" because otherwise they would still be living these spartan hunter lifestyles. Moreover, what is true for Native cultures is not transferable to mainstream American culture. Such people would better spend their time preserving Native rights than appropriating their culture.[56]

Although many indigenous cultures experienced their relationship with animals very differently than we do today, environmentalists further only their own self-interest when appealing to illustrations from Native American hunting cultures. Why not hold up as a counterexample to ecocidal culture gatherer societies that demonstrate humans can live well without depending on animals' bodies as food?[57] And why not work in solidarity with Native Americans rather than cannibalizing what is presumed to be their hunting model?

Furthermore, what method will allow us to accomplish the relational hunt on any large scale? Can we create as an ideal method one developed in a continent with many fewer people than today, and impose it upon an urban population that has by and large eliminated the wilderness in which Native American cultures flourished? The wilderness no longer exists to allow for duplication. As Rosemary Ruether poses the question: "Since there could be no return to the unmanaged wilderness, in which humans compete with animals as one species among others, without an enormous reduction of the human population from its present 5.6 billion back to perhaps 1 million or so, one wonders what kind of mass destruction of humans is expected to accomplish this goal?"[58]

I think too of other issues with hunting—the role of men as hunters, advocates of hunting, the connection of hunting with violence against women (see chapter 8), and the relationship, anthropologically, between hunting large animals and the subordination of women.[59] Even in traditional gatherer-hunter groups, women provide the majority of calories (and do so while only working what would be the equivalent of 3.5 days a week).

The problem with the relational hunt is that it is a highly sentimentalized individual solution to a corporate problem: what are we to do about the eating of animals? We either see animals as edible bodies or we do not. The hunting issue therefore is ultimately a debate about method.

6. But Plants Have Life Too

The argument that plants also have life is seen by ethical vegetarians as diversionary and a hideous trivialization of the suffering of intensively farmed animals. Yet it proves the necessity of an ecofeminist ethic on the eating of animals. In essence, the position articulated appears to be "If plants can be eaten, then animals can too," and conversely, "If not animals, then why plants?" Here the search for universals is clearly at work, disregarding the value ecofeminism sets on context.[60] Whereas ecofeminism emphasizes diversity and difference, the formulation of the plant argument relies on universalizing. Where ecofeminism would embrace solidarity and recognize that solidarity with animals requires different actions than solidarity with the plant kingdom, this argument presumes sameness. The place of plants in ecofeminist-vegetarian ethics is best understood by returning to the ecofeminist philosophy of contingency and the accompanying method of contextualization.

The current reality is that the greatest exploitation of plant foods, the accompanying deployment of pesticides and chemical fertilizers, the production of monoculture crops that neglect the needs of the soil are all related *not* to humans' need to eat plants but to creating foods for terminal animals to eat before they become flesh. The extensive exploitation of the plant kingdom arises because of the extensive exploitation of animals.

What does plant consumption consist of for humans? The majority of plant foods consumed by humans are from intrinsically renewable resources.[61] They are annuals. Or, as with sea vegetables, they benefit from being pruned if they have not been cast upon the shores by waves. Sea vegetables reproduce "by regeneration from fragments broken off parent plants and from spores."[62] Another category of plant food that provides a large portion of a vegetarian's diet are products of plants and not the plants themselves: the pulses, such as beans, lentils, garbanzos, are actually "fruits of leguminous plants."[63] Nuts and seeds, like all fruits and many vegetables, can be separated from the plant without violating the plant itself. Finally, there are sprouts and grasses that can be grown in anyone's windowsill.

In considering what it is exactly that vegetarians (should) eat the more appropriate question is, how do we minimize harm in the world?[64] There is much to be gained from approaching the plant world with a "feeling for the organism."[65] But this does not mean that we cannot get our nourishment from plants. It means we approach our food with questions such as these: do we affirm a process of life, the growth of a plant, or a process of suffering and death, the killing of an animal?[66] To equate the process of gathering with the process of killing is simply lying about violence and a distortion of women's past. Plant gathering has historically been women's activity; sustainable, organic agriculture, which relies on nature's capacity to renew itself, has been women's contribution.[67] Indeed, the historic model of gathering by women indicates that plants are not necessarily dominated by being harvested and consumed.

It could be argued that the position that "plants have life too and so we can eat animals" is implicitly patriarchal. To draw lines where lines should not exist (i.e., by claiming that eating an animal is essentially different from eating a human being) does not mean that we can't draw lines at all (i.e., distinguishing between eating a cow and eating a carrot). Questioning the appropriateness of drawing such lines is an example of Cartesian doubt. As Catharine MacKinnon argues, Cartesian doubt is a function of human male privilege. This privilege enables a standpoint that considers that everything is made out of ideas.[68] It collapses the epistemological and the ontological. It may be theoretically asked whether carrots are being exploited, but once we situate ourselves within the lived reality we know as this world, we must surely know or intuit that the eating of a horse, cow, pig, or chicken is different from the eating of a carrot. The apparent failure of environmentalists to stipulate this is a failure to participate in embodied knowledge; it reinforces the idea that we live by abstractions. Abstractions and the absence of embodied knowledge arise from the bias toward masculine reasoning that is as much a part of the logic of domination as the eating of animals. Those who disassociate corpses from the process of producing corpses and instead associate them with the plant world perpetuate a mind/body and rational/emotional dualism that ecofeminism seeks to eliminate.

7. Autonomy and Ecofeminist-Vegetarianism

As long as animals are culturally constructed as edible, the issue of vegetarianism will be seen as a conflict over autonomy (to determine on one's own what one will eat versus being told not to eat animals). The question, "who decided that animals are or should be food?" remains unaddressed.

After the Women and Spirituality Conference held in Boston in 1976, which offered only vegetarian food on-site, indignant letters to *off our backs* appeared from angry feminists who said they were forced to matronize nearby fast-food hamburger places due to the lack of flesh at the conference itself. Rather than being seen as agents of consciousness, raising legitimate issues, ecofeminist-vegetarians are seen as violating others' rights to their own pleasures. This may represent the true "daughter's seduction"—to believe that pleasure is apolitical and to perpetuate a personalized autonomy derived from dominance. The way autonomy works in this instance appears to be: "By choosing to eat meat, I acquire my 'I-ness.' If you say *I can't* eat meat then I lose my 'I-ness.'" Often the basic premise of the supposed gender-neutrality of autonomy is accepted, leaving both the notion of autonomy and the social construction of animals unexamined. As a result, animals remain absent referents.

The ecofeminist-vegetarian response to this idea of autonomy is: "Let's redefine our 'I-ness.' Does it require dominance of others? Who determined that a corpse is food? How do we constitute ourselves as 'I's' in this world?"

Giving conceptual place to the significance of individual animals restores the absent referent. This ecofeminist response derives not from a rights-based philosophy but from one arising from relationships that bring about identification and thus solidarity. We must see ourselves in relationship with animals. To eat animals is to make of them instruments; this proclaims dominance and power-over. The subordination of animals is not a given but a decision resulting from an ideology that participates in the very dualisms that ecofeminism seeks to eliminate. We achieve autonomy by acting independently of such an ideology.

Ecofeminism affirms that individuals can change, and in changing we reposition our relationship with the environment. This form of empowerment is precisely what is needed in approaching the issue of where animals stand in our lives. Many connections can be made between our food and our environment, our politics and our personal lives. Essentially, the existence of terminal animals is paradigmatic of, as well as contributing to the inevitability of, a terminal earth.

6

The Feminist Traffic
in Animals

Given the ecofeminist commitment to challenging patriarchal naturism, a naturism that includes the exploitation of animals, ecofeminism should incorporate vegetarianism both theoretically and practically. But should feminists who have not adopted an ecofeminist perspective be vegetarians? This question has appeared more and more frequently in recent years. Claudia Card sees it as a central issue: "Must we all, then, be vegetarians, pacifist, drug-free, opposed to competition, antihierarchical, in favor of circles, commited to promiscuity with women, and free of the parochialism of erotic arousal? Is this too specific? These values are not peripheral to analyses of women's oppressions."[1]

Another feminist, Joan Cocks, critically refers to the ideas that she sees informing feminist cultural practice: "The political strategies generally are non-violent, the appropriate cuisine, vegetarian."[2] Since feminists believe that the personal is political, the debates that have swirled around about vegetarianism indicate that many do not think their personal choice of animal foods reflects a feminist politics. But what if the values and beliefs embedded in the choice to eat animals are antithetical to feminism, so, that, in the case of corpse eating, the personal *is* political? In fact, feminist theory offers a way to examine and interpret the practice of eating animals so that vegetarianism is not reductively viewed as a "lifestyle" choice.

This chapter offers an interpretative framework against which the depoliticizing of feminist moral claims on behalf of the other animals can be perceived. It does so by providing a feminist philosophical examination of the dialectic between "the political" and "the natural," and contends that feminist conferences should be vegetarian. In focusing on the need for feminist conferences to be vegetarian, I am not required to address at this time the necessary material conditions for an entire culture to become vegetarian and whether all members of our society have the economic option to be vegetarian. Indeed, while tax subsidies, free natural resources, and the US-government's financial support of the animal industrial complex[3] keep the cost of animal flesh artificially low, vegetarianism has often been the only food option of poor people. Were government support to producers not available, animal flesh would be even more costly than vegetarian food. In the absence of neutrality on the part of the government, a grassroots resistance is demonstrating that, as more and more people adopt vegetarianism and de facto boycott the corpse industry, vegetable proteins are becoming more prevalent and less costly. In addition, as the fact of a coercive government policy on corpse eating is recognized, alternative political arrangements may become more feasible.[4]

Another reason for my focus on making feminist events completely vegetarian is the fact that most ecofeminists who include animals within their understanding of dominated nature have made this their position.[5] Furthermore, the conference proposal removes the vegetarian debate from the realm of personal decisions and relieves it of some of the emotional defensiveness that accompanies close examination of cherished personal practices. Moreover, the eating of animals is the most pervasive oppression of animals in the Western world, representing as well the most frequent way in which most Westerners interact with animals. Yet those living in the United States do not require animal flesh to ensure adequate nutrition. Lastly, this topic provides an opportunity to respond to feminists who challenge the movement that defends animals.

Defining the Traffic in Animals

Through the use of the term *feminist traffic in animals,* I wish to politicize the use of animals' bodies as commodities. The serving of animal flesh at feminist conferences requires that feminists traffic in animals—that is, buy and consume animal parts—and announces that we endorse the literal traffic in animals: the production, transportation, slaughter, and packaging of animals' bodies.

Trafficking in animals represents a dominant material relationship. As we have seen, the animal industrial complex is the second largest industry, and the largest food industry, in the United States. Currently 60 percent of American foods comes from animals, including eggs and dairy products or *feminized protein* and animal corpses or *animalized protein.*[6] These terms disclose that the protein preexists its state of being processed through or as an animal, that vegetable protein is the original protein.

Trafficking in animals relies on this vegetable protein as well, but requires that it be the raw material, along with animals, for its product.

For femi ists to traffic in animals we must accept the trafficking in ideas, or the ideology, about terminal animals. These ideas form the superstructure of our daily lives, a part of which involves the presumed acceptability of this traffic. The difficulty is that the coercive nature of the ideological superstructure is invisible and for trafficking to continue, must remain invisible.

When I use the phrase "traffic in animals," I deliberately invoke a classic feminist phrase, appearing in works such as Emma Goldman's "The Traffic in Women," and Gayle Rubin's, "The Traffic in Women: Notes on the 'Political Economy' of Sex."[7] By choosing the word *traffic* I imply that similarities in the treatment of "disposable" or "usable" bodies exist.

To "traffic in animals" involves producers *and* consumers. Whatever "objects" we determine to be worth purchasing become included within our moral framework, and the production of these objects, too, becomes a part of such a framework, even if this aspect remains invisible. While numerous books on the animal industrial complex are available,[8] they rarely are cited in feminist writings other than those by vegetarians, thus ensuring the invisibility of trafficking in animals for those who do so. The phrase "traffic in animals" is an attempt to wrest discursive control from those who wish to evade knowledge about what trafficking entails.

Discursive Control and Ignorance

As I argued in chapter 1, no objective stance exists from which to survey the traffic in animals. Either we eat them or we do not. No disinterested observer, nor impartial semantic space exists for discussing the issue. In a flesh-advocating culture, conflicts in meaning are resolved in favor of the corpse eating culture. No matter our individual actions, the place from which we stand to survey the eating of animals is overwhelmed by the normativeness of "meat" and the (supposed) neutrality of the term *meat*.

The contamination of the discursive space in which we might discuss the matter of cross-species consumption is further complicated by ignorance. Although vegetarians know a great deal more about the material conditions that enable corpse eating than corpse eaters do, discursive power, however, resides with the latter, not the former. Lacking specific information regarding the topic, people with the most ignorance still are able to set the limits of the discussion.[9] Thus, when Ellen Goodman argues that "people make choices in these matters [animal defense] from the first time they knowingly eat a hamburger or catch a fish" she makes an epistemological claim.[10] What exactly do corpse eaters know? That a hamburger comes from a dead animal? The details of the literal traffic in animals that has brought the dead animal into the consumer's hands? Goodman implies that people have specific knowledge about corpse production that in reality they do not have and usually do not want. She also assumes that this claim dispenses with the challenges of animal defenders.

Discursive Privacy

It is necessary to politicize the process of obtaining animal bodies for food by using terms such as *trafficking* because of the prevailing conceptual divisions of the dominant culture. The context for talking about the use of animalized and feminized protein is one of rigid separation between political, economic, domestic, and personal. As Nancy Fraser explains in *Unruly Practices:* "Domestic institutions depoliticize certain matters by personalizing and/or familiarizing them; they cast these as private-domestic or personal-familial matters in contradistinction to public, political matters."[11]

The result of this social division is that certain issues are banished to zones of discursive privacy rather than seen as foci of generalized contestation. For instance, purchasing, perparing, and eating food is cast as a private-domestic matter. A similar separation exists between economic and political:

> Official economic capitalist system institutions, on the other hand, depoliticize certain matters by economizing them; the issues in question here are cast as impersonal market imperatives, or as "private" ownership prerogatives, or as technical problems for managers and planners, all in contradistinction to political matters.[12]

Thus, while issues associated with *marketing* and *purchasing* dead animals become privatized to the domestic sphere of individual choice, issues involving the *production* of animals are *economized,* such as when the rise of "factory farms" is attributed solely to the demands of the market, or it is argued that we cannot interfere with the prerogatives of the animals' "owner."

When issues are labeled domestic or economic, they become enclaved, shielded from generalized contestation, thus entrenching as *authoritative* what are actually only *interpretations* of issues. Furthermore, "since both domestic and official economic institutions support relations of dominance and subordination, the specific interpretations they naturalize tend, on the whole, to advantage dominant groups and individuals and to disadvantage their subordinates."[13] This is precisely what happens with the consumption of animals' bodies: it has been naturalized to favor the dominant group—people who eat flesh—to the disadvantage of the consumed animals.

As feminism demonstrates, the divisions between politics, economics, and domestic issues are false. The problem that an analysis such as mine faces is that these divisions continue to be accepted even by many feminists when the issue is animals; and the response by dominant groups is to banish the issue back to a zone of discursive privacy. When the issue is people's oppression of the other animals, this tendency to enforce discursive privacy when issues are being politicized is further complicated. Another social division exists—that between nature and culture.

We do not think of the other animals as having social needs. Since animals are ideologically confined to the realm of nature, making any sorts of social claim on their behalf already introduces dissonance into established discourses. It appears that we are confusing the categories of nature and culture. But this in itself reflects a cultural classification enabled by predetermined ideologies that maintain a narrow, uncontextualized focus. Thus, any feminist animal defense position must challenge what has been labeled as "natural" by the dominant culture.

Ideology: Hiding the Social Construction of the Natural

Any debate about the place of animals in human communities occurs within a cultural context and a cultural practice. Here ideology preexists and imposes itself on individual perceptions, so that what is actually a problem of consciousness—how we look at animals—is seen as an aspect of personal choice and is presented as a "natural" aspect of our lives as human beings. Claiming human beings to be predators like (some of) the other animals (remember that less than 20 percent of animals are actually predators) is an example of the naturalizing of the political. Distinctions between people's carnivorism and carnivorous animals' predation are ignored in such a claim: human beings do not need to be predators, and there is no animal counterpart to human perpetuation of the grossly inhumane institutions of the animal industrial complex. Nel Noddings summons natural processes when she states that "it is the fate of every living thing to be eaten"[14] implying a similarity between the "natural" process of decay and the activity of slaughterhouses (which remain unnamed). Eating animals is also naturalized by glamorizations of hunting as an essential aspect of human evolution or as representing the "true" tribal relationship between indigenous people and animals. The result is that exploitation of animals is naturalized as intrinsic to people's relationships with the other animals. The "naturalization" of the ways we are socialized to look at animals affects how we act toward animals—that is, if we see animals as "meat," we eat them. Thus we can read in a letter responding to an article on "Political Correctness": "None of us has the whole picture. For one woman, vegetarianism is an ethical imperative; for another, eating meat is part of the natural world's give and take."[15]

Attempts to make the ideology and the material reality of corpse production visible, to denaturalize it, result in responses by feminists who through further promulgation of the superstructure and its importance for individual, or certain groups of, feminists, uphold the trafficking in (traditional) ideas about animals and actual trafficking in animal flesh. "Meat" is thus an *idea* that is experienced as an *object*, a *relationship* between humans and the other animals that is rendered instead as a *material reality* involving "food choices," a social construction that is seen as natural and normative. When the concept of species is seen as a social construction, an alternative social construction that recognizes animals as a subordinated social group, rather than naturally usable, becomes apparent.

To understand why feminists defend their trafficking in animals, we must perceive the dialectic that is at work between the political and the natural.

Naturalizing the Political: 1

In a flesh-advocating culture, decisions that are actually political are presented as "natural" and "inevitable." When Ellen Goodman argues that "we acknowledge ourselves as creatures of nature" in "knowingly" eating a hamburger or catching a fish, she presumes that her readers share with her an understanding that "creatures of nature" eat dead bodies. She also assumes that we will find it acceptable to be likened to the other animals when the issue is the consumption of animal flesh, even though so much of human nature (and justification for such consumption) is precisely defined by establishing strict notions of differentiation between humans and the other animals. Two prevalent conceptualizations assist in the naturalizing of the political choice to use animals as food and explain Goodman's confidence in her line of defense of such actions.

Meat as a Mass Term

The existence of *meat* as a mass term contributes to the naturalizing of the phenomenon of eating animals' bodies. Recall from chapter 1

(Quine) that objects referred to by mass terms have no individuality, no uniqueness, and that when we turn an animal into "meat," someone who has a very particular, situated life, a unique being, is converted into something that has no distinctiveness, no uniqueness, no individuality. The existence of *meat* as a mass term naturalizes the eating of animals, so that consumers do not think "I am now interacting with an animal" but instead consider themselves making choices about food.

Ontologizing Animals as "Naturally" Consumable

The prevailing ideology ontologizes animals as consumable, as mass terms. This ontology is socially constructed: there is nothing inherent to a cow's existence that necessitates her future fate as hamburger or her current fate as milk machine. However, a major way by which we circumvent responsibility for terminal animals' fate at the hands of humans is to believe that they have no other fate, that this is their "natural" existence, to be food. As a result, this ontologizing of animals that normalizes corpse eating may be embraced by people across the divisions of race, class, and sex. Unless some factor dislodges these positions and brings about a critical consciousness concerning corpse eating, these positions will continue to be held and, when under attack, fiercely defended as natural, inevitable, and/or beneficial.

The existence of *meat* as a mass term contributes to the ontologizing and thus "naturalizing" of animals as consumable. The ideology becomes sanctioned as eternal or unalterable, rather than suspect and changeable. To be a pig is to be pork. To be a chicken is to be poultry. When Nel Noddings raises the issue of the possible mass extinction of certain domesticated animals if humans were to stop eating them, she is reproducing this ontology. She continues to see the animals as being dependent on their relationship to us, as literally existing (only) for us. To be concerned about whether animals can live without us needing (eating) them continues their ontologized status as exploitable. Indeed, it clearly evokes this ontology: without our needing them, and implicitly, using them as food, they would not exist.

The current ontology requires that we acquiesce to the hierarchical structure that places humans above animals and defines "human" and "animal" antithetically. The current ontology continues to subordinate nonhuman nature—in this case, the other animals—to people's whims. Intensive factory farming is inevitable in a flesh-advocating, capitalist culture. It has become the only way to maintain and meet the demand for flesh products that currently exists and must be seen as *the logical outcome* of this ontology. Warehoused animals account for from 90 to 97 percent of the animal flesh consumed in the United States. Thus, those who argue that warehousing is immoral but alternatives to obtaining animal flesh are acceptable deny the historical reality that has brought us to this time and place. They conceive of some "natural" practice of corpse consumption that is free from historical influence, that is essentially atemporal and thus apolitical. Thus they naturalize the political decision to eat other animals.

Politicizing the Natural: 1

Animal-defense discourse refuses to see the consumption of dead animals as a natural act and actively asserts it to be a political act. It does so by refusing to accept the discursive boundaries that bury the issue as natural or personal. In doing this, animal-defense discourse exposes a matrix of relations that are usually ignored or accepted as implicit (the matrix that I call trafficking in animals) by proposing three interrelated arguments: a species-specific philosophy is limiting, our current ontology of animals is unacceptable, and our current practices are oppressive.

The Limitations of a Species-Specific Philosophy

As I argue in chapter 4, through the human/other dialectic "human" de facto represents Euro-American (human) maleness and "other" represents that which white maleness negates: other races, sexes, or species. This representation of otherness and the equation of it with animalness is central to the process of "naturalizing" the political. The traditional feminist resolution to the equation of any oppressed human group with animalness has been to break that association, to argue in a variety of ways for women's work and lives as representatives of culture rather than nature. It has most often left undisturbed the notion that animals represent the natural. While feminism works to liberate white women and people of color from the onerous equation with animals and otherness, it has not disturbed the equation of animals with otherness.

What we have for the most part in feminism is a species-specific philosophical system, in which (an expanded) humanity continues to negate the other animals precisely because their otherness is located in the natural sphere. Yet, we can find feminist philosophical voices that acknowledge the other animals. Elizabeth Spelman's important article on "Woman as Body," discusses the equation of women, slaves, laborers, children, and animals with the body and how this equation facilitates their oppression.[16] Barbara Noske points out that "as yet there exists in our thinking little room for the notion of a non-human Subject and what this would imply."[17] Nancy Hartsock wonders "why there must be a sharp discontinuity between humans and [the other] animals. Is this too an outgrowth of the masculinist project?"[18] As if in reply, Noske suggests that "even if there is such a thing as a species boundary between ourselves and *all* animals, might this discontinuity not exist on a horizontal level rather than on a vertical and hierarchical level?"[19]

Our Current Ontology of Animals Is Unacceptable

Resisting the current ontology of animals as consumable is central to animal defense. Once the human-animal division is perceived as corrupt and as inaccurate as the other dualisms closely examined by feminism, the resubjectification and denaturalization of animals can occur. This involves accepting them ontologically on their own terms and not on the basis of our interests.

The ontology of animals that accompanies animal defense theory involves distinguishing between reforms of certain practices that accept animals as usable and abolition of these practices. The goal is simply not bigger cages but *no* cages; not bigger stalls for veal calves, but *no* veal calves; not mandated rest stops but *no* transporting; not careful placement of downed animals (an animal who cannot get up, for any variety of reasons such as illness, broken bones, cancer, exhaustion, starvation, dehydration, or parasites) into front loader buckets to move them to be slaughtered (instead of tying a chain or a rope around the legs and dragging them) but *no* system that creates downed animals;[20] not "humane" slaughter, but *no* slaughter. Reform of the current system still subordinates animals to humans. Reform situates itself within the issue of animal *welfare* rather than animal defense and the concern becomes the *appropriate* use of animals rather than the elimination of human's use of animals.

Often when feminists respond to animal defense they attempt to dislodge its ontological claims and argue for the reformist acceptance of animals' exploitation. Ellen Goodman argues for the "intelligent, responsible use of animals." Mary Zeiss Stange wants hunters to "promote positive public images of animal use and welfare, as opposed to animal protectionism."[21] In upholding the dominant ontology, the promotion of responsible use of animals grants charity where liberty is needed. Or as Paulo Freire puts it, such paternalism—taking better care of terminal animals—enacts the "egoistic interests of the oppressors"[22]:

> Any attempt to "soften" the power of the oppressor in deference to the weakness of the oppressed almost always manifests itself in the form of false generosity; indeed, the attempt never goes beyond this. In order to have the continued opportunity to express their "generos-

ity," the oppressors must perpetuate injustice as well. An unjust social order is the permanent fount of this "generosity," which is nourished by death, despair, and poverty. That is why the dispensers of false generosity become desperate at the slightest threat to its source.[23]

An acceptance of the ontological integrity of those who are different from the "normative" human is needed, as well as the recognition of animals' consciousness and cultures. As much as men's accounts of women's li′es have been partial, false, or malicious lies, so too have humans' accounts of the other animals' lives. In resisting the naturalization of animals, we need, as Noske argues, to develop an anthropology of the other animals that encounters them on their terms. A false generosity only serves to restrict animals to the natural realm that enables their ontologizing as usable.

"Predation" Is Oppressive

Claiming that human consumption of the other animals is predation like that of carnivorous animals naturalizes this act. But if this predation is socially constructed then it is not a necessary aspect of human-animal relations. Instead it is an ongoing oppression enacted through the animal industrial complex.

Using the three-part definition of oppression proposed by Alison Jaggar,[24] we can see its applicability to the experience of the victims of the traffic in animals.

First, the "oppressed suffer some kind of restriction on their freedom."[25] Terminal animals suffer literal constraints upon their freedom: most are unable to walk, to breathe clean air, to stretch their wings, to root in the dirt, to peck for food, to suckle their young, to avoid having their sexuality abused, etc. Whether warehoused or not, all are killed. They are not able to do something that is important for them to do, and they lack the ability to determine for themselves their own actions.

Second, "oppression is the result of human agency, humanly imposed restrictions."[26] Humans have a choice whether to eat animals or not. Choosing to purchase flesh at a supermarket or have it served at a conference represents human agency; such human agency requires that the other animals lose their freedom to exist independently of us.

Third, "oppression must be unjust."[27] It includes the thwarting of an individual's liberty because of her or his membership in a group that has been targeted for exploitation. From the perspective of human-skin privilege, the oppression of other animals is seen as just, even though it arises from targeting for exploitation specific groups—in this case, the other animals. But why is human skin the sole referent for what is moral?

Viewed from a philosophical system that rejects the intertwined human/ animal and subject/object dualisms, humans' treatment of terminal animals is unjust. Beverly Harrison proposes "no one has a moral right to override basic conditions for others' well-being in order to have 'liberty' inconsistent with others' basic welfare."[28] This is what people are doing when they traffic in animals. As Alice Walker observes, "The oppression that black people suffer in South Africa—and people of color, and children face all over the world—is the same oppression that animals endure every day to a greater degree."[29]

Naturalizing the Political: 2

In response to efforts to resubjectify the other animals and label our treatment of them as oppression, people who do not wish to give up human-skin privilege seek ways to banish animal defense discourse from the political realm, to reprivatize and re-"naturalize" it. Reprivatization defends the established social division of discourses—that is, the personal is not the political, the natural is not the social, the domestic is not the economic—thus denying political status for animal defense. For instance, when Ellen Goodman contends that animal defense is "unnatural," she implicitly accepts discursive boundaries she otherwise finds disturbing. If animal defense is unnatural, then animal oppression is natural; if it is natural, it is not political. She is attempting to encase the debate once again in discursive privacy. Or, when a feminist refers to the "so-called animal liberation movement"[30] she implicitly denies political content to this movement. When Nel Noddings claims that domestic animals do not have meaningful relationships with other adult animals nor do they "anticipate their deaths,"[31] she delimits their lives within the sanctity of the "natural," which it is presumed we can identify (and control), rather than the social. It may be reassuring to believe that animals have no social network and do not object to their death; however these beliefs are possible only as long as we do not inquire closely into the lives of animals as subjects. Then we see that certain cultural structures facilitate these efforts at depoliticizing and renaturalizing animals' oppression.

The Flight from Specificity

Feminist theorist Nancy Hartsock observes that ruling-class ideas "give an incorrect account of reality, an account only of appearances."[32] The dominant discourse about animals has been determined largely by the appearance of flesh in animals' marketable form—T-bone, lamb chops, hamburger, "fresh" chickens—an appearance positing that "meat," like George Eliot's happy women, has no history. As long as a corpse has no past, its identity will come only from the constructed context of appetites and appearances. This permits a flight from specificity.

The flight from specificity favors generalities instead of engaged knowledge, mass terms over individual entities. To be specific would require confronting the actual practice and the meaning of what is done to animals. Generalities safely insulate one from this knowledge, keeping debates at a predetermined, unbloodied level. Most frequently they do not pinpoint the victim, the perpetrator, or the method. Just as most feminists would recognize that the statement "some people batter other people" or the term *family violence* as imprecise—who and how left undefined—so is the statement "we eat 'meat.'"

When, for instance, in her defense of eating animals, Nel Noddings refers to ensuring that domestic animals' "deaths are physically and psychically painless"[33] she presumes that such a practice exists and that we all sufficiently understand what she means so that we can *agree* that such a practice either exists or is attainable for terminal animals. In this, ignorance about the act of slaughtering prevails, though it remains unexposed.[34] In fact, such a practice neither exists nor is attainable.

Another example of the flight from specificity occurs when the term *meat eating* is applied transhistorically, transculturally, implying that the means by which flesh is obtained have not changed so much that different terms are needed, or else that the changes in the means of production are immaterial to a discussion. Consider Luisah Teish's encouragement to feed the ancestors flesh if this is what they want:

> I have said that cooking for your ancestors is simple. It is, with one exception. Do not think that you can *impose* your diet on them. It won't work for long.
>
> I knew a woman who tried to force her ancestors to keep a vegetarian diet. The oracle kept saying that they were not satisfied. I suggested she make some meatballs for them. She did and got "great good fortune" from the oracle. I could advise her this way because I'd tried to impose a pork-free diet on my ancestors, but much to my disgust they insisted on pork chops to accompany their greens, yams, and cornbread.[35]

How can the flesh obtained from mass-produced, warehoused, terminal animals in any way actually duplicate the flesh eaten by the ancestors when they were alive, when a different material reality constructed the meaning of "meatballs"? *Meat* is not an ahistorical term, though it functions here as though it is, as representation. Surely the ancestors know that "pork" obtained from a twentieth-century warehoused animal—

pumped full of chemicals, who never saw the light of day until transported to be butchered, whose relationship with other animals, including mother and/or children was curtailed, and who never rooted in the earth—is not at all the "pork" they ate.

In each of these cases, terms such as *painless* or *meatballs* or *pork* convey little specific knowledge about the production of flesh. Those aspects unidentified or misidentified are then presumed to be unproblematic or inconsequential. The result of this discursive control is that corpse eaters can set the limits on what types of information about corpse eating is allowed into a discussion.[36] What Sally McConnell-Ginet observes about the sexual politics of discourse holds true, too, for the debate over animal defense: "The sexual politics of discourse affects WHO can mean WHAT, and WHOSE meanings get established as community currency."[37]

The meanings that are established regarding flesh are almost always general, rarely specific. They recognize neither the specific animal killed to be food, nor the specific means for raising, transporting, and killing this animal. This flight from specificity regarding corpse production bars from the discourse matters that in other areas of feminist theory are considered the basis for making ethical decisions: material reality and material relationships.

Feminist Defenses of Trafficking in Animals

Before examining specific feminist defenses of trafficking in animals, some further problems of discursive control must be identified. Feminists, like nonfeminists, generally seek to banish animal defense by reprivatizing decisions about animals and renaturalizing animals' lives as subordinate to humans. In this, several factors function in their favor. They assume that their predefined understanding of the issue is adequate: for example, that it is correct to label animal defense as being in opposition to pluralism because their definition of pluralism excludes animal defense. Any predefined feminist principle that is established as in opposition to animal defense requires closer examination: does it presume that the socially authorized forms of feminist debate available for discussing this issue are adequate and fair? To paraphrase Fraser, does it fail to question whether these forms of public discourse are skewed in favor of the self-interpretations and interests of dominant groups (including human females)—occluding the fact that the means of public discourse themselves may be at issue?[38]

Hidden ethical stances prevail even in pluralistic feminisms. In an evolving community of individuals who share ideas and goals for changing a racist patriarchy, some values are so given, so taken for granted, that we never examine them. For instance, we agree that cannibalism is not a legitimate way to obtain nutrition, even though human flesh can be very tasty. Cannibalism is not a question of individual tastes, appetites, autonomy, or ritual; it is a forbidden activity whose forbiddenness appears obvious to almost everyone, and therefore this forbiddenness disturbs very few. Clearly this is not so when it comes to eating nonhuman animal flesh. In this case the flesh is considered both tasty and acceptable, based on a decision individuals and cultural traditions have made about nutrition and ethics. To suggest that nonhuman animal flesh be forbidden disturbs many.

The differing ethical stances regarding the flesh of human animals versus the flesh of nonhuman animals illustrates that the issue is not whether a community can forbid an action but who is to be protected from being consumed. Since a community-wide vegetarianism is seen as problematic but a community ban on cannibalism is a given, it is obvious that theorizing about species at this point in time is receiving different discursive space than theorizing about race, class, gender, and heterosexism.

Confusing Privilege with Autonomy

The invocation of autonomy—the insistence that enforcing vegetarianism at a conference restricts an individual's autonomy—presumes that no one else's liberty is at issue in food choices. This is simply not so. The invisibility of animals' oppression permits the debate to be about individual human's liberties, rather than making animals' oppression visible. Staking a preeminent claim for autonomy is an attempt at reprivatization. As Ruby Sales remarked during the 1990 NWSA Conference: "Privilege is not a condition. . . . It is a consequence of the condition of oppression."[39] From this politicized perspective, eating animals is a privilege humans have granted themselves, and this privilege is called "autonomy." The ideology that ontologizes animals as consumable preexists and provides the foundation for the easy confusion of privilege with autonomy.

Pluralism

The position that feminist conferences (and theory) should be pluralistic also is seen to be at odds with political claims for vegetarianism. Imposing one's dietary decision on all races or ethnic groups is viewed as racist, because the inability to exercise personal food choices severs an individual from her racial/ethnic tradition. I deeply respect the need to preserve nondominant cultures. However, I do not believe that pluralism requires siding with human-skin privilege in order to avoid white-skin privilege. We do not embrace nondominant cultural traditions that, for instance, oppress women. An unspoken "in-order-to" is buried in the assumptions about pluralism: We want feminism to be pluralistic; in order for this to be, we must be species-exclusive in our theory. From this context, we can see that a politicized issue, pluralism, is made to contest with a yet-unpoliticized issue, the traffic in animals. Moreover, we see that pluralism is defined in such a way that it applies only to other human beings. Conventional wisdom implies that for the one issue to prevail, the other must be kept in the realm of discursive privacy. Pluralism becomes a boundary enforcer rather than a boundary destabilizer. Pluralism in food choices, including eating dead animals, can be argued in this way as long as the dominant culture's current ontology of animals remains unchallenged.

Through reprivatization, vegetarianism is seen as a white woman's imposing her "dietary" concerns on women of color. However, since I am arguing on behalf of feminist-vegetarian conferences, let us agree that at present the foods offered at most conferences represent the dominant culture. They already ignore ethnic and racial traditions around food.

In addressing the right of racial and ethnic groups to eat animals we are not talking about food as nutrition but food as ritual. Poet Pat Parker argues that her "meat" eating is literally soul food.[40] But the ritual meaning of a meal may serve to reprivatize something that has broken away from discursive privacy. Alice Walker can see barbarity in her childhood diet in which "meat was a mainstay"[41] and yet still respect rituals that were not barbarous—her mother's gardening, for instance.

The "naturalizing" of the other animals as consumable is inimical to feminist pluralism—a true pluralism that seeks to recognize the other as a subject rather than an object. This pluralism would acknowledge that the social constructions of race, class, and sex are related to the social construction of species and must be confronted as such.

Politicizing the Natural: 2

A species-exclusive philosophy establishes *human* and *animal* as antithetical categories, and naturalizes human beings' use of the other animals. In contrast, a species-neutral philosophy would not exaggerate differences between humans and the other animals, or imply that singular human evils such as warehousing animals or rape represent some residual "natural" or "animal-like" tendency. As the "natural" is politicized and labeled oppression, "meat" will no longer be an idea that is experienced as an object. Trafficking will be destabilized by consiousness and solidarity.

The Politics of Consciousness

Consciousness of oppression requires responses. Alison Jaggar observes that "to talk of oppression seems to commit feminists to a world view that includes at least two groups with conflicting interests: the oppressors and the oppressed"[42] or to put it more bluntly in the terms of this book—corpse eaters and their flesh. Paulo Freire suggests that we can respond to these conflicting interests either as critics/radicals for whom "the importance is the continuing transformation of reality" or as naive thinkers/sectarians who accommodate "to this normalized 'today.'"[43] Naive thinkers/sectarians accept prevailing ideological barriers and discursive boundaries; critical consciousness can find no hold here: "sectarianism, because it is myth-making and irrational, turns reality into a false (and therefore unchangeable) 'reality.'" Ellen Goodman accepts an unchangeable "reality" when she argues that

> environmental purity, the ability to live a life without a single cruel act against nature, is impossible. . . . The only answer is to avoid the use—or exploitation—of any other species. . . . We acknowledge ourselves as creatures of nature. . . . The anti-fur extremists prefer to win by intimidation. They have staked out a moral position that leaves no room for the way we live. It is, in its own peculiar way, unnatural.[44]

Goodman both reprivatizes and renaturalizes the normalized "today." Why does Goodman think that the answer—to avoid the exploitation of other species—is unachievable, unnatural? She does not say. The alternative to this accommodation of and mythicizing of reality is to accept the process of radicalization, an actual engagement in the efforts to transform concrete reality. This transformation aligns one with the oppressed rather than the oppressor, the flesh rather than the corpse eater.

Breaking down ideological boundaries requires that those who are the oppressors must stop "regarding the oppressed as an abstract category,"[45] must stop seeing *meat* as a mass term, must be equipped to examine and challenge the way we live.

The Politics of Solidarity

Critical consciousness makes us aware of ourselves as oppressors. It transforms our understanding of reality in which the political has been naturalized. But then what? Freire observes:

Discovering her or himself to be an oppressor may cause considerable anguish, but it does not necessarily lead to solidarity with the oppressed. Rationalizing one's guilt through paternalistic treatment of the oppressed, all the while holding them fast in a position of dependence, will not do. Solidarity requires that one enter into the situation of those with whom one is identifying; it is a radical posture. . . . True solidary with the oppressed means fighting at their side to transform the objective reality which has made them these "beings for another."[46]

Trafficking in animals ontologizes them as "beings for another," making corpse eaters their oppressors.

The necessary precondition for animals to be free is that there be no trafficking in animals' bodies. The ontology will not collapse upon itself until the actions that the ontology upholds—for example, corpse eating—are stopped, and we stop being their oppressors.

Consciousness, Solidarity, and Feminist-Vegetarian Conferences

A feminist conference is an action—an action comprised of people gathering to plan, educate, and network around issues of justice for women. Alice Walker, reporting on her evolving feminist consciousness, comments: "I think about how hard it would be for me to engage in any kind of action now for justice and peace with the remains of murdered flesh in my body."[47] Walker's thoughts pose a question: should the remains of murdered flesh be available for consumption during feminist conferences? We live in a flesh-advocating culture. But should feminist conferences be flesh advocating? If I recall correctly, a letter to a feminist publication a few years back raised the issue, "Why are we going home for the holidays to watch our families eat dead animals?" No one has to go home for the holidays to see the traffic in dead animals—they can come to most feminist conferences.

The assumption that feminist conferences should have an all-inclusive menu has been tacit, a given, and thus untheorized. Feminist conference organizers often think they are assuming a neutral role in the debate about the consumption of animals by offering a vegetarian option that can be adopted personally if desired. In Freire's terms, they are naive thinkers. They wrongly conclude that there is such a thing as neutrality, that they are not de facto taking an ontological stance that aligns them with the dominant culture. A feminist conference that includes the vegetarian option presumes corpse eating as normative. As Nancy Fraser argues: "Authoritative views purporting to be neutral and disinterested actually express the partial and interested perspectives of dominant social groups."[48] An all-vegetarian conference thus destabilizes what is claimed to be neutral and comprehensive, demonstrating instead its partiality. It says that if feminists want to traffic in animal bodies they must be deliberate and not passive about it. It resists the naturalizing of the political.

The individual vegetarian option at a conference is inadequate because it perpetuates the idea that what we eat and what we do to animals (a simultaneous act if we traffic in dead animals) are solely personal concerns. It reprivatizes a political issue, making flesh the default diet. It removes the actions of a community from the consciousness of that community. Issues related to corpse eating such as the environment, women's health, and the politics and ethics of conflicting ontologies are rendered invisible. The Ecofeminist Task Force Recommendation to the 1990 NWSA Conference considered these aspects by calling attention to the environmental consequences (deforestation, soil erosion, heavy water consumption, the presence of unrecyclable animal excrement, immense demands on energy and raw materials) and the health consequences (identifying the correlation between corpse consumption and heart attacks, breast cancer, colon cancer, ovarian cancer, and osteoporosis).[49]

Trying vegetarianism at a feminist conference could be a catalyst for a changed consciousness about animals. The only way to experience vegetarian nourishment is by eating vegetarian food. The feminist-vegetarian conference proposal recognizes the practical hurdles to moving away from a flesh diet: many worry that they will not feel full after a vegetarian meal; that the dishes are unappetizing; or that insufficient protein will be ingested. Vegetarian meals therefore speak to practical fears: one *can* feel full; food *can* be tasty; vegetarians *do* get the same amount of protein each day that corpse eaters do—twice as much as our bodies require. As the Ecofeminist Task Force urged, conference organizers should "make every effort to provide meals that satisfy the health, conscience, and palate."[50]

Reprivatizers insist that the eating of animals is not a legitimate subject of feminist discourse, but a personal decision. Whether we eat blood and muscle or not is seen solely as an individual act, rather than a corporate one. This attitude toward corpse eating as solely personal is then actually enacted as individuals are given the choice to select competing meal options. Reprivatizers, keeping the debate at the personal level, also keep the debate about the issue of *food*. Animal defense discourse argues that the debate is a political one and the issue is *ontology*. Flesh at a meal automatically undermines a discussion of vegetarianism because the prevailing consciousness about animals—ontologizing them as consumable—is literally present.

The inappropriateness of this ontology, the naturalizing of it by humans' self-interest, the consequences of it for our health and the environment—the entire oppositional discourse that vegetarianism represents—can only become apparent in an atmosphere that respects animals. The current ontology will never offer this. It is an ontology at odds with feminism.

7

Reflections on a Stripping Chimpanzee: on the Need to Integrate Feminism, Animal Defense, and Environmentalism

I was a guest at a surprise birthday party that was being given for a [human] male friend. In the midst of the celebration, music began to play and a chimpanzee dressed as a stripper was brought into the room. As the poor little animal prodded by the owner began its [sic] act, I watched the faces of those witnessing this pathetic sight. Most of the guests were visibly embarrassed. I could hear scatterings of nervous giggles, the kind that come out when you're embarrassed and just don't know what to say. The guest of honor was so uncomfortable that he left the room.

The party was a miserable failure. The person who had arranged for this "entertainment" apologized and kept saying, "I had no idea it would be like this." He had paid one hundred dollars to watch a wonderful, intelligent animal be stripped of all dignity.[1]

What is the meaning for feminism that women are thought to constitute at least 75 percent of the animal defense movement? And what does it mean for the animal defense movement that some want to "feminize" it?[2] What is to be made of the charge by the Canadian fur industry and some feminists that the antifur movement is sexist?[3] What are the implications that for many years, a woman who was not a ball player's wife, but with whom the player was in a sexual relationship was called his "beast"? Why does someone train a chimpanzee to strip? Why is it that animal defense is not seen as an environmental issue? Applying the feminist critique of traditional philosophy to the evolving political discourse regarding animal defense offers answers to these questions.

The Need to Integrate
Animal Defense, Feminism, and Environmentalism

Animal defense and feminism, including environmental feminism or eco-feminism, are frequently seen to be independent (rather than interdependent) of and even in conflict with each other. As we have seen, feminism to a large extent has not explicitly incorporated animal-defense concerns into its activism and theory; while some feminists have been overtly critical of the animal defense movement, including charging it with sexism.[4] Other feminists explicitly reject the rights-based discourse that undergirded the theory of the animal defense movement in the 1980s.[5] Since animal-defense theory holds that animals are not mere instruments, it challenges the unquestioned use of research on animals by feminist scientists and raises important concerns about animal experimentation as a manifestation of sexist bias in science. It challenges feminists to see animals as deserving of moral consideration. Despite efforts by many to unite the issues of environmentalism (superficially conceived as a "holistic" concern for species preservation and other life forms besides animals) and animal defense (superficially conceived as an "individualistic" concern for the preservation of individual animals, usually mammals rather than bugs), many philosophical papers have been written in the past ten years that widen the gulf between the two rather than close it.[6] This, it seems to me, is a case of going in the wrong direction.

Three considerations suggest, instead, that the concerns of environmentalism, animal-defense theory, and feminism, particularly ecofeminism, can and ought to be brought together:

Feminist Analysis of the Status of Animals

First, a dialogue between feminist and animal-defense scholarship offers new ways for discussing women's experience, feminist theory, and the status of animals in a racist, capitalist patriarchy.[7] Like a chimpanzee made to strip, every category of animal exploitation reveals gender issues: descriptions of the hunting of animals that often use rape imagery in such a way that rape is seen as benign; animals incorporated either dead or alive as trappings in pornography; the equation of the eating of animals with human maleness so that a corpse-eating culture is called a "virile" culture; the killing of animals by batterers. It may be that, as some feminists argue, women's experience of exploitation equips us to understand what animals experience: "When I see the dominance/submission pattern of man's relation to animals, the way in which he reduces the animal to an object, a tool for his use, I understand the horror of that pattern for the dominated 'object.' I have lived it. I am living it."[8]

In reconstructing the history of the domination of nature, women, and colonized peoples, ecofeminists like Rosemary Radford Ruether have established a connection between the domestication of animals, the development of urban centers, the creation of slavery, and the establishment of the inequality of the sexes,[9] while some anthropologists have correlated human male domination with animal-based economies, i.e., hunting societies rather than gatherer societies.[10] Nancy Jay proposes that the sacrifice of animals in many religious ceremonies arises from the need of a patriarchal culture to purify itself from the fact of being born of women. The shedding of animals' blood—an action as serious as giving birth—provides a "ritual instrument" for maintaining a human male-dominated social order.[11] Animals' freedom from a religion that oppresses them will not occur until the need for animals to act as sacrificial lambs is eradicated. Animals' status and women's status is interdependent.

Animal Defense and Environmentalism

Second, the animal-defense movement should be seen as addressing environmental issues. There are several reasons for this. With regard to food production and consumption, both the untoward *consequences* of livestock production, which has been called "one of the major ecological disasters of our time"[12] and the *symbolic* role domesticated "food" animals play as emblematic of nature's fate—controlled, used as a resource, and annihilated—are environmental issues addressed by animal-defense theorists.[13] Although different issues are raised for so-called wildlife, environmental issues concerning the necessity, desirability, and justification for protecting and preserving wildlife are addressed by the animal-defense movement.[14] The work of ecofeminists such as Susan Finsen and Marti Kheel, among others, attempts to bridge the perceived gulf between "individualists" and "holists."

Voices have arisen from within the animal-defense movement that combine a theory of animal defense with theories about the environment and feminism to produce what is called a life-centered theology.[15] Feminist theory offers ways to examine environmental issues without sacrificing individual animals as environmentalists often seem to do. Moreover, environmental issues are often survival issues for people of color. Thus, they offer a way of addressing other social oppressions, and in particular, of challenging environmental racism. Finally, flesh foods are the paradigmatic capitalist product as they fulfill the capitalist demands for constantly expanding consumerism. Few things are more wasteful than corpse production. Because flesh production consumes so many resources, an animal-based agriculture can expand indefinitely. A socialist feminist approach to the issue offers valuable insights into the material nature of environmental exploitation.[16]

The Contributions of Ecological Feminism

Third, ecological feminism offers an interpretative framework for analyzing the domination of nature, including the domination of the other animals. As we have seen, ecological feminists claim that the dominations of women and nature are intimately connected and that any adequate feminism, environmentalism, or environmental ethic must acknowledge these connections.[17] The contribution of ecofeminism's insights into social "isms of domination" such as sexism, racism, classism, and naturism and the ways these sanction and perpetuate a "logic of domination" that (falsely) assumes that the superiority of (some) humans provides a theoretical basis for recognizing the intersectional nature of oppression.[18] Furthermore, drawing on the insights of various strands of feminist ethics, ecofeminism also offers a critique of the strictly philosophical rights and interests arguments that cause many environmentalists unease. Thus ecological feminism provides a philosophical framework for analyzing the connections among feminism, environmentalism, and animal defense. It also acknowledges the interrelated aspects of social domination and domination of nature, and through its global manifestations, demonstrates the possibility of multicultural theory and action.

Five Questions/Five Vantage Points

Feminists in all fields have pointed out that the questions one asks often affect what one takes to be significant to an issue, the methodology one uses to determine answers, and even the answers one gets or countenances. This is certainly so in the present case. Consider five questions that suggest interconnections among the issues raised by feminists, environmentalists, and the animal-defense movement.

1. Are Animals to Humans as Women are to Men? Exploring a Variety of Cultural Dualisms.

As previous chapters indicate, many contemporary feminist theories address a variety of conceptual sets that are historically characterized by these opposing terms: subject/object; self/other; domination/agency; culture/nature, sameness/difference; male/female; white/nonwhite; human/animal. We have seen how these dualisms mediate power and value hierarchies of domination: man dominates woman; culture dominates nature; whites dominate people of color whom they label "nonwhite"; a subject dominates an object; humans dominate animals. The eradication of a logic of domination as it is sustained, perpetuated, and enacted through these cultural sets becomes one of the goals of ecofeminism.[19]

Clearly identifying the cultural set of human/animal and the meaning of this cultural set, in terms of both anthropomorphic views of animals and the use of animals as "inferior" or "subordinate" beings to further the interests of humans, is a logical extension of any feminist discussion of dualisms and the way they are institutionalized. Furthermore, as with the chimpanzee forced to perform a traditional female action, one way in which animals are oppressed is by associating them with women's lesser status, and vice versa. That is, linking the subordinated aspects of patriarchal dualisms (animal/woman) reinforces the subjugation of each. (For an example of this intersectional reinforcement of subordination, see Figure 8 "The Hardest Part Is Getting in"—an image reproduced on a T-shirt for a graduating class of a veterinary school, and marketed by their "Food Animal Club.")

Animal exploitation encapsulates several dualisms simultaneously, for instance, the human "mind" studying the animal "body" in animal experimentation; the human "male" hunting the animal who is called "female" when seen as prey; the human whose "selfhood" is defined against the animal "other" who is "beast," the "cultural" human watching the "natural" animal in the settings of zoos, circuses, rodeos; the voice of "reason" telling us that our "feelings" about animals should not determine ethical positions about corpse eating, animal experimentation, or other forms of exploitation.

"Is species difference, like sex difference, socially constructed and experienced, and if so, how?" This question raises a host of issues about what the categorizing of species entails[20] and how those categorizations reflect assumptions regarding power relations, human self-definition, and

Figure 8: The Hardest Part Is Getting in

the role one's race, ethnicity, sex, and class play in the social construction of species. This question is a logical step in the challenges feminism offers a racist patriarchy and an important direction for feminist theory.

2. What Is the Role of Reason and Rationality in Determining the Situation of Women and Animals in Western Philosophy?

When Thomas Taylor parodied Mary Wollstonecraft's *A Vindication of the Rights of Woman* by writing his *Vindication of the Rights of Brutes,* his motives were not solely to say, "what will be next if we give women rights, *animals?"* Wollstonecraft's text was heavily invested with the goal of demonstrating women as reasonable beings, *unlike* animals. Wollstonecraft wanted to break the historical association of women with nonrational animals, e.g., the one found in Aristotle. Recall the epigraph to the preface describing Aristotle's position: "Aristotle does not merely posit the general inferiority of women but describes them as 'incomplete beings' . . . creatures in a gray area between beast and man."[21] Taylor wanted, in a sense, to affirm Aristotle's position by demonstrating that women *are* no more reasonable than animals.[22]

The issue of the extent to which women are or are not unlike animals raises several pertinent questions: what is meant by "reason" and "rationality"? Leading philosophers have held that "woman is not rational, at least not in the same way as man."[23] In Western thought, "a lesser, immature, or defective rationality consistently has been attributed to women."[24] Gender metaphors, of necessity, are embedded in patriarchal understanding of rationality.

The animal-defense movement has at times reinforced a rationalist bias that belittles women. This can be seen particularly in the antifur movement. That women wear fur coats is embedded in malestream culture's image of femininity. Here we find the "arrogant eye" in full glory. Advertisements for fur coats depict women as objects who are gazed upon. But the advertisements "promise" that women who wear fur coats become subjects ("What becomes a legend most? Blackgama" or "The Little Fur Stole That Went to Bifano's and Became a Star"). Women's subjectivity is hinted at because of the de facto objectifying of animals that frames the motivations—to sell parts of animals' bodies. However, women's subjectivity is never achieved. They can be only stars or legends.

Fur coats, like pornography and striptease, speak a human male language of exchange. And so does the antifur campaign. Or at least one prominent aspect of it. Illustrative of the antifur campaign is the advertisement "It takes up to 40 dumb animals to make a fur coat; but only one to wear it" showing a woman holding a fur coat that leaves a trail

Figure 9: Forty Dumb Animals. Photograph © 1985, Jill Posener

of blood. Granted, women wear the majority of fur coats, but why do they wear them? Who buys them? What is the role of malestream culture in creating the feminine look that requires fur on women? Putting on a fur coat and stripping one's clothes off to display a female body exist on the same continuum, as this ad implicitly conveys: only the lower half of the woman is shown and she holds the fur coat as though she had just taken it off. She is pure body—wearing high heel shoes, a skirt with a hemline above her knees, while one hip juts out, a sexually suggestive pose. The billboard ratifies the "arrogant eye." Calling women "dumb animals" is reminiscent of the Western political tradition that has viewed women precisely as dumb animals. And it is fairly obvious that a headless woman cannot be a man of reason.[25] (See Figure 9 for one feminist response to this billboard.)

According to feminist epistemological insights, before we can begin discussions about reason or rationality, we need to inquire, "Whose knowledge are we talking about?"[26] When we see that men have controlled philosophical and political discourse, we must next inquire, "How has human male experience structured/delimited the threshold issues regarding the social contract and inclusion within the moral order?"[27] Might not concern about what constitutes being human and rational arise from a basic though unexamined elite human Euro-

American male experience? Positing the issues in this way helps us to see that inadequate theories of the social contract based on elite human Euro-American male experience have been taken as adequate. They are flawed not only by omission (of women) but also by commission (i.e., development of theory from the perspective of a masculinely gendered person). The same observations can be applied to the antifur campaigns that err by omission and commission.

3. What Is the Place of Emotion and Feeling in Morality?

Feminist philosophers have struggled with the message and history of Cartesian thought and brilliantly pinpointed its androcentricity.[28] Cartesian thought also is of central concern to animal-defense philosophy since it is seen as providing the carte blanche for invasive scientific experimentation on animals[29] and for animal "machines" and "factory" farms that characterize current corpse production.

Feminist theory has raised important questions about the Western philosophical tradition's emphasis on rigorous logic and its simultaneous devaluing of emotions as legitimate sources for decision making. This devaluing has been seen as intimately connected to the devaluing of women. Yet, animal-rights discourse currently emphasizes rationality and reason in its arguments on behalf of the sentience and moral rights of other animals.[30] Meanwhile, the response to the animal-defense movements of both the nineteenth and twentieth century is to use terms such as *anti–intellectualism, obscurantist, irrational,* and *antihuman.* As Roberta Kalechofsky points out, these same words "were used to describe women in the nineteenth century, and most particularly intellectual women who were regarded as desexed."[31] The accusation that people concerned about animals are merely sentimental builds upon the equation of the emotional with the sentimental, irrational, feminine, and womanish. In upholding the rational/emotional dualism, animal rights theory *appears* to disallow humans' feeling about other animals into the realm of ethical decision making.

If animal-rights theory—perhaps defensively at times—upholds a rigorous rationality to spare it the accusation of being simultaneously emotional and feminine, this may signal a failure to recognize how deeply the Cartesian dualism of feeling and reason impacts both gender-based notions of rationality and the resistance to seeing the sentience of animals as an issue. Yet typically our empathy for the plight and well-being of animals is grounded in the recognition of their sentience. While some ecofeminists and environmentalists—perhaps defensively at times— shrug off animal-defense arguments on behalf of animals' sentience on the grounds that it depends on traditionally male-defined notions of both reason and rights, an alternative dialogue suggests itself.

To begin with, one could build on feminist ethicists who develop a theory of embodiment. For instance, Beverly Harrison writes: "If we begin, as feminists must, with 'our bodies, ourselves,' we recognize that all our knowledge, including our moral knowledge, is body-mediated knowledge." She continues, "We know and value the world, *if* we know and value it, through our ability to touch, to hear, to see."[32] When I argue that animals are absent referents, in one sense of that term I mean that they are disembodied entities, beings whom we never touch, hear, or see. Disembodied knowledge literally brings about disembodied animals who have little potential of being touched, heard, or seen, except as means to our ends.

A strength of writings such as that of Singer's and Regan's is that a part of their discussion is devoted to describing exactly what is happening to animals—they restore the absent referent. While this does not mean that as readers we are touching, hearing, or seeing the animals, our imagination provides the opportunity to link the knowledge we have gained about animals' current extensive suffering with animals we have known, heard, and seen, and further, to reflect on what this means. Despite their disclaimers concerning reason in the forewords of their books, in recognizing the necessity of setting out precise information about animals' current state of existence, they affirm embodied knowledge. One could ask: Do Regan and Singer and other animal-defense theorists have the analysis correct—they understand and act upon the problem of animals' instrumentality—but incorrectly attempt to fit it within a framework delimited by its own human male bias?

Integrating Harrison's understanding of embodiment with the issue of animals in contemporary society requires that we situate ourselves. Alice Walker's articles on her interactions with animals provide a challenging and effective starting place for each of us to begin asking: How do I feel about animals? How are animals present in my life, e.g., alive (companions, "wildlife") or dead (as food, garment)? How do I feel when reading about animals' suffering and what should be the ethical and philosophical responses to this feeling? Do I feel differently about different types of animals? How do I decide personally how I should act toward animals? What have I learned and what is actively repressed about animals' lives? How are the conflicts between feeling and knowing resolved for myself when the issue is animals?

Moving from an introspective examination to the theoretical implications of animals' experiences, other questions arise: Do the various feminist challenges to malestream conceptions of moral reasoning also effect and transform the debate about animals? Does the question of the use of animals gain legitimacy only if one redefines the relationship between reason and emotions and the role of each in moral theory and decision making?

4. What Is Knowledge and How Do We Gain It?

Feminist philosophers have identified ways in which the methodology of science both arises from and valorizes human male experience. Evelyn Fox Keller, Sandra Harding, and Carolyn Merchant have argued that science is not value-free, that the scientific concept of objectivity is itself a value—a value that remains unexamined by science's claim to be value-free.[33] Feminist philosophers also have described science as generally characterizing individuals as autonomous, independent, and solitary, and the scientist as one who is and should be a disinterested human observer.

Scientists offer three reasons why the knowledge gained from experimenting on animals is justified: that knowledge is valuable; it is unreproducible without animals; and the complexity of the issues makes it difficult for laypeople to comprehend. These reasons suggest that the issue of animal experimentation is primarily a question of epistemology and secondarily one of hermeneutics. It is a question of epistemology because issues associated with the acquisition of knowledge are primary in the debate: What is it? How do we get it? It is a question of hermeneutics because issues associated with meaning are also pertinent: How is knowledge interpreted or applied? Through feminism the issues of epistemology and by extension hermeneutics are unresolved and destabilized rather than made static and apolitical in nature.

If the feminist critiques of science are correct, animal experimentation seems less a scientific question than a power issue filtered through the current, malestream power discourse. Gendered notions of knowledge acquisition mean that disenfranchised bodies are used to gain knowledge.

5. Is "Rights" Right?

Contemporary animal-defense theory has been deeply dependent on the dominant philosophical traditions that feminism seeks to expose. Some feminist philosophers have argued that rights theory rests on social contract theories that are at the very least inadequate and biased.[34] Many ecofeminists experience a double uneasiness with the notion of rights: there is the general uneasiness expressed by some feminist theorists that our current philosophical inquiry about rights, interests, and the status of the individual over-and-against others, as well as what constitutes being human, arises from a traditional male rather than female experience. It also posits a liberal subject, the idea of which is no longer tenable in postmodern theory. And, there is sympathy with environmentalists' concern that rights discourse on behalf of animals is a form of ethical extensionalism that recognizes only some animals (especially other mammals) while neglecting other animals and the environment as a whole. Unfortunately, the tendency for feminists to dismiss the defense of animals because of the contaminated notion of "rights" means that animals themselves become absent referents. The virtue of animal-rights theory is that it recognizes individual animals and argues against their instrumentality. In light of feminist critiques of rights language, the task becomes one of searching for language that can just as effectively say that each individual animal's life matters, that people should see their treatment of animals as ethical issues.

Embodied knowledge is an alternative that emerges as the dialogue among feminists, environmentalists, animal-defense advocates and others continues. Beverly Harrison, for instance, argues that feminist behavior will arise not from truths grounded in abstract knowledge (as is suggested by the question, "Do animals have rights?") but in refusing complicity in destructive social forces and resisting those structures that perpetuate life-denying conditions.[35] The problem becomes then that of making visible the invisible—explaining why the current treatment of animals is a destructive social force. Feminist theories about "different voices" (Gilligan), "maternal thinking" (Ruddick), and connectional selves (Keller) offer the grounds for exploring the meaning of our connection to the other animals and how we act morally upon these connections or lack of them.[36]

Interrelated oppressions cannot be eliminated if they are attacked separately; chimpanzees who strip, furbearing animals needed to uphold the feminine look, dead animals required as "virile" food—and all the animals they represent—will not be free if women, people of color, nondominant men, and children are not.

Once the elite Euro-American male bias of Western theory is acknowledged, the question becomes: Do we begin from this position of biased male experience or first redefine the threshold issues based on human experience that consciously includes (and tests itself against) women's experience? Do we then find ourselves at a different point of departure for discussing the status of animals; i.e., might we be in a culture in which animals were already included? In suggesting this, I am not positing any essentialist attitude toward women as theorists; it is not the female psyche or our biology as such that will determine the development of an alternative theory, but a discourse that evolves from the experience of beings who have been excluded from most of the powerful positions in Western culture.

Feminism and environmentalism should not simply dismiss animal defense and the theories that accompany it because of a reliance on philosophical concepts of rights and interests; instead a more sophisticated response is called for, one that is able to separate this solution from the illuminating analysis that animal defense offers of the destructive social forces against animals. Identifying these destructive social forces and interrogating them from a "nonimperialistic and life-affirming" ethic that respects "nonhuman life forms"[37] is an important next step in integrating feminism, animal defense, and environmentalism. In the concluding section of this book, I attempt such integration.

Part 3

From Misery to Grace

She decides she will not eat any sort of meat ever again. . . .
She makes a silent vow to be a vegetarian from now on even
if she has to starve to do it. Better that than even the remote
possibility of eating one's friends and fellow sufferers. . . .
Pooch wonders, does not some atavistic need exist in all of
us to save the world, exactly to the degree that we would
save ourselves, for aren't we "the world" as much as any
other piece in it? Perhaps the more animal we are . . . that is,
Pooch thinks, that I should keep my basic nature even while
becoming (or rather, hoping to become) an intellectual . . . if
I could retain strong links to my animal past. Never forget
what I am and where I come from.

—Carol Emshwiller, *Carmen Dog*

Merely by ceasing to eat meat, merely by practising restraint,
we have the power to end a painful industry. We do not have
to bear arms to end this evil, we do not have to contribute
money, we do not have to sit in jail or go to meetings or
demonstrations or engage in acts of civil disobedience. Most
often, the act of repairing the world, of healing moral
wounds, is left to heroes and tzaddikim, saints and people of
unusual discipline. But here is an action every mortal can
perform—surely it is not too difficult!

—Roberta Kalechofsky

Figure 10: *Vestiges*, (Human/Cow) by Susan kae Grant

8

Bringing Peace Home: a Feminist Philosophical Perspective on the Abuse of Women, Children, and Pet Animals

I have been a vegetarian since 1974. In 1978, I started a hotline for battered women in rural upstate New York where I lived at that time. Because my vegetarianism was motivated by a concern for animals, I began to notice that animals—as well as the batterer's female sexual partner—were often victimized by violent men. For instance, one day a woman whom we had been helping to leave her violent husband called to report what had happened when he returned the children after his visitation was over. The children, the husband, and the wife were all sitting in his pickup truck in the driveway. Something occurred that enraged him. Simultaneously, the family dog appeared in the driveway. He plunged the truck forward so that it ran over the dog. He then threw the truck in reverse and backed over the dog. He repeated this forward-backward motion many times. Then he got out of the truck, grabbed his shotgun, and, in front of his devastated family, shot the dog several times.

Empirical evidence indicates that acts of sexual exploitation, including physical battering of sex partners, often involve violence against other animals as well. Drawing on a model provided by Karen J. Warren[1] I will make explicit the variety of connections between sexual violence and injury to animals. Then I will demonstrate the importance to feminism and animal defense of taking seriously these empirical connections because of their implications for conceptual analysis, epistemology, political philosophy, environmental philosophy, and applied philosophy. In doing this, I hope to set a standard and provide a set of suggestions about what must be included in any adequate feminist peace politics. It is not my goal in what follows to use the examples of the abuse of animals solely to illustrate how women and children are made to suffer. Then I would recapitulate on a philosophical level what the abuser actually does, using animals instrumentally. Instead, I seek to broaden the reader's worldview about what counts as "feminist peace issues" to include concern about the connections between abuse of animals and women, and to see the experience of animals as legitimate concerns in and of themselves.

This essay takes Elizabeth Spelman's implicit understanding that somatophobia—hostility to the body—is symptomatic of sexism, racism, classism, *and* speciesism, and demonstrates how hostility to despised and disenfranchised bodies, that is, those of animals, children, women, and nondominant men, becomes interwoven.[2] To avoid somatophobia, feminist philosophy must take the connections between abuse of animals and abuse of women seriously.

Terminology

Several terms that feature in my argument deserve attention upfront.

I will use the conventional term pet to describe animals who are a part of a household.[3] Those involved in the animal-defense movement prefer the term *companion animal*. While I find this term helpful, the word *pet* suggests some commonalities between sexualized behavior and animals: the term *pet* also connotes sexual activity, specifically, fondling and caressing.

Battering is a component or kind of sexual violation, since it occurs against one's sexual partner. Catharine MacKinnon's insights on this matter are helpful: battering "is sexually done to women. Not only in where it is done—over half of the incidents are in the bedroom. Or the surrounding events—precipitating sexual jealousy. . . . If women as gender female are defined as sexual beings, and violence is eroticized, then men violating women has a sexual component."[4]

I am uncomfortable with the term *battered woman* although it is one that the movement against violence against women has itself adopted. I agree with Sarah Hoagland (whom I quoted in chapter 5), that the term elides the agency of the batterer, while also ascribing an unchanging status to his victim.[5] However, because it is the commonly adopted term, and is used by the scholars and activists from whom I draw my empirical data, I use the term.

One might suggest that the violence examined in this chapter is really "male violence." But the minute we widen the scope of inquiry to include the other animals, we must proceed with sensitivity to the way language may be inaccurate. The anthropocentric presumption that "male" and "female" can be used interchangeably with "men" and "women" is erroneous. What is actually being discussed is *human*-male violence. While in what follows I am vigilant in using the adjective *human* to qualify male, I will abide with convention in discussing animal abuse, allowing that meaning to exclude human animals.

Empirical Evidence

Karen J. Warren argues that understanding the empirical connections between women and nature improves our understanding of the subordination of women while also establishing the practical significance of ecofeminist philosophy.[6] Empirical connections that reveal the intersection of the abuse of animals and the abuse of women expose another layer of intentional infliction of suffering by violent men, another way of comprehending the phenomenology of sexual violation. I am concerned about what this control and terror mean for women and our subordination, *and* for animals and their subordination.

Testimony from survivors and their advocates indicate two significant configurations in which sexually violent men harm women, children, and animals. There is a threat or actual killing of an animal, usually a pet, as a way of establishing or maintaining control over women and children who are being sexually victimized. And, there is a use of animals in sexually violating women or children, or the use of animals to gain some sort of sexual gratification. Of concern is a third way in which sexual exploitation influences behavior toward animals: anecdotal evidence suggests that child victims of sexual abuse sometimes injure animals. These configurations will be discussed under the specific phenomenological forms that the sexual exploitation takes: battering, marital rape, pornography, child sexual abuse, ritual abuse, serial killing, and sexual harassment. Taken together, this evidence, as we will see, has striking implications for feminist philosophical considerations.

Battering is one form of human male sexual violence that victimizes women, children, and animals. Threats and abuse (often fatal) of pets by a woman's sexual partner occur in his attempts to establish control. As with other forms of battering, the killing of a pet is "done to show control and domination."[7] Lenore Walker points out, "As a way to terrorize and control their women, batterers have even been known to hold pets hostage."[8] According to guides for battered women, behaviors that are commonly shared among batterers include hunting, owning of guns, threatening, harming, or killing a pet.[9] "Abusers are often cruel to animals. Many kill them for sport, and this should not be minimized. Anyone who beats a dog or other pets should be considered a potential batterer."[10] Bonnie Burstow, a radical feminist therapist warns that the killing of a pet by a human male heterosexual partner is one of the signs that "the woman is in an imminently life-threatening situation and immediate action is called for."[11] For instance, one man slashed two pet cats to death and then threatened to turn the butcher knife on his wife and her dog.[12] In another incident, Molly, after a brutal battering by her husband that lasted several hours, "realized he was laughing. Molly had seen him beat a dog like that once, slowly until it [*sic*] died. She remembered that he had laughed then, too." Shortly after that, Molly killed her husband in self-defense.[13]

Diana Russell describes an incident that occurred in California:

> [Michael] Lowe casually pumped a shot into the dog. The sheepdog ran under the family's truck, cowering in pain as Lowe went back into the house and returned with a .30-.30 Winchester rifle. He called to the animal and made her sit in front of him as he fired five more shots, killing the family pet [in front of the family]. Three months later he did the same to his wife. Then he killed himself.[14]

Anne Ganley, a psychologist who has pioneered in victim-based counseling for batterers, identifies "the destruction of property and/or pets" as one of four forms of battering (along with physical, sexual, and psychological battering). She observes that:

> Typically, the offender and the victim do not identify the destruction of property/pets as part of the battering; yet it is. The offender's purpose in destroying the property/pets is the same as in his physically attacking his partner. He is simply attacking another object to accomplish his battering of her. Sometimes we minimize the seriousness of this form of battering by saying that at least it is better than hitting her. Unfortunately, it often has the same psychological impact on the victim as a physical attack.[15]

(And we need to remember that battering an animal *does* injure someone.)

Angela Browne found that many of the women she interviewed who had killed their husbands in self-defense frequently reported destruction of animals: "These incidents often seemed to the women a representation of their own death."[16] The killing of pets often resulted in the loss of a battered woman's last hope.

> The kitten was sitting in the yard. Billy got his rifle, walked up to it [sic], and shot it [sic]. Then he hunted down the other two cats and shot them. Kim was hysterical—following him around, tugging on him, jumping up and down and screaming. She begged him not to kill the cats, and after he had, she begged him not to leave them there. So he picked them up and threw them over the fence. After Billy went to sleep that night, Kim crept out, found the cats, and buried them. Then she lay down in the field and cried.[17]

When the husband murders a pet, he may be destroying the woman's only source of comfort and affection.[18]

A little-studied form of battering involves the use of animals for humiliation and sexual exploitation by batterers and/or marital rapists. This is the second form of sexual violence victimizing women and animals. Batterers and *marital rapists* (and the two groups are neither mutually exclusive nor completely inclusive of each other) may train dogs to "have sex with" their wives[19] or force their wives to have sex with a dog: "He would tie me up and force me to have intercourse with our family dog. . . . He would get on top of me, holding the dog, and he would like hump the dog, while the dog had its [sic] penis inside me."[20] The batterer's/rapist's control is amplified by requiring humiliating acts of his victim. This is a form of torture. Linda Marchiano (Linda "Lovelace") threatened by her batterer, Chuck, with death, was subjected to sex with a dog: "Now I felt totally defeated. There were no greater humiliations left for me." She explained, "From then on if I didn't do something he wanted, he'd bring me a pet, a dog."[21] As with the preceding cases, the threat or actual use of a pet to intimidate, coerce, control, or violate a woman is a form of sexual control or mastery over women by men, as well as an indication of how extensively abusive men sexualize their actions, including their relationships with other animals.

A third linking of violence against women, children, and animals to human male sexual violence is *pornography*. One genre of pornography features sexual activity "between" humans and animals. (I qualify this term since I believe this activity to be coercive.) Bears, snakes, and dogs—to name just a few of the species of animals incorporated into pornographic films—are shown in a variety of sexual and sexualized positions with women. Linda "Lovelace's" sexual violation with a dog was filmed and became a popular pornographic loop, that is, a brief film. This loop—often cited by reporters and others in response to her book *Ordeal* ["Many who have seen *Deep Throat* or another, even sleazier film in which her co-star was a dog, will argue that Linda Lovelace liked what she was doing, and liked it a lot."[22]—depicts what Marchiano considers "the worst moment of my life."[23] There is some evidence that some viewers of pornography have attempted to duplicate such scenes in abusing their partners.[24]

My fourth case-in-point concerns *child sexual abuse*. The testimony of survivors of child sexual abuse reveal that threats and abuse of their pets were often used to establish control over them, while also ensuring their silence, by forcing them to decide between their victimization or the pet's death. Sylvia Fraser poignantly describes the dilemma this threat by her father-rapist presented to her as a child:

> Desperation makes me bold. At last I say the won't-love-me words: "I'm going to tell my mommy on you!" . . .
> My father needs a permanent seal for my lips, one that will murder all defiance. "If you say once more that you're going to tell, I'm sending that cat of yours to the pound for gassing!"
> "I'll . . . I'll . . . I'll . . ."
> The air swooshes out of me as if I have been punched. My heart is broken. My resistance is broken. Smoky's life is in my hands. This is no longer a game, however desperate. Our bargain is sealed in blood.[25]

This type of threat is not restricted to father-daughter rape. Alice Vachss, formerly a prosecuter of sex crimes, reports on this phenomenon in *Sex Crimes:* Children "are threatened with huge, child-oriented consequences if they tell. The molester kills a kitten and says the same thing will happen to the child."[26] One chilling example involved a two-and-a-half-year-old girl whose abuser claimed to have killed the pet rabbit, then he cooked the rabbit, and forced her to eat some of the flesh, warning her that if she reported the abuse, the rabbit's fate would be hers.[27]

Besides physical abuse of animals by child sexual abusers, there is the sexual use of animals by some child sexual abusers. In these cases, the sexual use of animals seems to enhance or expand or extend the abuse of the genuinely powerless and unsuspecting victim. For instance, one colleague reported a case in which a veterinarian, upon discovering that the dog had a sexually transmitted disease, made a referral that resulted in the discovery that the father was also sexually abusing his two preadolescent daughters. And there are other cases.[28]

A child may injure animals or pets or "stuffed animals" as a sign or signal or expression that something is very wrong.[29] Abuse of animals is recognized in the most recent revision of the *Diagnostic and Statistical Manual of Mental Disorders of the American Psychiatric Association* (DSM-III-R)[30] as one of the symptoms indicative of Conduct Disorder. A preadolescent boy who had been brutally raped by his father described how he would tie a firecracker around a cat and watch as it exploded. Brohl reports that "an adult survivor tearfully related that when she was seven years old she drowned her cat."[31] While Frank Ascione, who has conducted extensive research on this issue, cautions that "much of the information we have on the relation between sexual abuse of children and children's cruelty toward animals is derived from retrospective research," he is also able to provide some information drawn from a more reliable methodology:

> William Friedrich (April, 1992, personal communication) provided data from a large-scale study of substantiated cases of sexual abuse in children 2–12 years of age. Most of these children had been victimized within twelve months of data collection that included administration of the Child Behavior Checklist (Achenbach 1988). Parental reports of cruelty to animals were 35 percent for abused boys and 27 percent for abused girls; the percentages were 5 percent for nonabused boys and 3 percent for nonabused girls, a highly significant difference based on clinical status.[32]

Though the incidence and specificity of *ritual abuse* continues to be debated in the social science literature and in the popular press, mutilated animals have been found in various parts of the country, and victims and some perpetrators describe the central role that killing animals has in ritual abuse.[33] Consequently, reports of ritual abuse indicate a fifth pattern of patriarchal violence against women and other disenfranchised adults, children, and animals in which all aspects of abuse of animals is evident.[34] To review, there are threats, abuse, torture, and killing of pets and other animals to establish control. Additionally, there is the use of animals for humiliation and further sexual exploitation. For instance, Elizabeth Rose reports forced sexual contact with animals as one aspect of ritual abuse.[35] Last, injury to animals is one way that a child signals that something is wrong. Psychologists who have worked with survivors of ritual abuse indicate that, along with several other specific actions, physical symptoms, and preoccupations, harming animals or describing animals that have been hurt can be a warning sign that a child has been a victim of ritual abuse.

A sixth linking of violence against women, children, nondominant men, and animals to human male sexual violence is the killing of animals by *serial murderers* and other murderers who rape and mutilate. Serial killers share some common features: they are likely to report their crimes, are almost always men and usually younger than thirty-five, and "the earliest acting out of sadistic impulses often occurs in the early teens in the form of torturing and killing animals such as cats and dogs."[36] For instance, as a child, serial killer Jeffrey Dahmer searched the neighborhood for roadkills that he kept in a toolshed; kept the bones of racoons, dogs, cats, groundhogs, squirrels, and chipmunks inside formaldehyde-filled pickle jars; kept an animal graveyard with skulls on top of crosses; and collected stuffed owls, rabbits, and small birds. According to one psychologist, David Silber, "His behavior didn't change. The objects changed."[37] Cruelty to animals in childhood was one of the significant differences in behavioral indicators between sexual murderers who were themselves abused before they became abusers and murderers without such a history.[38]

Last, *sexual harassment* often includes pornographic material involving explicit depictions of human-animal sexual activity or reference to this material. Since an adequate discussion of sexual harassment takes me beyond the scope of this chapter, I mention it here only to be sure it is included in the patterns of ways human male sexual violence has operated to subordinate women, children, and animals in interconnected ways. According to the testimony of their victims, sexual harassers incorporate this pornography that depicts animals with women into their victimization activities. Moreover, again according to victims and akin to Marchiano's experience, it is this aspect of sexual harassment that is the most humiliating. For instance, during the hearings to review the nomination of Clarence Thomas to the Supreme Court, held in October 1991 before the Senate Judiciary Committee, we heard from Anita Hill of Thomas's references to pornography: "I think the one that was the most embarrassing was his discussion of pornography involving these women with large breasts and engaged in a variety of sex with different people or animals. That was the thing that embarrassed me the most and made me feel the most humiliated."[39]

Philosophical Implications of the Empirical Connections

We have seen how animals are victims, too, through a variety of acts of sexual violence and exploitation. Truly this material on the connection between abuse of women, children, and nondominant men and abuse of animals is painful to encounter. But only by taking this material seriously can we expand our knowledge about sexual violation. The intersection of abuse of women and animals has implications for feminist philosophy in the specific areas of conceptual analysis, epistemology, political philosophy, environmental philosophy, and applied philosophy.

Conceptual Analysis

The empirical evidence cited above details a shocking hostility to the bodies of disenfranchised others—women, children, nondominant men, and animals. As Elizabeth Spelman recognized when she proposed the concept of somatophobia (hostility to the body), one of the important reasons for feminists to recognize somatophobia is to see the context for women's oppression and the relationship it has with other forms of oppression. Clearly, women's oppression is interwoven with that of animals, so that women and animals are both trapped by the control exercised over their own *and* each other's bodies (i.e., women and children who stay silent because of abusers' threats to their pets; pets who are killed to establish a climate of terror).

Spelman believes that it is important for feminists to recognize the legacy of the soul/body distinction and its use in denigrating women, children, animals, and "the natural," who are guilty by association with one another and with the body.[40] The problem is not only that women are equated with animals' bodies, for instance in pornography, but also that *animals are equated with their bodies.* The soul/body split that concerns Spelman and that she identifies as a part of Western philosophical tradition is acutely evident in notions of animals having no soul, and in the current secular period, of animals having no consciousness, undergirding the instrumental ontology of animals as usable.

Spelman recognized that somatophobia is enacted in relationships such as men to women, masters to slaves, fathers to children, humans to animals;[41] now we see that it is actually often enacted in relationships such as men to women *and* animals, fathers to children *and* animals. The connections between the abuse of women and the abuse of animals make explicit that somatophobia applies to species as well as gender, race, and class interactions. It also requires that we rethink philosophical arguments that rely on anthropocentric notions of harm from sexual objectification.[42]

The testimony of Anita Hill about the humiliating experience of hearing about pornography that included women with animals illuminates Spelman's formulation of somatophobia, particularly the insights that it applies to gender, race, class, and species, and that oppression is interwoven. Consider, for instance, Kimberlé Crenshaw's brilliant article on how feminist and antiracist narratives are structured in such a way as to exclude understanding the experience of a black woman such as Anita Hill. Crenshaw describes the working of interwoven oppressions of race and sex in the racializing of sexual harassment: "While black women share with white women the experience of being objectified as 'cunts,' 'beavers,' or 'pieces,' for them those insults are many times prefaced with 'black' or 'nigger' or 'jungle.'"[43] The sexual aggression experienced by women of color often will simultaneously represent their subordinate racial status. (Consider this example from Lorene Cary's memoir, *Black Ice,* of the racialized sexual politics of meat: Cary worked as a waitress with white waitresses and black cooks: "A few customers told me with a leer that they preferred dark meat."[44])

In her discussion of the representation of African-American women in pornography and the way such representation enabled the pornographic treatment of white women, Patricia Hill Collins ties together the racialization of sexual aggression against black women with the racist view that equated black women with animals:

> Within the mind/body, culture/nature, male/female oppositional dichotomies in Western social thought, objects occupy an uncertain interim position. As objects white women become creations of culture—in this case, the mind of white men—using the materials of nature—in this case, uncontrolled female sexuality. In contrast, as animals Black women receive no such redeeming dose of culture and remain open to the type of exploitation visited on nature overall. Race becomes the distinguishing feature in determining the type of objectification women will encounter. Whiteness as symbolic of both civilization and culture is used to separate objects from animals. . . . The treatment of all women in contemporary pornography has strong ties to the portrayal of Black women as animals. . . . This linking of animals and white women within pornography becomes feasible when grounded in the earlier denigration of Black women as animals.[45]

As Collins points out, race and gender have been inscribed *onto* species: the pre-existing division upon which pornography imposes its images is of animals—beasts, bodies not redeemed by souls—and animal nature, the notion that there is some pure, unmediated bodily sexuality that is not socially constructed. Sander Gilman writes that Buffon, for instance, "stated that this animallike sexual appetite went so far as to lead black women to copulate with apes."[46] Pornography that features black women and animals together may function specifically as a racializing of both sex and species hierarchies. In fact, it may be that women of color are more likely to be used in pornography that shows bestiality.[47] Thus, sexual harassment of women of color by reference to such pornography will carry an added dimension to its demeaning and controlling message. Given the view of black women as animals, and the white pornographic imagination that cast black women sexually with animals, Anita Hill may have experienced a specific form of racialized sexual harassment in Thomas's references to bestiality. Only by including animals within the lens of feminist analysis can the extent and effect of somatophobia in a culture be made visible.

Epistemological Issues

If something is invisible we do not have access to it for knowledge. Much of the sexual victimization of women, children, and animals takes place in such a way as to be invisible to most people. In addition, there is the general invisibility of culturally accepted forms of animal abuse, such as corpse eating, hunting, animal experimentation. What will overcome the invisibility of animal abuse and of the connection between abuse of animals and abuse of women? A relational epistemology helps overcome this culturally structured invisibility. To the person who has a relational epistemology, who has significant relationships with animals, *and* who values these interactive relationships, animal abuse will be less invisible. A relational epistemology also means that a woman experiencing abuse does not isolate her experience, but empathetically may see one's experience as like, rather then radically different from, another's.

As a feminist speaker in the animal-defense movement, I have been approached by many sexual abuse survivors throughout the country who tell of how they made connections between their own sexual abuse and the use and abuse of animals. In 1990, one woman told me how the experience of being choked by her abusive husband transformed her relationship with animals. Suddenly she realized that just as her husband claimed to love her yet was trying to kill her, she claimed to love animals yet she ate them. She survived his attack, left the marriage, and became active in vegetarian and animal-defense activities in her community.

A relational epistemology, in itself, does not automatically result in concern for animals. Aspects of animals' lives and their experience of oppression may remain invisible because of a dominant metaphysics that views animals instrumentally and accepts a value hierarchy. But if one starts to extend out a relational epistemology, this value hierarchy breaks down a little more and a metaphysical shift may occur.[48]

Second-person relationships provide the foundation for such a metaphysical shift. The concept of second persons, introduced by Annette Baier and amplified by Lorraine Code, recognizes that our knowledge is never atomistically individualistic or "self-made." Instead we become persons through our dependence upon other persons from whom we "acquire the essential arts of personhood."[49] Lives begin in communality and interdependence; thus in our acquisition of knowledge, "persons are essentially second persons."[50] The connections between the abuse of animals and the abuse of women suggests that second-person relationships exist between humans and animals as well as between humans and humans. Women and children victimized by abusers reveal intense second-person relationships with animals as well as humans. Otherwise how could control be so inexorably established by the brutalization of pets? How else could they see their death prefigured in the death of the pet?

This second-person relationship can serve as a catalyst to change one's metaphysical stance vis-à-vis the other animals. As happened with the woman being choked by her husband, she suddenly recognized through second-person relations that she had accepted a value hierarchy that failed to protect or value animals. As Code explains: "Imposing meaning on someone else's existence from a position removed from it and ignorant of, or indifferent to, its specificities is at the furthest remove from second-person relations in their normative dimension."[51] Second-person relations enable second-person thinking, from which the metaphysical shift evolves. With second-person thinking "knowledge claims are forms of address, speech acts, moments in a dialogue that assume and rely on the participation of (an)other subject(s)."[52] Significantly, for the battered woman and many others, these other subjects are/include animals.

A relational epistemology paves the way for a metaphysical shift because it acknowledges the value of relationships, and of thinking relationally. Given this position, it is harder to say that our relationships are only with human beings, because many of us have significant relationships with animals. Thus seeing ourselves as born into relationships rather than as atomistic, self-made individuals allows for an important metaphysical shift too: no longer seeing humans as radically other than nonhuman life forms, no longer erecting a boundary between the presumably "self-made human" and the presumably "nature-made animal." Someone who has a relational epistemology is in a position to see what the dominant culture in its metaphysics has constructed as invisible and acceptable; the relational epistemology disables the functioning of somatophobia and its undergirding of animal oppression. This metaphysical shift involves valuing animals as other than objects or bodies and repudiating a subject-object relationship premised on domination rather than respect. It acknowledges that animals have a biography not just a biology, and that what is required is an anthropology, not an ethology, of animals.[53]

Feminist philosophers may distrust the activism of animal defenders because animal-rights philosophy is not based on a relational epistemology. However what may be going on is that many animal defenders (75 percent of whom, let us recall, are estimated to be women) become committed to animal defense based on a relational epistemology that enables a metaphysical shift that repudiates somatophobia. However, in the absence of a well-developed and popularized defense of animals based on a relational epistemology, they seek for a way to verbalize that which has not been bridged—their knowledge stance with an activist language. Philosophical defenses of animals that draw upon either Tom Regan's explication of animal rights or Peter Singer's explication of animals' liberation have so far gained currency in the animal advocacy movement as the appropriate activist language. The result is that because the animal-defense movement has been thought to have been begotten in the image of its "fathers" (Regan and Singer), feminism may have misread what is happening epistemologically.

Political Philosophy

The gender-specific public/private distinction is a conceptually flawed one. Historically, in Western culture, female gender-identified traits have been associated with the private ("domestic," "home") sphere, while male gender-identified traits have been associated with the public ("civic," "political") sphere. According to Catharine MacKinnon, the private sphere is, for women, "the distinctive sphere of intimate violation and abuse, neither free nor particularly personal."[54] Carole Pateman argues further that the subordination of women in the private sphere, ("the sexual contract") is what enables the construction of modern political theory ("the social contract").[55] Not only does the public/private distinction inscribe sexual difference and domination, it keeps invisible the empirical connections between human male sexual violence and violence toward women, children, and animals that this chapter identifies. This prevents feminist philosophy from recognizing the importance of ecofeminist insights into what Karen Warren calls "women-nature connections" as being at the heart of feminist philosophy.

If we review the features of an oppressive conceptual framework that Warren has identified,[56] the way that the public/private distinction operates in the abuse of women and animals will become clearer. Among the features of an oppressive conceptual framework is value-hierarchical thinking or "up-down thinking" that places higher value, status, or prestige on what is up rather than what is down. Abuse enacts a value hierarchy—through abusive behavior a person establishes control, becoming "up" rather than "down"—while originating in value hierarchies: those who are "down" in terms of (public) status—women, children, nondominant men, and animals—are more likely to be victimized.

Warren also identifies value dualisms as part of an oppressive conceptual framework. Disjunctive pairs such as human/animal, male/female, adult/child, white/nonwhite are seen as oppositional rather than as complementary, and exclusive rather than inclusive. Higher value is accorded the first item in each dyad. Until recently, violence in the "private" home was not closely scrutinized by the public sphere (women, children, and animals having less value than men, adults, and humans respectively). Feminist peace politics seeks to change this. As Sara Ruddick observes, "As there is no sharp division between the violences of domestic, civic, and military life, there is also no sharp division between the practices and thinking of private and public peace."[57] It is essential for feminist peace politics to recognize the human/animal dualism central to public/ private distinctions. From Aristotle on, the conception of "manhood"— the public, civic man—depended heavily on seeing women not merely as "lesser humans than men but less-than-human." As Wendy Brown reminds us "it was precisely the sharpness of the Athenian conception of manhood that bore with it a necessary degradation and oppression of women, a denial of the status of 'human' to women."[58] Thus, women were devalued through association with devalued animals. While we have progressed from this theoretical equation of women with animals, we have not eliminated the value dualism that undergirded such public/ private separations, the value dualism by which biology determines who is "mind" and who is "body." We have just removed the human species from this debate. Whereas biology is no longer acceptable for determining human value, it remains acceptable for determining animals' less-than-human value. The role of biology as a central determining factor in the perpetuation of the human/animal dualism is similar to and interrelated with the way that privacy perpetuates the male/female dualism: that is, biology and privacy provide alibis for abuse.[59]

Finally, the "glue that holds it all together"[60] is a logic of domination: "a value-hierarchical way of thinking which explains, justifies, and maintains the subordination of an 'inferior' group by a 'superior' group on the grounds of the (alleged) inferiority or superiority of the respective group."[61] The idea of the private/public division protects the private domain from being the focus of certain ethical and philosophical concerns, concerns such as justice, that are often presumed to pertain only to the public realm.[62] This private/public division functions as a part of the logic of domination: the "I-have-a-right-to-do-what-I-want-in-my-own-home" patriarchal justification for abusive behavior against those constructed as "inferior"—adult female partners, children, and animals.

Through the operation of value hierarchies, value dualisms, and the logic of domination, the public/private distinction has functioned historically within patriarchal oppressive contexts to keep human male sexual violence toward women, children, and pets out of the higher-status "political" areas and in the inferior, out-of-police-concern private arena. This is to the detriment of women, children, pets and other animals, and the entire culture.

Environmental Philosophy

One could argue that environmental abuse is a form of somatophobia, that abuse of the earth is an expression of the hatred of the earth's body. For this reason alone environmental philosophy should be attentive to the conceptual issues raised by the connection between the abuse of animals and the abuse of women. In addition, and very specifically, information about the association between guns, hunting, and battering suggests that any environmental philosophy that defends hunting or offers a hunting model must be reevaluated.[63] Environmental and ecofeminist philosophers who appeal to a hunting model of any culture need to rethink the implications of applying it to the dominant Western cultures where battering is the major cause of injury to adult women, and hunting and owning guns is implicated in this battering. In fact, some advocates for battered women argue that battering incidents increase just prior to hunting season. Moreover, at least one batterer's program requires batterers to relinquish all their guns and firearms in order to participate in the program.[64]

Applied Philosophy

Several areas of applied philosophy are affected by these empirical connections between human male sexual violence toward women, children, and animals. In what follows I touch on a few of these areas.

Public policy. Because of Health Department regulations and liability insurance requirements, shelters for battered women cannot generally allow pets in the shelters. The movement to protect battered women needs to establish relationships with local veterinarians and animal advocates so that pets can be sheltered. Shelters need to inquire: "Do you have a pet that lives with you? Are you afraid to leave the animal? Do you need shelter for your pet?"[65]

Training humane workers and animal control officers to check for child abuse when following up on animal abuse has begun in some places, such as Florida, Ohio, Washington, DC, and parts of California. But humane workers and animal control officers should also be trained about woman-battering since injury to pets occurs not only in relationship to child abuse and neglect but also in cases of battering. Veterinarians, too, need to be trained along these lines, and the question of mandatory reporting of animal abuse needs to be addressed by the veterinary profession. But I am in no way advocating that a woman's decisions about whether to remain or leave should be overridden by intervention by these professionals. Instead, their role as allies should be established. And information about pet injury as itself being a form of battering needs to be publicized.

Homeless shelters and battered women's shelters are often offered surplus animal flesh from hunters. In fact, hunters, including the well-known celebrity bow-hunter Ted Nugent, often organize giveaways to these shelters. (We should be reminded that battered women make up about 40 percent of homeless people.)[66] But given the association of hunting and violence against humans, and batterer programs that require batterers to stop using any guns, accepting flesh from hunters to feed battered women and other homeless individuals presents ethical problems. (I know of at least one battered women's shelter that refused to accept flesh from hunters and of some animal activist and vegetarian organizations who adopt a battered women's shelter at which they periodically serve vegetarian meals.)

Biomedical ethics. The relationship between being a survivor of child sexual abuse and anorexia (which is receiving more attention)[67] needs more exploration by those sensitive to the ethical legitimacy of vegetarian claims. One private-practice dietitian and counselor observed that "the animalistic nature of meat and dairy might seem particularly disgusting to patients recovering from sexual abuse."[68] This is, in fact, one of the symptom clusters associated with ritual abuse survivors: "Did the child suddenly develop an eating disorder, e.g., refuse meat, catsup, spaghetti, tomatoes?"[69] I have argued elsewhere that young girls might have a problem with food while also being vegetarians for ethical reasons.[70] In one location in Los Angeles, 90 percent of the anorexics being counseled were vegetarian (with 50 percent considered to have good reasons for their vegetarianism, i.e., they are not doing it solely to diet or restrict their fat intake because of "obsessive" concern for calories), while another program in Indiana estimated that 25 percent of "patients" at its program were vegetarian. Interestingly, "some dietitians and counselors insist that eating meat is integral to recovery."[71] Rather than having their motives for vegetarianism pathologized, anorexic young women could benefit from a recognition that a relational epistemology may have catalyzed a metaphysical shift regarding terminal animals.

Philosophical psychology. Some programs offer healing to survivors of sexual victimization, including formerly battered women, through "animal-assisted therapy." Alice Vachss describes the comforting presence of a dog she brought to work at the sex crimes prosecutors' offices; some child victims only testified on videotape with the dog present: "With Sheba there to make her feel safe enough, the little girl was able to tell what had been done to her."[72] A social worker at a battered women's shelter in Boston told Jay McDaniel, "The more my clients learn to trust animals and the Earth . . . the more they begin to trust themselves. And the more they trust themselves, the better they can free themselves from exploitive relationships."[73]

Implications for Feminist Peace Politics

The connections between the abuse of animals and the abuse of women have important implications for a feminist peace politics.

The connections between the abuse of animals and the abuse of women call attention to the effect of war and patriarchal militarism on relations between humans and animals and on the lives of animals. Like abusers, occupying forces may kill animals as an expression of control, to instill terror, and to ensure compliance. I have been told such stories: in one case, in the 1970s, after capturing the adult men in a household, the occupying military force very deliberately shot the pet canary in the assembled presence of the family. Just as with battery, such actions are reminders of how mastery is both instilled and exhibited. In addition, the destruction of animals, like rape, is a part of wartime actions.[74] Moreover, as Ascione reports (drawing on the work of Jonathan Randal and Nora Boustany), anecdotal evidence suggests that "children exposed to chronic war-time violence display violent and cruel behavior toward animals."[75]

Sexualized violence takes on new dimensions in the light of the connections between the abuse of animals and the abuse of women. "The sadistic murderer derives sexual pleasure from the killing and mutilation or abuse of his victim. . . . The act of killing itself produces very powerful sexual arousal in these individuals."[76] Thus, sex-crime offenders might relive their crime through animal surrogates. Arthur Gary Bishop, a child molester and murderer of five boys, relived his first murder by buying and killing as many as twenty puppies. (Most frequently the movement is in the other direction.)

After doing an extensive literature review of children who are cruel to animals, Frank Ascione queries, "What is the effect on the child who sexually abuses an animal and that animal dies? (such as boys having intercourse with chickens)?"[77] That the sadistic attacks on horses, often involving sexual mutilation, that have occurred in southern England since the mideighties are called "horseripping" suggests the sexualizing of animal abuse.[78]

Making animal abuse visible expands feminist peace politics. Instead of the glorification of anonymous death in massive numbers that we encounter in heroic war writings, the connections between the abuse of animals and the abuse of women remind us of the specific embodiment and agonizing painfulness of every single death. In the place of unnamed troops, there are named individuals, including animals. These names remind us that all victims—the pets as well as the troops—have a biography. In addition, we now see that biologisms, and the racism such biologisms give rise to, are involved in attitudes toward "animals" and "the enemy."[79] The militaristic identity, like the abuser's control, is dependent on others as objects, rather than subjects. Moreover, it has been observed that "women are more likely to be permanently injured, scarred, or even killed by their husbands in societies in which animals are treated cruelly."[80] Finally, our growing understanding of the commodification of bodies in conjunction with militarism[81] can benefit from insights into the commodification of animals' bodies.[82] Dismantling somatophobia involves respecting the bodily integrity of all who have been equated with bodies.

In response to the conceptual connections between women and animals, feminists as diverse as Mary Wollstonecraft and Simone de Beauvoir have attempted theoretically to sever these connections. Clearly, in the light of the connections between the abuse of animals and the abuse of women, this theoretical response is inadequate because it presumes the acceptability of the human/animal value dualism while moving women from the disempowered side of the dyad to the dominating side. Any adequate feminist peace politics will be nonanthropocentric, rejecting value dualisms that are oppositional and hierarchical, such as the human/animal dualism.

In her discussion of feminism and militarism, bell hooks refers to "cultures of war, cultures of peace."[83] We have seen how the connections between the abuse of women and the abuse of animals both enact and occur within cultures of war. It remains for feminists to define clearly and specifically how animals will be included in cultures of peace.

9

Feeding on Grace: Institutional Violence, Feminist Ethics, and Vegetarianism

> Better is a dinner of vegetables
> where love is
> than a fatted ox and hatred
> with it.
>
> Proverbs 15:17
> (*New Revised Standard Version*)

The day after I arrived home from my first year at Yale Divinity School, an urgent knocking summoned me from my task of unpacking. There stood a distressed neighbor reporting that someone had just shot one of our horses. We ran through the pasture to discover that indeed, one of my horses was lying dead, a small amount of blood trickling from his mouth. Shots from the nearby woods could still be heard. One horse lay dead and the other frantically pranced around him.

That night, upset and depressed, I encountered a hamburger at dinner. Suddenly I flashed on the image of Jimmy's dead body in the upper pasture, awaiting a formal burial by backhoe in the morning. One dead body had a name, a past that included my sense of his subjectivity, and was soon to be respectfully buried. The other dead body was invisible, objectified, nameless, except in his or her current state as hamburger, and was to be buried in my stomach. At the time I realized the hypocrisy of my actions. The question confronting me was: "If Jimmy were meat would I, could I, be his meat eater?" And the answer was: "Of course not." Having recognized his individuality, his subjectivity, having been in relationship with him, I could not render him beingless. So why could I do this to another animal, who, if I had known him or her, would surely have revealed a similar individuality and subjectivity?

The invisible became visible: I became aware of how I objectified others and what it means to make animals into meat. I also recognized my ability to change myself: realizing what flesh actually is, I also realized I need not be a corpse eater. Through a relational epistemology I underwent a metaphysical shift.

This experience in 1973 catalyzed the process by which I became a vegetarian, as noted in the preceding chapter, slightly more than a year later. It also catalyzed a theoretical and theological search to understand why the dominant society invests so many economic, environmental, and cultural resources into protecting the current metaphysical status of animals as edible objects.

The eating of animals is a form of institutional violence. The corporate ritual that characterizes institutional violence deflects or redefines the fact that the eating of animals is exploitative. This is why conscientious and ethical individuals do not see corpse eating as a problem. As this book has pointed out, the most frequent relationship the majority of Americans have with the other animals is with dead animals whom they eat. Because of institutional violence, corpse eating is conceived of neither as a relationship nor as the consuming of dead animals. We require an analysis of institutional violence to identify just why it is that feminist ethics ought to reconceptualize corpse eating. This chapter offers such an analysis and reconceptualization.

The Institutional Violence of Eating Animals

Through an understanding of institutional violence we will come to see the dynamics of exploitation vis-à-vis the other animals, and begin to recognize their suffering as ethically relevant in determining our own actions.

For something to be *institutional* violence it must be a significant, widespread, unethical practice in a society. As the second largest industry in this country, corpse production is both widespread and vitally important to the economy. Though corpse eating is now the normative expression of our relationship with other animals, a close examination of the functioning of institutional violence will reveal why I call it unethical.

Institutional violence is characterized by:

(1) An infringement on or failure to acknowledge another's inviolability

(2) Treatment and/or physical force that injures or abuses
(3) Involving a series of denial mechanisms that deflect attention from the violence
(4) The targeting of "appropriate" victims
(5) Detrimental effects on society as a whole
(6) The manipulation of the public (e.g., consumers) into passivity.

Corpse eating fits this definition of institutional violence. In fact, the word *meat* itself illustrates several of these components. It renders animals appropriate victims by naming them as edible and deflects our attention from the violence inherent to killing them for food.

The Institutional Violence of Eating Animals Is an Infringement on or Failure to Acknowledge Another's Inviolability

Some individuals recognize the inviolability of animals; they believe that animals are not ours to use, abuse, or consume. They believe that if animals could talk, farmed animals, vivisected animals, furbearing animals, circus, zoo, and rodeo animals, hunted animals, would all say the same thing: "Don't touch me!" Yet animals cannot proclaim their inviolability in our language. Moreover, because we have no adequate language for emotions, we have no framework into which our feelings about animals' current violability can be fit. In the absence of such language, it is important that we widen feminist ethical discourse to address the problem of the use of animals.

Corpse eating, in almost all cases, is an unjust use of another for one's own profit or advantage. It is unjust because it is *unnecessary* (people do not need to eat animals to survive), *cruel,* and perpetuates inauthentic relationships among people and between people and the other animals. As such, it enacts the first component of institutional violence—the failure to honor another's wholeness and the interposition of one's will against another's self-determination. Through the term *inviolability* I assert that animals should have a "don't-touch-me!" status in relationship with people. Institutional violence tramples these claims and arrogates to humans the right to dominate and violate animals' bodies.

The function of institutional violence toward animals is to uphold and act upon the violability of animals. At the individual level it wrenches any notion of animals' inviolability from one's sense of ethics. Even if many children object upon learning where flesh comes from, this objection is rarely respected. And even if adults are discomforted by some form of flesh—whether it be because of the animal it is stolen from, a dog, a horse, a rat, or the part of the animals being consumed, the brain, the liver—they may feel they have no ethical framework into which these objections might be placed. The absence of such a framework means that any reminders that animals have to be killed to be consumed, experienced by children explicitly and by adults implicitly, remain unassimilated and repressed. Institutional violence interposes an ethics of exploitation for any burgeoning ethic of inviolability.

Institutional Violence Involves Treatment and/or Physical Force That Injures or Abuses

By treatment I mean *ongoing* conditions that are abusive or injurious. Factory farming involves such treatment. Intensively farmed animals fare poorly, being raised in enclosed, darkened, or dimly lit buildings. Their lives are characterized by little external stimulus; restriction of movement; no freedom to choose social interactions; intense and unpleasant fumes; little contact with human beings; ingestion of subtherapeutic doses of antibiotics to prevent diseases that could tear through an entire population of imprisoned animals. Laying hens live with two to four others in cages slightly larger than this opened book. When being cooked in an oven, the chicken has four or five times more space than when she was alive. Veal calves are kept in their tiny crates, where they cannot turn around since exercise would increase muscle development, toughen the flesh, and slow weight gain. Standing on slatted floors causes a constant strain. Diarrhea, a frequent problem because of the improper diet that is meant to keep their flesh pale, causes the slats to become slippery and wet; the calves often fall, getting leg injuries. When taken to slaughter, many of them are "downers," unable to walk.

As I pointed out in chapter 6, factory farming is inevitable in a flesh-advocating culture, because it is the only way to maintain and meet the demand for flesh products. Moreover, no matter where the animals to be slaughtered have been raised, it is the custom to withhold feed for the last twenty-four hours of their life. As the authors of *Raising Pigs Successfully* reveal: "Withholding feed is usually done for the sake of the butcher (less mess when the intestines and stomach are empty) and to save wasted feed. Some raisers don't do it because they say that it upsets the animal to miss feedings and adds to the stress level on butchering day."[1] This is clearly abusive treatment.

By physical force, I mean *specific* actions that cause injuries, in this case death by violence. While raising an animal in a loving family-farm situation may mean that the conditions described above are not evident, this condition—that of force that injures or abuses—will always be present, because the animal does not become flesh food without being violently deprived of his or her life. This violence can come in one of three ways: death at the hands of the family farmer, death by a hired gun who comes to the farm, or, as with animals intensively farmed, death at a slaughterhouse. This last option requires the transporting of the animals—often the only time that an animal will travel—a strange, sometimes uncomfortable, and perplexing if not alarming experience. At the slaughterhouse, smells and sounds alert the animal that something frightening is happening.

Clearly, animals prefer to live rather than to die and when given the opportunity they tell us so.

As a child growing up in a small village, I lived down the street from the town butcher. He allowed us to watch him kill and butcher the animals. These animals did not go merrily to their deaths. Several times, rather than face his rifle, cows escaped from the truck and went running down the street. Pigs let out high squeals, moved frantically, and upon having their throats slashed, tossed and turned while being yanked heavenward so that bleed-out could begin.

The killing of animals is physical force that injures and abuses animals against their will.

Institutional Violence Requires a Series of Denial Mechanisms

Denial of the extent and nature of violence is an important protective device for maintaining institutional violence. It communicates that the violence that is an integral part of the existence of some commodity, some benefit, is neither troublesome nor severe. In the language of "meat" and "meat eater" the issues of animal suffering and killing are neutralized. This language reveals the difficulty of naming the violence. Why do we eat animals and yet, through language, deny that this is what we are doing? Adrienne Rich offers one answer: "Whatever is unnamed, undepicted in images. . . whatever is misnamed as something else, made difficult-to-come-by, whatever is buried in the memory by the collapse of meaning under an inadequate or lying language—this will become, not merely unspoken, but unspeakable."[2]

The truth about raising and slaughtering animals is both unspoken and unspeakable. It is especially not to be discussed when animals' bodies are being consumed. As a consequence *false naming* is a major component of institutional violence. Indeed, false naming begins with the living animals. Whether they are to be found on family farms or in factory farms, the advice is the same: Do not give animals to be eaten by human beings any names that bestow individuality. Family farmers advise: "If you're going to eat it [sic], don't give it [sic] a pet name. Try something like 'Porky' or 'Chops' or 'Spareribs' if the urge to name is too strong."[3]

False naming means that we can avoid responsibility. False naming creates false consciousness. We communicate something different about our relationship to animals when we speak about "meat" than when we speak either about living animals who enjoy relationships or about the eating of slaughtered, cooked, and seasoned severed animal muscle and blood.

False naming enacts the structure of the absent referent. The structure of the absent referent is fulfilled in intensive or factory farming, but did not originate with it. Indeed in *The Sexual Politics of Meat,* I gave little attention to factory farming per se because I see the problem as the ontologizing of animals as edible, not any single practice of producing flesh foods.

False naming means that corpse eaters are people of the lie. They are lying about their actions, which, because of the screen of language, they do not even see as actions. Someone, in fact, must be acting as a perpetrator of violence for there to be someone else called "meat." False naming announces that there is no call to accountability for the eating of animals. In the absence of accountability, abuse continues.

The lack of any direct involvement with or consciousness of the violence of the slaughterhouse keeps us unaccountable. Again, as the family farmers reveal:

> We usually send our hogs out to be slaughtered simply because we don't want the work of preparing the meat ourselves and because, emotionally, we tend to grow attached to the porkers. It is far easier to pat them good-bye as they leave in the truck and welcome them back in white paper wrappers. The act of killing something [*sic*] you have raised from a baby is not an easy task.[4]

Killing, except for the ritual of the hunt, remains distasteful to most consumers. Since the institutional violence of corpse eating requires killing, at the rate of at least nineteen million a day, a cloud of denial surrounds this.

Denial is enacted at the financial level as well. As I argued in chapter five, corpse eaters do not have to pay the true costs for the flesh that they eat. Federal government support of corpse production, for instance, of "welfare cowboys," who are allowed to graze their cattle on federal land, perpetuates the cheapness of animals' bodies as a food source. Consequently corpse eaters are allowed to exist in a state of denial. They are not required to confront corpse eating as a "pocketbook" issue. Federal support of an animal-based diet protects it from close scrutiny from budget-conscious households.

Institutional Violence Targets "Appropriate" Victims

I have referred to two different experiences I myself have had with the violence of corpse eating. In one, I watched with fascination and excitement as animals were slaughtered, bled, dunked into boiling water to rid them of their hair, skinned, disemboweled, and halved. In the other, I became upset by the death of my horse and connected that to the "hamburger" I was about to eat. How could I go home as a child from watching the bloody slaughter and contentedly eat flesh foods, but as a young adult, greet the recognition that I was eating animals as a contradiction? Several answers come to mind; they revolve around the notion of the appropriate victim. When cows and pigs were butchered, they had no names and no prior relationship with me. I had not affectionately combed their hair, bestowed attention upon them, recognized their individuality and personality, or felt that my individuality was acknowledged by them. While their deaths were very vivid, indeed, the reason for our attendance at this ritual of slaughter, they remained absent referents. Images construct pigs and cows as appropriate victims—their sociability denied, given neither a past, present, nor future upon which we base our knowledge of them. I had little other understanding of them, except that as pigs and cows they were meant to be killed and eaten. As children, my friends and I recognized this and accepted it. I honestly cannot remember meeting with any qualms the pork chops or T-bones served at home the same night as the butchering we had watched. At this young age I had already separated myself from identifying with or understanding these animals.

However, horses are not generally meant to be killed and eaten in US culture. As a child, I begged that dogfood made from horses be banned from our home.

Through my personal loss when Jimmy died, I came to see the meaning of institutional violence *for the victims rather than the consumers*. This painful experience allowed an ethics of inviolability to enter my consciousness. There were no longer any appropriate victims.

Ideology makes the existence of "appropriate victims" appear to be natural and inevitable. Everything possible is done to keep us from seeing terminal animals as subjects of their own lives, and to keep us from seeing ourselves in any sort of relationship with a living, breathing, feeling, other-than-human animal. Such animals are objectified in life and in death. We ignore our radical biological similarity with these animals. The other animals become appropriate victims for corpse eating simply because they are not humans. Their inferiority established by a logic of domination that attributes moral significance to their differences from humans, they become subordinated to humans' interests.

One pertinent difference between my arrogant-eye gaze upon the butchering of animals as a child and my loving-eye engagement with Jimmy's death, was not only my age—in one I was a child and in the other a young adult—but my feminist consciousness that had for several years been alerting me to the function of "appropriate victims," specifically, the making of women as appropriate victims for rape, battering, and sexual harassment. In addition, my relationship with Jimmy was what I referred to in the previous chapter as a second-person relationship. Because of this second person relationship *and* my feminist consciousness that questioned the construction of appropriate victims, I was enabled to see that just as there are no appropriate victims in sexual violence, so there were no appropriate victims in speciesist violence.

Unlike malestream thinking that seeks knowledge in order to control, deprives "objects" of study of the opportunity to speak for themselves, is reductive, and does not place the knowing subject as accountable to that which she or he is studying, this process of questioning corpse eating that I described above represented "second-person" thinking.[5] This "second-person" thinking was possible because of my relationship with a nonhuman animal. Through friendship with a horse, hamburger was no longer an object, able to be possessed and controlled; it was the end result of a process of objectification. Through Jimmy, I began to imagine what the hamburger might say to me, so that I was prompted to consider that this object of consumption had had a voice and an identity. I began to restore the complexity of the individual animal rather than accept that which the dominant culture had reduced them to. And finally, I began to see myself as accountable to those who were being consumed.

Institutional Violence Has Identifiable Detrimental Effects on the Society as a Whole

Institutional violence is culturally protected and seen as beneficial, even though it is actually harmful in several ways besides the killing of billions of animals. There are three areas of concern here: the consequences to the environment, to the health of eaters of animals, and to the workers who produce dead animals for consumption.

Consequences for the environment: As we saw in chapter five, corpse eating is a major contributor to environmental exploitation because of its immense demand on limited water supplies, its role in polluting water, causing the desertification of land, the loss of topsoil and habitat, deforestation, in contributing to the greenhouse effect, and the inordinate amoung of fossil fuels and other raw materials consumed.

Consequences for corpse eaters' health: Dr. Joan Ullyot in a book on women and running, ranked people according to their health. The healthiest were found to be vegetarian runners. Surprisingly, the second healthiest were not runners, but vegetarians who did not run. The third healthiest were runners who were not vegetarians.[6] Numerous examples of the health benefits of vegetarianism can be found in the pages of the major medical journals these days.

The body is a locus of control and authority, of autonomy and independence, of pleasure and pain, of oppression and liberation. All of these are implicated in a discussion of the health consequences of corpse eating. In the light of increasing evidence of the healthfulness of vegetarian eating, we must speak of our own material reality, and of health of soul as well as of body: what happens when we take someone else's flesh into our own? What is the relationship between flesh that we eat and our flesh? What is the conception of the self when we eat that which is like us, when we eat flesh?

Consequences for the workers who produce flesh foods: With the institutional violence of slaughtering, the animal must be treated as an inert object, not as a living, feeling, breathing being. Similarly the worker on the assembly line becomes treated as an inert, unthinking object, whose creative, bodily, emotional needs are ignored. They must view the living animal as the "meat" that everyone outside the slaughterhouse accepts it as, while the animal is still alive. Meanwhile, as we saw in chapter four, they, too, are viewed as living meat by antiunion corporations.

The Final Condition of Institutional Violence Is That Consumers Are Manipulated into Passivity Regarding This Practice

This manipulation occurs in several ways. Children become convinced that eating animals is good and proper. Objections are quelled at the dinner table. Since the 1950s the four basic food groups have contributed to consumers' passivity as beneficiaries of the institutional violence of corpse eating. Because of the four basic food groups and their emphasis on flesh foods and dairy products, many people continue to believe erroneously that they need to eat flesh to survive. Free recipes sent to newspapers around the country by the Dairy Council, the Egg Council, the Beef and Pork lobbies keep the idea of eating animals and their feminized products firmly in place, so firmly that many who perceive its deficiencies despair of changing their diet.

It may seem to be a tautology to say that if we believe some other beings are meant to be our flesh (the appropriate victims) then we are meant to be corpse eaters. Conversely, if we are meant to be corpse eaters then we also believe that someone else is meant to die to be our "meat." These are interlocking givens, ontologies that become self-perpetuating and breed passivity. Either no problem exists; it is unchangeable; or it is changeable, but simply too difficult to do so.

Genesis and the Institutionalized Violence of Eating Animals

I have described the nature of institutional violence and demonstrated how it is that corpse eating is a form of institutional violence. With this framework established, we can now turn to the way that the Bible, specifically the early chapters in the book of Genesis, functions to sacralize animals' oppression. In the context of the United States in which Christian interpretations have insinuated themselves into much cultural discourse, including ostensibly secular discussions, it is necessary for feminist ethics to acknowledge the way the early chapters of Genesis are appropriated to sanctify the institutional violence of eating animals. These chapters are invoked as an authorizing myth of dominance. Despite the secular nature of American culture, the early chapters of Genesis, mediated by a specifically Christian interpretation, offer a legitimization for the eating of animals that seems to let individuals off the hook. It functions as a myth of origins, explaining our nature as corpse eaters.

Feminist biblical scholar Elisabeth Schüssler Fiorenza describes a hermeneutics of liberation that sees the Bible both as "a thoroughly patriarchal book written in androcentric language," and "a source of empowerment and vision in our struggles for liberation." This hermeneutics requires "a dialectical process of critical readings and feminist evaluations."[7] Such a dialectic is rarely engaged for understanding or interpreting our relationships with the other animals, especially that we eat them. The early passages of Genesis in which it is thought that God gives permission to dominate animals and nature in Genesis 1 and authorizes corpse eating in Genesis 9 are often uncritically accepted as a cultural myth.

The same passage that establishes that humans are in the image of God, appears to bestow legitimacy on the exploitation of the other animals. Genesis 1:26 reads: "Then God said, 'Let us make humankind in our image, according to our likeness; and let them have dominion over the fish of the sea, and over the birds of the air, and over the cattle, and over all the wild animals of the earth, and over every creeping thing that creeps upon the earth.'" Genesis 1:26 is seen to be God's permission to dominate the other animals and make them instruments for human's interests, thus de facto allowing corpse eating. By interpreting *dominion* to mean "God gave us permission to exploit animals for our tastes," several denial mechanisms are enacted. We are deflected from concern about animals by believing that we are absolved from the decision that has cast animals as flesh. The comforting nature of this belief derives from the fact that the onus of the decision to eat animals is shifted from individual responsibility to divine intent. (Someone, but not me, is responsible for these animals' deaths. If I am not responsible, I do not need to examine what I am doing and its consequences.) In this viewpoint, God as the author of and authority over our lives has created us as corpse eaters. In one act of authorization two ontological realities are simultaneously created: corpse eater and flesh. As Walter Bowie, the commentator in *The Interpreter's Bible*, remarks on this passage: "Fish and fowl and animals have been his [*sic*] food."[8]

This interpretation of Genesis 1:26 requires associating dominion and exploitation. Some believe that the clue to this association is found in the choice of words in this passage. Gerhard Von Rad opines that "the expressions for the exercise of this dominion are remarkably strong: *rada*, 'tread,' 'trample' (e.g., the wine press); similarly *kabas*, 'stamp.'"[9] But others see a less-harsh meaning to the concept of dominion. Because of the growth of environmental theology, a dialectical hermeneutic process is taking place that challenges the absolute claims to dominance associated with this passage. James Barr suggests that *rada* was generally used about kings ruling over certain areas. "For instance in 1 King v. 4 the verb is used to express Solomon's dominion (expressly a peaceful dominion) over a wide area." He believes that *kabas*, "subdue," refers not to animals but to the tilling of the earth.[10] C. Westermann suggests that the use of *rada* ("have dominion, govern") "can be compared with what is said in 1:16 about the sun and moon, which are to 'govern' the day and night."[11] According to this viewpoint, dominion carries no idea of exploitation, indeed, "man would lose his 'royal' position in the realm of living things if the animals were to him an object of use or of prey."[12]

When dominion is equated with exploitation, people are finding in the Genesis passages an origin myth that confirms their own preconceptions concerning their relationship with animals. This gravitation to a sacralized dominance reveals its own inconsistencies, however, for it requires separating Genesis 1:26 from the instructions to be vegetarian that follow three verses later: "See, I have given you every plant yielding seed that is upon the face of all the earth, and every tree with seed in its fruit; you shall have them for food." *The Interpreter's Bible* notes the difficulty of reconciling these two passages when it explicates Genesis 1:29: "Man is thus to be a vegetarian. This is something of a contradiction to verse 26, according to which he was to *have dominion over* all living creatures."[13] For others "the human 'dominion' envisaged by Genesis 1 included no idea of using the animals for meat and no terrifying consequences for the animal world. Human exploitation of animal life is not regarded as an inevitable part of human existence, as something given and indeed encouraged by the ideal conditions of the original creation."[14]

Genesis 1:26 does not supersede the meaning of creation that extends to include Genesis 1:29. When severed from the meaning of creation and the direction to be vegetarian, the passage becomes a historically justificatory defense of actions. This is a denial mechanism at the theological level.

These defenses continue when considering God's explicit permission to consume animals in Genesis 9:3, "Every moving thing that lives shall be food for you; and just as I gave you the green plants, I give you everything." On a certain view of Genesis, one must argue that corpse eating is a consequence of the fall. The end of vegetarianism is "a necessary evil,"[15] and the introduction of corpse eating has a "negative connotation."[16] In his discussion of the Jewish dietary laws, Samuel H. Dresner argues that "the eating of meat [permitted in Genesis 9] is itself a sort of *compromise*," "*a divine concession to human weakness and human need*."[17] Adam, the perfect man, "is clearly meant to be a vegetarian."[18] In pondering the fact that Isaiah's vision of the future perfect society postulates vegetarianism as well, Dresner observes:

> At the "beginning" and at the "end" man is, thus, in his ideal state, herbivorous. His life is not maintained at the expense of the life of the beast. In "history" which takes place here and now, and in which man, with all his frailties and relativities, lives and works out his destiny, he may be carnivorous.[19]

What is interposed between Genesis 1:29 and Isaiah is human history. In this sense, history is the concrete, social context in which we move. Moreover, history becomes our destiny.

Through a corporate sacred myth, the dominant Christian culture offers the idea that because an action of the past was condoned by God and thus the ethical norm of the time, it may continue unchanged and unchallenged into the present time. History becomes another authority manipulating and extending our passivity. It allows us to objectify the praxis of vegetarianism: it is an ideal, but not realizable. It is out of time, not in time. When Genesis 9 is used to interpret backward to Genesis 1 and forward to our own practice of corpse eating, history is read into creation, and praxis is superseded by an excused fallibility. History will then immobilize the call to praxis—to stop the suffering, end institutional violence, and side with the oppressed animals. If vegetarianism is placed out of time, in the Garden of Eden, then we need not concern ourselves with it.

Objectifying the praxis of vegetarianism makes it ahistorical, outside of history and without *a* history. This may explain one reason vegetarianism throughout the ages has been called a fad despite its recurrence. Corpse eating has not constituted a large part of the diets of humankind and most individuals at some point experience some discomfort with the eating of animals. Moreover, in the light of the sexual politics of meat whereby women, second-class citizens, are more likely to eat what are considered to be second-class foods in a patriarchal culture—vegetables, fruits, and grains rather than flesh—the question becomes who exactly has been eating the flesh after Genesis 9? Consider, for instance this terse comment on Leviticus 6 by Elizabeth Cady Stanton, a leading nineteenth-century feminist: "The meat so delicately cooked by the priests, with wood and coals in the altar, in clean linen, no woman was permitted to taste, only the males among the children of Aaron."[20]

Feminist ethics needs to ask of Genesis 9 and the idea that humans are unable to avoid eating flesh: Is this true for us now? What feminist theology advocates for men—a "theology of relinquishment"[21]—animal defenders advocate for people who exploit animals. Isn't reconstructing relationships the most authentic and ethical response available to us?

Resisting Institutionalized Violence

We are estranged from animals through institutionalized violence and have accepted inauthenticity in the name of divine authority. We have also been estranged from ways to think about our estrangement. Religious concepts of alienation, brokenness, separation ought to include our treatment of animals. Eating animals is an existential expression of our estrangement and alienation from the created order.

Elisabeth Schüssler Fiorenza reminds us that "the basic insight of all liberation theologies, including feminist theology, is the recognition that all theology, willingly or not, is by definition always engaged for or against the oppressed."[22] To side with history and posit vegetarianism as unattainable is to side against the oppressed animals; to side with the praxis of vegetarianism is to side with the oppressed and against institutional violence.[23]

We are not bound by our histories. We are free to claim an identity based on current understandings of animal consciousness, ecological spoilage, and health issues. No more crucifixions are necessary: animals, who are still being crucified, must be freed from the cross. (See Figure 11.) The suffering of animals, our sacrificial lambs, does not bring about our redemption but furthers suffering, suffering from the inauthenticity that institutional violence promotes. Feminist ethicist Beverly Harrison offers important insights into this process of resisting institutional violence, which can be readily connected to the eating of animals. (I add these connections in brackets.)

Figure 11: *Vestiges* (Cross) by Susan kae Grant

> Each of us must learn to extend a critical analysis of the contradictions affecting our lives in an ever-widening circle, until it inclusively incorporates those whose situations differ from our own [such as animals]. This involves naming structures that create the social privilege we possess [to eat animals and make them appropriate victims] as well as understanding how we have been victims [manipulated into passivity so that we believe that we need to eat dead animals]. . . . Critical consciousness and, therefore, genuine social and spiritual transcendence, do not and cannot emerge apart from our refusing complicity in destructive social forces and resisting those structures that perpetuate life-denying conditions [including eating animals].[24]

Perhaps our greatest challenge is to raise the consciousness of those around us to see the institutional violence of eating animals as an ethical issue. But how does something become an ethical issue? Sarah Bentley has described the process by which woman-battering became an ethical concern.[25] She does so by drawing on Gerald Fourez's *Liberation Ethics* that demonstrates that "'concrete historical struggles'" are the basis for the development of "the discipline called 'ethics.'" For something to become an ethical issue we need "'a new awareness of some oppression or conflict.'" This is critical consciousness.

The defense of animals and its identification of the eating of animals as inhumane and exploitative is an example of this critical consciousness. As Bentley explains, after a time of agitation by a group living with the critical consciousness of this oppression, others besides the group with the critical consciousness will begin to question the oppression as well. The social consciousness of a community or a culture is transformed by this agitation. "Ethical themes, therefore, are *historically specific,* arising from 'the particular questions that certain groups are asking themselves.'"

Responding to the insights from the defense of animals, individuals must ask questions about the institutional violence that permits them the personal satisfaction of eating flesh. "In effect, the [particular] questions represent 'problems *raised by practices* that have to be faced.'" Farming and slaughtering practices such as caging, debeaking, liquid diets for calves, twenty-four-hour starvation before death, transporting and killing animals are all troublesome practices and they raise particular questions that need to be addressed.

Ethical statements "always evolve 'as particular ways of questioning in which people, individually or in groups, *stake their lives* as they decide what they want to do and what their solidarity is.' Thus, *if no one questions,* if no *practical engagement* takes place, no problem exists." False naming and other denial mechanisms I have mentioned cannot be overcome at a merely theoretical level. Practical engagement is required.

Unless we acquaint ourselves with the *practice* of farming and slaughtering animals, we will not encounter the *problems* raised by these practices, such as the abuse of animals, the environment, our health, and workers in the corpse industry. If the problem is invisible, in a sense mirroring the physical invisibility of intensively farmed animals, then there will be ethical invisibility.

An ethical stance that would challenge the institutional violence of eating animals involves three connected parts: certain practices raise problems; practical engagement and solidarity with the oppressed ensues when these problematic practices are perceived; an ethical position arises from this ongoing solidarity that forges critical community consciousness. As we become personally aware of the contradictions between feminist ethics and the practice of eating animals, we find that we must enter into a struggle regarding our own and this culture's practice.

To overcome our failure to acknowledge another's inviolability we need to find alternative ways of relating to animals rather than eating them. Recall Beverly Harrison's insight that "we know and value the world, *if* we know and value it, through our ability to touch, to hear, to see."[26] This sensual knowing involves calling upon second-person relationships with animals. The epigraph to the book offers a model for this type of knowing and its consequences: Alice Walker describes an experience when she touches, hears, and encounters an animal, when she has a second-person relationship with an animal. With the horse Blue the depth of feeling in his eyes recalls something she feels adults fail to remember: "Human animals and nonhuman animals can communicate quite well."[27] Shortly after regaining that knowledge, Walker experiences the injustice of a steak: "I am eating misery" she thinks. Walker touches, hears, sees, and describes interactions with very specific animals with whom she has second-person relationships, and she is changed by this, called to authenticity.

We all have an option to dispense with the consumption of misery, we can feed instead on the grace of vegetables. Virginia de Araújo describes such a perspective, that of a friend, who takes the barrenness of a cupboard, filled only with "celery threads, chard stems, avocado skins" and creates a feast, a grace

> & says, On this grace I feed, I wilt
> in spirit if I eat flesh, let the hogs,
> the rabbits live, the cows browse,
> the eggs hatch out chicks & peck seeds.[28]

The choice is institutionalized violence or feeding on grace. Can one feed on grace and eat animals? Our goal of living in right relationships and ending injustice is to have grace *in* our meals as well as *at* our meals. Feminist ethics must recognize that we are violating others in eating animals and in the process wilting the spirit. There are no appropriate victims. Let the hogs, rabbits, cows, chicks live. In place of misery, let there be grace.

10

Beastly Theology: When Epistemology Creates Ontology

Mortals deem that gods are begotten as they are, and have clothes like theirs, and voices and form . . . yes, and if oxen and horses or lions had hands, and could paint with their hands, and produce works of art as men do, horses would paint the forms of gods like horses, and oxen like oxen, and make their bodies in the image of their several kinds . . . The Ethiopians make their gods black and snub-nosed; the Tracians say theirs have blue eyes and red hair.

—Xenophanes

Calvin and **Hobbes**   by Bill Watterson

Figure 12: Eternal Consequences (*Calvin and Hobbes* Copyright Watterson. Reprinted with permission of Universal Press Syndicate. All rights reserved.)

> Talking about whether or not animals feel pain, is like talk-
> ing about the existence of God.
>
> —an animal researcher

Similarities exist between discussing the other animals and discussing
God, and no, it is not just that *dog* is *God* spelled backwards. Granted,
some of the similarities are actually expressed in opposition: the idea of
God as an unembodied, disincarnate force, while animals are seen as
soulless and solely body. (Recall the discussion of somatophobia, [see
pp. 152–53]). The charge of anthropomorphizing, often laid at the feet
of animal defenders, originally referred to language about God. As Mary
Midgley points out, anthropomorphism "may be the only example of a
notion invented solely for God, and then transferred unchanged to refer
to animals."[1]

Our concepts of God, ourselves, and how we relate to animals are all
bound together. Theologically as well as culturally positioned under
man's control, animals have been devalued. While all language about
God is metaphorical, animals often become reduced to metaphors that
reflect human concerns, human lives.[2] The term *beast* functions in this
way. Beastly theology is Christian patriarchal theology about animals,
in which they are seen as "beasts" in a pejorative sense—categorized as
less than, as representing the opposite of human beings.

We will explore some of the problems inherent in this Christian beastly
theology, because it has influenced and interacted with Western philosophy in positing animals as usable. In this chapter, I raise some of the
philosophical issues that theology must attend to so that it is not used
to uphold institutional violence. I place epistemological issues central to
beastly theology, both to explore the problems of Christian beastly theology and to help shape theology that does not marginalize the other
animals, but affirms relationships with them, treats them according to a
transvaluation of their status, and that ultimately retires the word *beast*
from the English language.

Anthropomorphism can go either up or down, humanizing either the
deity or animals; but if the vertical distance is closed in any way, i.e.,
between God and humans or humans and animals, many are discon-
certed. Curious, then, that one of the few feminine images of the divine
presented in the New Testament moves downward past humans entirely,
drawing instead on an image from the world of animals. It is actually
pollo-morphic: "How often have I desired to gather your children to-

gether as a hen gathers her brood under her wings, and you were not willing!" (Luke 13:34; see also Matthew 23:37). In talking about the other animals, including whether or not they feel pain, we must bring the theological attention and skills we would bring to talking about the existence of God. We must, in other words, attend to this with as much care as a hen gathering her brood under her wings.

What Is Beastly Theology?
The Patriarchal Christian Answer

> The tame animal is in the deepest sense the only natural animal. . . . Beasts are to be understood only in their relation to man and through man to God.
>
> —C. S. Lewis[3]

C. S. Lewis accepts a hierarchy of value that determines where on the continuum God, men, and beasts fall. The vertical boundaries that divide human and animal are related to the boundaries that have been inscribed between maleness and femaleness, God and humans. This results in a patriarchal beastly theology that contradictorily knows that something invisible exists (God), while denying the sensory information available that indicates any sorts of relevant connections between humans and animals. Barbara Noske points to the contradictions of anthropocentric theory, and by implications, beastly theology: "I have always wondered how humans (Marxists and others) can be so sure about their own *ability* to judge animal *inabilities*. Humans pretend to know *from within* that they themselves possess certain faculties and to know *from without* that animals do not."[4] How do we explain beastly theologies that know from within that God exists, but similarly know from without that animals' consciousness does not exist, or that it is not ethically relevant? Feminist theologian Paula Cooey offers one answer: it is "way too easy to project a God in our own image because it is simple to commit idolatry and way too difficult to project pain and pleasure on actual sentient nonhuman creatures. Thus we can project a conscious being and call it God because we perceive it as a linguistic being, but it is much harder to do this with animals because it is hard to attribute consciousness, pain, and suffering to a nonlinguistic being."[5]

Certainly the theological centrality of the Word in Christian thought militates against recognizing animals as subjects of their own lives. Whether used literally (in the sense of valuing spoken and written words over other forms of communication), or metaphorically (in the identification of Jesus Christ as God's definitive "Word"), it has the effect of marginalizing and objectifying those who have no words. Although God speaks in other, nonverbal ways in Scripture—whirlwind, fire, political upheaval, military victory or defeat—God's definitive communication is in the form of words: the Decalogue, the Law, Scripture, etc. Speaking thus becomes identified with holy power. Language provides us with both a sense of affinity with God and subject status, while simultaneously confirming the object status of those who have no speech.[6]

But this focus on language may deflect our attention from the knowledge claims that are presupposed in patriarchal beastly theologies. Language may be one of the methods for acquiring knowledge, but to stake one's knowledge claims solely on language becomes self-referential, as Cooey implies when she points to how easy it is to commit idolatry. Moreover, "the most eloquent signs of pain, human *or* animal, are non-linguistic."[7] Why, when projected God-ward, is one form of inner knowledge acceptable, but projected animal-ward, is this form of knowledge rendered unacceptable, and the external knowledge we can gain from animals eloquently expressing pain distrusted? Because anthropocentricity is inherently circular, arising from and referring to human beings. As Donald Griffin, a leading ethologist, remarks:

> I believe that with due caution it is reasonable to make some use of such analogies between human and animal behaviour and mental experience, for the simple reason that central nervous systems are so similar in all their basic attributes, as far as we know. Against the charge that such reasoning by analogy is mistakenly anthropomorphic, I have pointed out that such anthropomorphism is mistakenly only if there are indeed fundamental and absolute differences between human and non-human mental experiences. Since this is the question under discussion, it is prejudicial to assume, even by implication that one of the possible answers to the question is necessarily correct.[8]

Anthropocentric theology is inherently circular too. When theology is modeled upon the traditional, self-referential conceptualizations of the God–human relationship, knowledge claims on behalf of the other animals are most likely to be excluded.

Value Hierarchies and Dualisms

Previous chapters have drawn on ecofeminist philosopher Karen J. Warren's description of the components of an oppressive conceptual framework to place animals conceptually within feminist philosophy and theory. Here Warren's work illuminates patriarchal beastly theologies.

As we have seen, value-hierarchical thinking or "up-down thinking" places higher value, status, or prestige on what is up rather than what is down. In Christian theology, God has been up, animals have been down. And though humans are seen to be in between, both the notions of *imago dei,* that humans are in the image of God, and the idea that animals do not have souls place humans much closer to God than to the other animals.

Warren also identifies value dualisms as part of an oppressive conceptual framework. We have seen how disjunctive pairs such as human/animal, male/female, adult/child, white/nonwhite, culture/nature, mind/body, subject/object, humans/nature are seen as oppositional rather than as complementary. Dualisms reduce diversity to two categories: A or Not A. They convey the impression that everything can then be appropriately categorized: *either* it is A *or* Not A. These dualisms represent dichotomy rather than continuity, enacting exclusion rather than inclusion. Feminist theologian Catherine Keller explains how the identification of the separative self is based on emphasizing differences: "It is *this,* not *that.*"[9] This phenomenon is especially true in the ontological assumptions concerning humans and the other animals. We structure this ontology by saying we are *this,* not *that*; humans, not animals. We are people, they are beasts. We go to heaven, they do not.

Higher value is accorded the first item in each dyad. Moreover, the second part of the dualism is not only subordinate but *in service* to the first. Women serve men, nature serves culture, animals serve humans, people of color serve white people. Theologically, traditional conceptions of heaven and earth work in this oppositional, dualistic way that discourages earth consciousness. Restrictive dualisms uphold a logic of domination. Central to a logic of domination is language that normalizes this domination. The hierarchical nature of the traditional conception of the Godhead sacralizes a logic of domination in our relationships.

Let us recall certain characteristics of the prevailing, fossilized "God-talk" that relies on hierarchical images: God is imaged as a human male (father, lord, king), and as a male with authority and power; human maleness is conceptualized as being higher up on the hierarchy than human femaleness. In my research on people's attitudes to animals for *The Sexual Politics of Meat,* I discovered why animals of prey are called "she" no matter what their sex. Because, according to linquists, the word *she* connotes a "minor power."[10] Will "she" always be a "minor power" as long as resistance exists to seeing God—about as major a power as one can be—as anything but "He"?[11] Will animals be a "minor power" and exploitable as long as the traditional conception of God ratifies hierarchy in our relationships?

Yes, according to Catherine Keller:

> The association in this epoch between separatism and masculinity is

so tight that as long as God is imagined in mainly masculine metaphors, there is simply no chance for conversion to a fundamentally relational spirituality. And the reverse holds equally true: as long as divinity is externalized by the traditional perfections of self-sufficiency, omnipotence, impassionability and immutability, "God"—even were she made in name and image a woman, an androgyne, or a neuter—will support the oppression of women. . . . As long as separation itself is deified, women of faith will end up in the doubly dependent role of subjugation to God and the male, who is himself subjugated to God.[12]

Human authority over the other animals is modeled after the notion of divine authority over humans, and men's authority over women. We recapitulate a hierarchy of control, playing God, lord, ruler, regent, dominator toward the other animals. This role is one of dispensing decisions rather than egalitarianism; it enforces rather than enhances; it highlights separation and difference rather than relationship and similarity. Concepts of God as father and animals as beasts fall at either ends of this value-hierarchical continuum. Metaphors announce and reinforce this placement.

Metaphors of Domination

Metaphors are and are not true, depict and yet cannot depict reality. As Sallie McFague explains it: "Metaphor always has the character of 'is' and 'is not.'"[13] This is especially true with theological metaphors. When *metaphors* for God that offer models of relationship with God become instead *definitions* of God, they become frozen, inadequate, anachronistic. While the metaphor of "God the father" provides one way of thinking about our relationship with God based on relationships we know and understand, it is not a definition of God. God may be like a father in some ways, but God is not a father. When metaphor becomes definition, limits on relationships occur.

Metaphors for God become frozen and outdated; so, too, do metaphors for animals. When metaphors like "beast," "bestial," "brutal," "beastly," "animal desires," "animal-like" are used uncritically to provide contrast with and to glorify human behavior, we have allowed our ideas about animals to be frozen and outdated. Let us remember, as Keith Thomas points out, that "it was as a comment on *human* nature that the concept of 'animality' was devised."[14] What we consider to be their reality becomes our metaphor. We respond to animals as though these metaphors about *our* behavior are true for them. In the process, a distancing akin to the distancing accomplished by envisioning a separate, individualistic, regent in the sky is accomplished. Our metaphors seem to say that God is not us; we are not animals. But much feminist theology suggests that God is us, is in us, is revealed by us, is a part of our relationships. And animal defenders declare, we are animals. As philosopher Mary Midgley says emphatically: "*They are the group to which people belong.* We are not just rather like animals; we *are* animals."[15]

Maureen Duffy observes: "The truth is that we have always used animals not simply for practical purposes but as metaphors for our own emotional requirements, and it is this that we are unwilling to give up by considering them as creatures with rights and lives of their own. We refuse to recognise the sentience of other species in order that we may go on treating them as objects, projections and symbols."[16] Similarly, while it may have helped believers of previous centuries to say that God was like a lord, king, ruler, these metaphors are not helpful today as they uphold the idea of God being separate from creation. As Sallie McFague explains:

> We live in our imaginations and our feelings in a bygone world, one under the guidance of a benevolent but absolute deity, a world that is populated by independent individuals (mainly human beings) who relate to one another and to other forms of life in hierarchical patterns. But this is not *our* world, and to continue doing theology on its assumptions is hurtful, for it undermines our ability to accept the new sensibility of our time, one that is holistic and responsible, that is inclusive of all forms of life, and that acknowledges the interdependence of all life.[17]

Metaphors of a triumphant, monarchical "God" are not true for our time. But they help to explain why we see animals as exploitable. A value hierarchy that is upheld by a logic of domination places animals so low on the hierarchy that their bodies can be viewed instrumentally. Moreover, as long as the main images in Western culture are of "God" as ruler, lord, king of creation, and this metaphor is derived from the experience of some (predominantly white male) human beings, then animals cannot be ruler, lord, kings of creation. By anthropomorphizing God, we exclude animals from the Godhead. In addition, the value dualisms of spirit over body, maleness above femaleness, heaven above earth become sacralized.

If images of God as king and male are incomplete, partial, and inadequate, so too are *animal* metaphors.

The "God" of the Man of Reason

> The very beginning of Genesis tells us that God created man in order to give him dominion over fish and fowl and all creatures. Of course,

Genesis was written by a man, not a horse. There is no certainty that God actually did grant man dominion over other creatures. What seems more likely, in fact, is that man invented God to sanctify the dominion that he had usurped for himself over the cow and the horse. Yes, the right to kill a deer or a cow is the only thing all of mankind can agree upon, even during the bloodiest of wars.

—Milan Kundera[18]

As we have seen in earlier discussions, feminist philosophy challenges the notion of an atomistic subject, "the man of reason" who splits subject from object, and whose mode of being is marked by transcending the body. Just as animals are defined precisely as what humans are not, so, traditionally, "femaleness was symbolically associated with what Reason supposedly left behind."[19] Feminists have demonstrated that a knowing subject cannot transcend the social structures in which he or she lives, or become abstracted from one's own history. However, the idea of the man of reason was that he could overcome body, history, social situations, and thereby gain knowledge of others he examined as objects. This idea of the man of reason was accompanied by the Western idea of a disembodied, ahistorical God the father. The Man of Reason and his God created categories for animals, categories that arise from knowledge claims about what we *believe* to know that animals are.

Human male dominance may be having a parallel influence on both the assumption of who the knower is *and* the assumption of who an animal is. As feminist philosopher Alison Jaggar explains: "Several feminist theorists have argued that modern epistemology itself may be viewed as an expression of certain emotions alleged to be especially characteristic of [human] males in certain periods, such as separation anxiety and paranoia, or an obsession with control and fear of contamination."[20] According to this insight, modern epistemology and its suspicion of emotions, dualist ontologies, rationalist bias, and concern for achieving objectivity, may represent not some universal response, but a very specific one: the response to the experience of being an elite human male. Similarly, feminist theorist Barbara Noske points out that "it is really the straight Western male whose strongholds are threatened by human-animal continuity. Physical closeness, grooming, nurturance and companionship are so much part of the female *and* male primate behavioural pattern that the lack of these among heterosexual Western males is genuinely surprising."[21]

The patriarchal knower's fear of his own body may account both for the enlightenment epistemology that objectifies others and the delineation of a complete and utter chasm between human and animal.

In a vertically organized world, in which spatial hierarchies denote value or lack thereof (the traditional God-human-animals hierarchy) beastly theological categories are maintained. Pulsating out from the humanocentric view of the world, we both wish to make and resist making the Other in our image. The "Man of Reason" traditionally transcended both femaleness and beastliness, while viewing many female traits as linking women to other animals.[22] Anxious about charges of expressing sentiments for animals if they were acknowledged to have forms of consciousness, sociality or other human-allied concepts, the man of reason deemed these emotions untrustworthy and invalid sources of knowledge. The positivistic scientific views of the other animals that arise from "men of reason," i.e., traditional scientists, is one that Barbara Noske calls the "de-animalized animal." Since it is equipped only to measure observable phenomena, and its explanatory apparatus of natural selection focuses on the individual organic level, this scientific view discounts animals' culture. It strips the other animals of consciousness, inventiveness, and cultural context. What we have is "a de-animalized biological construct rather than a mirror of animal reality."[23] It becomes, however, the prevailing viewpoint. This illustrates an "objectifying epistemology," as Josephine Donovan calls it, "which turns animals into 'its.'"[24] The positivist tradition simultaneously denies animals their context and the knowing subject her emotions.

Many who experience a metaphysical shift toward animals, refusing to ontologize them as usable, discover a feeling of abiding anger contrary to the reasonable standard of patriarchal culture. Anger is a frightening and much-misunderstood expression, an "outlaw emotion" in Alison Jaggar's terms. According to Jaggar, outlaw emotions

> may enable us to perceive the world differently from its portrayal in conventional descriptions. They may provide the first indications that something is wrong with the way alleged facts have been constructed, with accepted understandings of how things are.... Only when we reflect on our initially puzzling irritability, revulsion, anger, or fear may we bring to consciousness our "gut-level" awareness that we are in a situation of coercion, cruelty, injustice, or danger.[25]

While the knowledge claims arising from men of reason would disown such emotions, Jaggar points to the importance of such outlaw emotions for challenging dominant conceptions of the status quo. She perceives intertwined influences in which "appropriate emotions may contribute to the development of knowledge" and "the growth of knowledge may contribute to the development of appropriate emotions."[26] In light of Jaggar's insights, we can see that anger may well be an appropriate response to the knowledge of monkeys in stereotaxic chairs, minipigs being developed for animal experimentation, debeaking so that hens do not commit cannibalism in their stressful and overcrowded cages, the capture and breeding of dolphins and whales for humans' entertainment, the transporting of one-or two-day-old feeble male calves (awkwardly walking and still with wet umbilical cord) to slaughterhouses, the dragging of old, crippled dairy and beef cows by skid steer loaders or the scooping up of downers into buckets to get them to the slaughterhouse door, and any number of creatively cruel interactions that humans have with animals. *These emotions are not only appropriate, but appropriate sources of knowledge.* By occluding these acts we hide from the truth.

In February 1994 the California Board of Education banned the use of Alice Walker's "Am I Blue?" from a statewide English test because it was "anti-meat-eating." Marion McDowell, president of the California Board of Education reportedly said that the conclusion of the short story—when the narrator spits out the steak she had been eating because she is eating misery—"could be rather disturbing to some students who would then be expected to write a good essay while they were upset."[27] Fascinating in this decision is the epistemological control exercised here: no one challenges the fact that Alice Walker's essay may be speaking the truth; it is eliminated because the truth might be upsetting. Again, we see that emotions are related to truth and, as McDowell implies, that the growth of knowledge may contribute to the development of appropriate emotions, truly outlaw emotions.

*The Categorization of Animals
and the "God" of the Man of Reason*

What results from an anxious knowledge stance that objectifies animals and disowns outlaw emotions is an ahistorical and disembodied view of animals. The knowledge claims gravitate to categories that would apply in most, if not all cases, across history and specific individual situations. And this is exactly their problem. The debate about what is uniquely human, and what it is about animals that makes them nonhuman, takes place precisely in the zone that theologies of liberation have shown to be false—the zone of absolutes. Definitions or categorizations regarding animals function as absolute truths. Such absolute or universal knowledge claims represent the logic and interests of the oppressor. Grounding one's claims in ahistorical absolutes demonstrates bad faith. To cling to certainty in categories such as *animals* represents a political decision and avoids a risky and potentially destabilizing discourse.

In discussing the way categories of knowing influence perceptions, Michel Foucault described a passage from the writer Jorge Luis Borges that provides a different ordering of things. Borges wrote about a Chinese encyclopedia in which animals are divided into "(a) belonging to the Emperor, (b) embalmed, (c) tame, (d) sucking pigs, (e) sirens, (f) fabulous, (g) stray dogs, (h) included in the present classification, (i) frenzied, (j) innumerable, (k) drawn with a very fine camel's hair brush, (l) etcetera, (m) having just broken the water pitcher, (n) that from a long way off look like flies."[28] According to Foucault this passage "shattered . . . all the familiar landmarks of my thought." Because these categories are alien to our experience, this example provides the vehicle for Foucault and Sharon Welch—who cites it in her feminist theology of liberation—to explore the relativity of truth claims and of ordering experiences. Foucault points out that the dominant culture, too, may be relying on categories that function as absolute but are actually as contingent as Borges's fabulous organization of animals. Pushing this insight, I would argue that such absolutes as our current categorization of animals may be as contingent and false as Borges's example. Seeing Borges's categorization of animals only as the vehicle to expose the falsity of absolutes is one option. While this fictional classification may operate to disrupt one's notion that existing categories can be adequate or accurate, it could also direct us to the fixed categorizations that still operate when we think of and interact with the other animals. I would turn such insight about absolutes and universals back toward that which prompts such insight—the categories we cling to in oppressing animals.

What we perceive here is that the fabulous categorizations of animals reflects on another level—a level that has so far been unacknowledged—the actual situation of animals who have been categorized by humans. While there appears to be a logic to these familiar animal categories, they may simply represent the arbitrary logic of the oppressor:

> (a) animals who are edible; (b) animals who are not edible; (c) animals who produce food for us while living (cows, goats, chickens, bees); (d) animals living as companions in households; (e) animals living in households but not wanted (vermin); (f) animals whose bodies can be experimented upon; (g) animals who can be worn; (h) animals who have social networks but no consciousness; (i) animals who use tools but are not humans; (j) animals who can be hunted; (k) animals who no longer exist; (l) animals who are in danger of extinction; (m) etcetera.[29]

These examples are not fabulous and fictional, they represent everyday relations that are predicated on acceptable boundaries arising from universal truth claims of what is uniquely human. These boundaries and the structure of relations they legitimize are as suspect as any other form of traditional knowledge posited as universal and absolute. They result from what Donna Haraway calls "the god trick."

The God Trick

The *god trick* refers to the positioning of those who hold to a traditional notion of objectivity: that one can transcend body, personal and cultural history, and thereby acquire "pure knowledge." In Marilyn Frye's terms, the god trick sees with an arrogant eye. According to Donna Haraway, "those occupying the positions of the dominators are self-identical, unmarked, disembodied, unmediated, transcendent, born again."[30] In dualistic patriarchy, those occupying the positions of the subjugated, therefore, are marked, embodied, mediated, imminent. Haraway argues further that knowledge arising from this positioning of the subjugated is situated knowledge, and because situated, therefore responsible, whereas knowledge arising from a place where one has the illusion of a view of infinite vision produces unlocatable and thus irresponsible—that is, unable to be called into account—knowledge claims:

> The standpoints of the subjugated are . . . preferred because in principle they are least likely to allow denial of the critical and interpretive core of all knowledge. They are knowledgeable of modes of denial through repression, forgetting, and disappearing acts—ways of being nowhere while claiming to see comprehensively. The subjugated have a decent chance to be on to the god trick and its dazzling—and therefore, blinding—illuminations. "Subjugated" standpoints are preferred because they seem to promise more adequate, sustained, objective, transforming accounts of the world.[31]

Virginia Woolf provides an excellent example of someone engaging in the god trick in her classic feminist text, *A Room of One's Own*. She demonstrates the way absolute and universal categories work, the way one claims to see comprehensively:

> I thought of that old gentleman, who is dead now, but was a bishop, I think, who declared that it was impossible for any woman, past, present, or to come, to have the genius of Shakespeare. He wrote to the papers about it. He also told a lady who applied to him for information that cats do not as a matter of fact go to heaven, though they have, he added, souls of a sort. How much thinking those old gentlemen used to save one! How the borders of ignorance shrank back at their approach! Cats do not go to heaven. Women cannot write the plays of Shakespeare.[32]

How comforting to hold such firm beliefs as the bishop! Yet, in Donna Haraway's words, how irresponsible are such knowledge claims. Irresponsible precisely because they appear unable to be called into account. (How does one, after all, prove who does go to heaven?) How much thinking patriarchal beastly theologies used to save us! Once we believe that any authority or our theology has decided the question of the status of the other animals, then we can, without any qualms, safely abdicate thinking, feeling, responding to the issues that arise concerning the exploitation of animals. The surest way to short-circuit justice is to believe that the question of exploitation has already been settled and we are not the responsible parties in the debate. We let someone else perform the god trick and then chose it as our own methodology.

The God Trick and Animals

In Woolf's description of the bishop's knowledge claims the traditional spatial hierarchy of heaven and earth recalls the literal hierarchy of humans and animals, men and women, since, as Virginia Woolf reminds us through the bishop's self-proclaimed authority, humans may go to heaven, but animals are earthbound. Of course his opinion represents a defensive position: there is self-interest in believing that animals (at least those who are consumed) do not go to heaven. To imagine that we would meet animals in heaven, may be a disquieting thought for those who eat them.[33] Yet, whether cats or farm animals go to heaven is not the point, to imagine heaven as separate from and above earth decenters our here-and-now relationships with all that live on earth. The parallel hierarchies of space and power (heaven over earth, humans over animals), enact a distancing that allows us to become disengaged from animals and the earth. This distancing allows us to become godlike—in Haraway's terms, "unmarked, disembodied, unmediated, transcendent."

While we may be godlike in the way we can create and dispose of animals, we actually are marked, embodied, mediated. The choice before us is to cling to the God–human–animal hierarchy and inevitably continue to see God as an old gentleman, or affirm the relevance of our own—and animals'—sensory experiences. Options other than an objectifying epistemology exist.

Agreeing Not to Play the God Trick

Among other things, theologies of liberation interpret sin as domination, and direct our attention to *structures* of domination and exploitation. Traditional, universal truth claims are exposed as false. Whereas there is a tendency to universalize animals, actually no one animal nature exists. Animals are particular, embodied, social creatures, not representatives of a measurable and thus "timeless" or disembodied quality. Moreover, developments in ethology and the other sciences are undermining the human/animal dualism by pointing to evidence of animal consciousness, language, tool use, and other attributes previously considered the sole province of human beings. Our capabilities are continuous with those of the other animals, not discontinuous.

Patriarchal beastly theologies derive from an epistemological stance that presumes universal categories and removes the knowers from any position of responsibility at all. But the god trick is an illusion. As Lorraine Code argues, we do not know "the world" as objective observers who are separate from the world. Hopefully, we wish to know the world as "moral and epistemic subjects who know and understand by positioning themselves within a situation in order to understand its *implications* and see in those implications contextualized, situated reasons for action."[34] But in order to so position ourselves we must be willing to reexamine universal categories.

Not only is the dominant culture coercive—constructing universal categories and absolutes where they do not exist—it has an ability to absorb a radical viewpoint, an epistemological challenge, and eviscerate it so that it looks like the argument is about ontology. As long as we are debating ontology, the epistemological is invisible. This serves the dominant culture's perspective. What should be suspect, and a question of consciousness—for instance, universal categories that cast animals as consumable—is rendered valid and inevitable.

An Excursus on Ontology and Epistemology

Epistemological and ontological issues recur throughout this book. They are particularly pertinent to theological discussions. When feminist theologians devoted close attention to the Genesis 2 story of creation they did so in part because it provided theological justification for an ontological situation—women's subjugated status. To get at the ontological, these theologians reinterpreted Genesis 2. They argued that the story of Eve's heeding the serpent and disobeying God, thus being told that she would be subject to her husband, was not actually about the woman being untrustworthy and sinful, nor did it mandate women's subordination. Similarly, as we saw in the previous chapter, attempts are made to interpret Genesis 1 to break the ontologizing of humans as dominators of animals and the rest of nature.

But these defenses keep the debate on the ontological level, when what is needed is a focus on knowledge claims and therefore on epistemology.

The epistemological is always framing a discussion, an approach, a theology. It is often invisible or actively concealed.

In the previous chapter I described the death of Jimmy, and how it precipitated ontological questions: Why are some animals seen as consumable? What I had previously "known" rationally, that I ate animals, I now "knew" as an embodied truth—and one with serious moral implications. I felt the fact that I consumed animals resonating throughout my bodily self in a shock wave of horrified fascination and irredeemable immediacy. And a realization radiated from this felt truth, this embodied knowing: what I am doing is not right, this is not ethically acceptable. In a sense I began to ask myself: On what grounds have I accepted the ontologizing of animals as edible?

What I "knew" through my bodily self was, as Josephine Donovan states: "We should not kill, eat, torture, and exploit animals because they do not want to be so treated, and we know that."[35] This embodied knowledge involved recognizing that whereas I had ontologized animals as consumable, exploitable, violable, I could do so only through the god trick, by following the methods of any oppressor in believing the illusion that this was a universal perspective, i.e., that no other ontological possibility existed such as that the other animals might want to be treated otherwise, as inviolable. As Donovan recognizes, another perspective exists, that of the animals so violated. Integrating this perspective within the reality of my life required me to change my diet and my moral framework. In this sense, mine was the sort of knowledge that feminist philosopher Lorraine Code describes when she envisions knowledge that does not seek to control "nature" but instead lets "nature" speak for itself.

I questioned the ontology that permitted oppressive actions and controlled "nature," and began to seek an alternative ontology. But I also began to recognize that what has been cast as an issue of ontology—i.e., are animals "meant" to be eaten?—is much more centrally a question of epistemology. The epistemological questions feminists explore regarding the social construction of "women," knowledge, science, and culture address knowledge claims that are pertinent here. What do we know about animals? about human beings' differences from the other animals? about how the other animals experience their relationships with human beings? and how do we know it? How do we know, for instance, that animals do not suffer when being killed to become food? that animal experimentation is the only way to advance medical knowledge? Who is making these knowledge claims about the other animals and on what grounds? What do we actually know about animal consciousness? about the standpoint of animals? about what commonalities we truly share with the other animals? about the ways animals experience themselves and other animals? Questions such as these problematize the knowledge claims that accompany the acceptance of the value dualisms and value hierarchy of patriarchal beastly theology.

From questions such as these we begin to see that the current ontological condition of animals as violable has less do with *their* beingness, than with *our* consciousness. Animals need not be destined to become humans' food (ontology). That we see them as food or clothes is a construct of perception, cultural intervention, a forced identity (epistemology). The representation "animal" is what we are given to know.

The epistemology of the "human" who sees "animals" as usable creates the world of the human/animal dualism. The way we humans look at animals literally creates them as usable.[36] This means that in life "human" and "animal," like "woman" and "man" are "widely experienced as features of *being,* not constructs of perception, cultural interventions or forced identities." Both *species* and *gender* are "lived as ontology, not as epistemology."[37] As Catharine MacKinnnon observes, what is occuring is a "transformation of *perspective* into *being.*" And if it succeeds ontologically, human dominance does not look epistemological: "Control over being produces control over consciousness."[38] This is why so many debates focus specifically on animals' beingness: because the shift from perspective to being (from epistemology to ontology) is, if successful, hidden from view. The role our consciousness plays in all of this remains concealed.

Catharine MacKinnon points out further that "when seemingly ontological conditions are challenged from the collective standpoint of a dissident reality, they become visible as epistemological."[39] Animal defenders offer such a dissident reality, saying, "Animals aren't meant to be eaten or experimented upon! Eating animals and experimenting upon them is not inevitable! Their meaning in life does not come from their being consumed!" Those who challenge animals' exploitation are knowing subjects who have recognized their position in, and accountability to, the animals' world. What has been hidden is brought into view.

Transforming Beastly Theology

Because women's roles were declared to be subordinate to men as a matter of God's will, a part of the feminist theological task has been the breaking of the authoritative/ontological association that predetermines questions of authentic being. Feminist theology begins with experience as a corrective to the authority/ontological situating of women as other. A similar process of beginning with experience opens new possibilities of relationships with animals. As testimonies of numerous people reveal, when people experience the realities of the slaughterhouse or the factory farm, they are less likely to want to see themselves as corpse eaters and the other animals as flesh. Outlaw emotions may prompt epistemological shifts.

Many defenders of the other animals came to their positions through radical intersubjectivity, through the second-person relationship of knowing another animal. Here, too, is the sort of knowledge that does not seek to control "nature" but instead lets "nature" speak for itself. Such resituating of nature as a speaking subject is illustrated in Vicki Hearne's *Adam's Task:* "It occurs to me that it is surprising that 'I don't know, I haven't met her' is rarely the response given to 'Can Washoe [the chimpanzee] talk?'"[40]

Second-Person Theology

In chapter 8, I described the concept of second persons. We become persons through our dependence upon other persons from whom we "acquire the essential arts of personhood."[41] Lives begin in communality and interdependence; thus in our acquisition of knowledge, "persons are essentially second persons"[42] and our knowledge is never atomistically individualistic or "self-made." In chapter 9, I described my own metaphysical shift in relationship to animals that resulted from a second-person relationship with an animal. Second-person theologies are needed to upend patriarchal beastly theologies. Like second-person thinking in which "knowledge claims are forms of address, speech acts, moments in a dialogue that assume and rely on the participation of (an)other subject(s),"[43] second-person theology derives from encountering the other animals as subjects. As Vicki Hearne suggests, our knowledge claims are inadequate if in discussing animals we have not included them within the dialogue.

God unfolds in relationships. Most animals are excluded from experiencing this notion of "God-in-relationship" because we use them precisely in ways that sever relationships. Many forms of animal exploitation involve caging and confining them, restricting their ability— no, their need—to enjoy social relationships, and bestow upon animals an expectation that they can exist inanimately even while alive. Does the creation of some beings solely for the purpose of being objects make sense in the face of an intrinsically and radically relational divinity? If God is process, *being,* and revealed through relationship should we not situate all beings within that divine relationship, seeing with loving eyes?

It is said that talking about whether animals suffer pain is like talking about the existence of God. But, let's push this further. What if trying to have a conversation with an animal is like trying to have a conversation with God? Would we then bring a discipline of attending to our relationships with animals? Vicki Hearne refers to Martin Heidegger's suggestion of "listening to the dog's being."[44] Sally Carrighar in *Home to the Wilderness: A Personal Journey* offers an example of such listening to an animal's beingness: "I talked to the birds and animals and I talked sense, in a normal voice. . . . [I would say] to a very shy grouse, 'Have you thought of taking a dustbath? Look here where the earth is so fine and dry.' I knew they did not understand the words, but to such sensitive creatures a tone may convey more than we realize. . . . It seemed that they had to feel a true sense of warmth, not sentimentality but concern.[45] Need it be observed that such conversations are impossible with one's "steak" dinner or leather coat?

Second-person theology incorporates animals both directly through acknowledging them as subjects rather than objects, and also in its care to create knowledge claims that assume and rely on the participation of these other subjects. The result would be not only the destabilizing of flesh and leather and other forms of animal exploitation, but the retiring of the word *beast,* recognizing that its function is restricted to a vertically organized world.

Liberating animals from the appellation of beast, we would also be liberated from the need to label humans as "not beasts." *Beast* would appear in dictionaries with the label *archaic* appended to it.

From Beastly Theologies to Second-Person Theologies

> I do think that one's fellow animals of other species are aware of the change in one's own attitude when one becomes vegetarian. . . . I do think that the psychological act of deciding to be a vegetarian frees one from a lot of guilt towards animals and I think they are aware of this. My impression is that one's relationship to them becomes very much less ambiguous and ambivalent and one is freer to think of them as equals. I think it's this property that they respond to. I definitely have the impression that I have a different relationship with animals since I became a vegetarian.
>
> —Brigid Brophy[46]

With second-person theologies, animals would no longer be absent referents in theological discourse—metaphors for human beings—nor absent referents in theological praxis, objects whom we do not know anything about, or whom we assume to know categorically and universally. Second-person theologies are inimical to the structure of the absent referent. When animals are absent conceptually, we have eliminated the space in which our embodied knowing could encounter relationship, there is nothing for our loving eye to engage with. Whatever limits there are to knowing the viewpoints of the other animals, we can know that what matters to them is that we stop defining them and using them. We can never be in relation with all animals nor need we be, but we can work to release all animals from being ontologized as usable.

In dismantling the structure of the absent referent, second-person theologies resituate animals, resubjectifying them, acknowledging that each animal is a subjective presence in the world. As Barbara Noske argues, we need to move to a descriptive rather than definitional discourse about animals, recognizing a species boundary that is horizontal rather than vertical and hierarchical.

Second-person theologies offer alternatives to the dualistic reduction of human versus animal claims. By challenging the dualism, we refuse to accept the oppositional nature of the definitions of humans and animals. In this we are not making "animals" like "humans," only less so. We are, however, releasing both humans and animals from this reductive dualism. We may discover that our concepts of ourselves will change as our concepts of animals change. In fact, feminist challenges to the notion of the autonomous human subject will benefit from the liberating of the other animals from the category of "animal." As Barbara Noske explains:

> Nature had to be devaluated to a state where it could be useful economically and technically, though harmless ideologically. But nature could only be devaluated if and when humanity detached itself from nature and ceased to feel part of it. The Dutch philosopher/anthropologist Ton Lemaire makes clear that the two developments, namely, the objectification of nature and the autonomization of the human subject, go hand in hand, "reality could only fully become an object after humanity had collected its personality out of the unconscious intertwinement with external nature."[47]

In recognizing that we can be second persons to animals, we reinsert our personality within creation. We are not separated, autonomous "knowers" in a dominating culture but second persons with the rest of nature. The process of reengaging with creation, and particularly with the other animals, will produce a different subjectivity and a different theology.

In a culture that ontologizes animals as exploitable we must address current behavior that is predicated on this ontology. A few centuries from now people might have to do something actively to cause the harm of animals, now they must actively do something to impede the harm of animals (i.e., bag vegetarian lunches instead of buying school cafeteria lunches, inquire into the contents of soap, shampoo, etc.). As long as "meat" or "fur" or "leather" are available in stores, people have to intervene actively against the consumerism of producing, procuring, or purchasing these "products." We must resist doing something we have been taught to do.

What remains for all of us is a task of personal and mythic archaeology, the reinspection of old terrain. We ourselves are buried under layers of categories that construct species difference as a meaningful ethical determinant. We can no longer allow the bishop and other patriarchal knowers to determine our knowledge. Those issues identified by feminist theology as central to patriarchal religion—issues such as the subordination of experience to authority, the rigid conceptualization of "God" as Father and monarch, the notion of the separate, atomistic self—are also central to the idea that animals can be objects or instruments, and that our relationship with the divine trumps their inviolability. Catherine Keller proposes that "the pull toward connection, when coordinated with feminist sensibility, can and does generate a new meaning of what it is to be a self."[48] Would this pull toward connection, this new meaning of being a self, and its relationship to the ultimate in life, would this deep affinity with all beings condone using animals instrumentally, experimenting on their live bodies, and consuming their dead bodies? Given the nature of the interlocking system of oppression, can we continue to ignore this question?

Coda

The day after the 1990 March for Animals in Washington, the *Washington Post* carried an article about it in its local edition. The article described the march, and quoted one animal defender who said, "We're no longer just little old ladies in tennis shoes."

I am hoping to live long enough to qualify to be a little old lady. Since, unlike the person who made the comment, this category is something I actively aspire to, I wondered about this backhanded compliment.

After all, one thing that was being said was "before the rest of us discovered the legitimate and important issues about humans' oppression of animals, little old ladies had." Perhaps when they started agitating on behalf of animals they were not little old ladies. But people's refusal to face the facts about what we do to animals made them old in the process.

We know that the British antivivisection movement of the nineteenth century would have collapsed without women. We know that an estimated 75 percent of animal rights activists today are women.

This is what I know about little old ladies:

As women age they often become more radical. As men age, they are likely to become more conservative.

Apparently, according to Dr. Gideon Seaman and Barbara Seaman, as women age they leave flesh out of their diet. They have learned to listen to their bodies.[1] Listening to our bodies is something our culture actively works against. In a sense we have an ethic of disembodied domination: an ethic that disregards the effects on our bodies and the earth's body of consuming animals, and an ethic that disdains to consider animals and their bodies as legitimate concerns.

Other cultures respect the older generation and especially women: women were known as wise women. But Western culture hurls numerous epithets at old women: calling them for instance crones, "an ugly, withered old woman," or "hag." Crone can also mean "a cantankerous or mischievous woman." What feminist does not quarrel and disagree with the dominant culture as it now exists? Mary Daly suggests that crones are the long-lasting ones.[2] That's what feminists will have to be to defeat animal exploitation.

Another meaning of the term *crone* is "a withered, witchlike old woman." Just a few hundred years ago, hundreds of thousands of women were accused of being witches during a massive antiwoman campaign:[3] many of them were little old ladies,[4] or single women who were herbal healers and midwives. Many were said to have "witches' familiars," i.e., companion animals who were said to be equally bewitched. As Keith Thomas describes it:

> But whether these domestic pets or uninvited animal companions were seen as magical is another matter. These creatures may have been the only friend these lonely old women possessed, and the names they gave them suggest an affectionate relationship. Matthew Hopkin's victims in Essex included Mary Hockett, who was accused of entertaining "three evil spirits each in the likeness of a mouse, called 'Littleman,' 'Prettyman' and 'Daynty,'" and Bridget Mayers, who entertained "an evil spirit in the likeness of a mouse called 'Prickeares.'" More recently the novelist J. R. Ackerley has written of his mother that: "One of her last friends, when she was losing her faculties, was a fly, which I never saw but which she talked about a good deal and also talked to. With large melancholy yellow eyes and long lashes it inhabited the bathroom; she made a little joke of it but was serious enough to take in crumbs of bread every morning to feed it, scattering them along the wooden rim of the bath as she lay in it."[5]

When flies and mice are invested with the qualities of personhood—given names, seen as individuals, interacted with—we have the basis for an ethic that would challenge their oppression.

Animal suffering is mostly invisible to the average consumer. Flesh departments in supermarkets never show films about animals being imprisoned in intensive farms or butchered, and household products never carry on their label a picture of the animal experimentation that was conducted as part of product testing. What people take for granted about their lives requires the invisibility of animals and of their experience of oppression. We face the challenge of making the invisible—and that which people actively wish to keep invisible—very visible. When we make animals' experiences visible, we expose traditional ethical, moral, and religious discussions that ignored animals.

Traditionally, concern about animals has been seen as individual and emotional—something equated with little old ladies. Who, remember, like all women, were not allowed to contribute to the original discussions about what is ethical, moral, or religious in the first place. Let's recall what Spinoza said: "The objection to killing animals was 'based upon an empty superstition and womanish tenderness, rather than upon sound reason.'"[6] The mischievous, cantankerous crone inside myself asks, who decided what is "sound reason"? Why is tenderness considered a negative quality, equated with effeminacy? Animal defenders are actively dismantling the dominant philosophies, and that, of necessity, will involve a feminist approach that acknowledges these outlaw emotions as appropriate.

Louise Armstrong, in examining the problem of what freedom meant to nineteenth-century women who proposed what some condescendingly call "protectionism," argues that "what women were seeking was freedom *from* what men were free to (and wanted to) do to them: abandon them to poverty and disrepute and take possession of their kids along with everything else; beat them; rape them; thrive on images that reflected and normalized female degradation as justified." She continues: "And for a class of people (women) to want to be free *from* institutionalized and legalized abuse and exploitation by another class (men) is not necessarily a lesser or weaker goal than wanting equal power to abuse and exploit." Then she offers this example of what she means: "(If people feel free to kill and eat chickens, maybe the first thing the chickens want is not their own place setting at the table, but the freedom not to be on the platter.)"[7] When factory-farmed animals are consumed, we do not see them directly; they are not sitting next to us. If their dead selves are on our platter, their living selves have been given little place in our conceptual framework. And if they actually occupy a place in our conceptual framework they will probably not appear on our platter.

I was already a vegetarian when I began to learn about factory farming. Yet, it was, and still is, disturbing to spend much time reading about the lives of terminal animals. It is painful to encounter descriptions of imprisoned, bored, hungry, disfigured, diseased animals, at times stressed to the point of cannibalism, in numbers difficult to conceptualize. We soon realize that it is not our own individual vegetarianism that is the solution; though this is necessary. A revolution in how our society conceptualizes itself is required.

I began by reviewing the journal articles that are used as sources in books on factory farming. As I read through these articles, couched in scientific language—and I realized that entire journals are devoted to "Animal Science"—the massive industry that they are writing about became more apparent. The question so many of these articles explore, though in objective language, is, in my paraphrase: "Now that we have completely deprived the animals of everything they instinctively need to live—social organization, the feel of the earth for rooting or dust bathing, the mother's teat for a newborn calf to suck, how do we manage the responses that occur in these animals?" They are concerned with responses like the "social vice" of cannibalism, a calf licking his or her stall, pregnant animals about to deliver, desperately attempting to create a nest on concrete. Everything that requires study seems to scream "look at the results of treating animals like machines and putting them in artificial environments!"[8]

Just as the animals have no flesh in disembodied, objective writings, so I find that I, the narrator, must not become a disembodied voice, as though I had no flesh. Our feelings matter. Resisting the structure of the absent referent requires learning the facts about animals' lives and responding to those facts. But to do this requires confronting information we usually ignore and experiencing discomforting feelings. When something repressed is brought to the surface a certain degree of anxiety and much energy is released. This is what happens when the issue of people's treatment of the other animals is raised.

Reading the journal articles about terminal animals, I realized how painful it is to maintain a critical consciousness about how humans treat other animals. When writing about the thwarting of all the essential aspects of each animal's self by factory farming, I find that I cannot describe it too closely. I cannot, like Peter Singer detail "the skin [of hens] rubbed bright red and raw" by rubbing against the wire of their cages. This may be why many choose not to give conceptual place to animals. If animals are conceptually disembodied, their bleeding or raw flesh need not be considered.

What happens when a group who is supposed to be invisible tries to make animal issues visible? What happens when little old ladies work to give conceptual place to animals, talking about the bleeding or raw flesh of animals? Sexism will effect the dominant culture's dismissive judgment of them. But many of us see ourselves following in their tradition, in leather-free tennis shoes, of course.

bell hooks argues persuasively that feminist theory needs to address both margin and center. Theory that comes only from the center—from a position of privilege—"lacks wholeness, lacks the broad analysis that could encompass a variety of human experiences."[9] Theory from those who have lived on the margins—where the oppressed live—is oppositional in nature: looking both from the outside in and from the inside out, focusing "attention on the center as well as the margin." hooks's metaphor *from margin to center* has resonated with feminists since her book first appeared in 1984.

Animals can be found at both margin and center of the dominant culture, but this presence is not a reflection of their status as independent beings, but more often a statement of the status of the humans with whom the animals lived. I remember cringing when reading a biography of Fannie Lou Hamer as it recounted that the dog, belonging to the white farmer for whom Hamer worked, had his or her own inside bathroom, whereas Hamer lived in a small house with no working indoor toilet.[10] But just as a fur coat often announces the wealth of a woman's husband, so the dog's bathroom made a statement about the white family who benefited from the status their elite white privilege bestowed.

Although animals can be found at both margin and center, the task of feminist theory in response to the oppression of animals is different from the task of working toward the eradication of the oppression of humans. Whereas oppressed humans live on the margins, moving to the center in service capacities but not through positions of power or to live there, animals are everywhere, yet nowhere truly free. They are everywhere but in an unseen way—as commodities. For instance, besides clothing many people, dead animals' bodies are in camera film, videotapes, marshmallows, Jell-O, rubber tires, house paints, tennis racket strings, emery boards, car antifreeze, and countless other products.[11]

Pushing the margin metaphor, we could argue that while oppressed people are on the margins of the pages of culture, dead animals have been the pages on which an anthropocentric culture has written its self-justifications. Metaphorically, we define ourselves over and against what we decide animals are. Literally, animals' bodies were the raw material for the transformation from papyrus to book, from a more transitory material to a longer lasting one. The Dead Sea Scrolls, for instance, are collections of leather rolls. Parchment, from the skins of various animals (most frequently cattle, sheep, and goats) refined the use of leather rolls. The development of this new material (and vellum, which is a finer quality parchment made from calf skins), revolutionized the form of the book. The papyrus roll was replaced by the parchment codex (the modern form of the book) with folded leaves bound together.[12]

Our theoretical and theological task is to get animals off the pages on which we inscribe our own anthropocentric ideas about them. Frankly, it would be nice not to be a little old lady working for the animals. It would be nice if the work of getting animals off the pages of our anthropocentric culture was done by then. That is the challenge those little old ladies present to our culture.

Appendix 1

Vestiges: 1992–93 / Susan kae Grant

This work consists of a limited edition artist's book and installation. It questions the issues of animal welfare and addresses the misrepresentation and commodification of animals through language and detachment by juxtaposing appropriated medical illustrations of animal hearts with the human heart. Through the use of computer, a backdrop of text was created for each heart containing words associated with each animal. Visually, the words become a patterned backdrop with little significance until they are apparent, then they are haunting and provocative in their subtleness. The lush textural quality of the hearts themselves are equally compelling, creating a seductive veneer that deliberately overpowers the text. The combination of the two suggests a critical consciousness that focuses on moral and ethical principles while questioning traditional cultural belief systems.

The installation is multidimensional. The walls are constructed of metal studs and chicken wire skinned with plastic tarp covered with text consisting of animal names repeated 31,000 times juxtaposed randomly with the word murder. The repetitive rows of text are subtle yet overwhelming in their symbolically vulnerable and translucent state.

Six large segmented crosses each representing a different animal and 72 electric votives are mounted on top of the studs, wire, and wall text. Each cross measures roughly 6'(H) x 5.5'(L) x 4"(D) and consists of five 20" x 24" photographic panels mounted on aluminum. The photographs in the book and installation are manipulated silver prints using a variety of processes including sand paper, solvent transfers, and conté crayon on handmade silk paper.

An altar and four small benches are placed in the center of the installation. Emanating quietly from the altar is a short version of a language piece consisting of a computer synthesized sound track created by Paul DeMarinis and Laetitia Sonami for the collaborative project, "Mechanization Takes Command." While the computer synthesized voice is difficult to decipher, once obvious its haunting mechanical sound and message is confrontational. The mood of the environment is dark, impersonally industrial, evocative and ritualistic. It creates an undeniable spiritual quality which brings the issues of animal welfare to the forefront of public discourse.

This work, like my others is autobiographic, but in a less personal sense. It deals more specifically with outward questions and societal issues associated with the welfare of animals, while at the same time, childhood memories were also inspirational. My father's wealth came from the meat industry, he ran a meat packing plant. As a teenager in the summer I worked packing meat. Childhood memories of visiting the plant and later working in the industry remain haunting and unsettling. In 1981 I became a vegetarian and have been supportive of the animal welfare movement ever since.

Appendix 2

Feminists for Animal Rights

Feminists for Animal Rights (FAR) is dedicated to ending all forms of abuse against women and animals. Because exploitation of women and animals derives from the same patriarchal mentality, FAR attempts to expose the connections between sexism and speciesism whenever and wherever we can. We feel that the common denominator in the lives of women and animals is violence—either real or threatened—and we work in nonviolent ways to change that.

FAR attempts to raise the consciousness of the feminist community, the animal-rights community and the general public about the connections between the objectification, exploitation, and abuse of women and animals in patriarchal society. As ecofeminists, we are concerned about cultural and racial injustice and the devaluation and destruction of nature and the earth. We view patriarchy as a system of hierarchical domination, a system that works for the powerful and willing against the powerless and unwilling.

In addition to publishing a semiannual newsletter, FAR has regional chapters in close to a dozen cities across the United States and Canada. FAR volunteers are engaged in a number of ongoing projects.

One of the projects that FAR volunteers have coordinated in a number of locations is a foster care program for the companion animals of women in battered women's shelters. Companion Animal Rescue Effort (CARE) has been initiated in an effort to address the rampant violence against women and animals in our society. Our safe houses provide the companion animals of battered women with the security they need while the women are working to make their own lives more secure. We provide foster care, veterinary care, lots of TLC for animals who may be traumatized, and respectful assistance for women who need support.

FAR also provides speakers for school, activist, professional, community, and religious groups. Our most popular program is the slide presentation "Animal Liberation through an Ecofeminist Lens" created by FAR cofounder Marti Kheel. The show provides a history of the portrayal of women's relationship to other-than-human animals before and after patriarchy in art, religion, and mythology. It goes on to explore the connections between the objectification, exploitation, and abuse of women and animals in contemporary society, from pornography to the vivisection lab to the slaughterhouse.

For information concerning membership and joining or starting a group in your area, please contact FAR, P.O. Box 16425, Chapel Hill, NC 27516.

Notes

Epigraph to book: Alice Walker, "Am I Blue?" *Living by the Word: Selected Writings, 1973–1987* (San Diego: Harcourt Brace Jovanovich, 1988), pp. 7–8.

Preface

Epigraph to preface: Wendy Brown, *Manhood and Politics: A Feminist Reading in Political Theory* (Totowa, New Jersey: Rowman & Littlefield, 1988), pp. 55–56.

1. Denise Webb, "Eating Well," *New York Times,* January 23, 1991, p. C3.
2. Thanks to Emily Culpepper and her friend for calling this image and its feminist implications to my attention.
3. *Malestream* was coined by Mary O'Brien. See *The Politics of Reproduction* (Boston: Routledge & Kegan Paul, 1981), p. 5. The use of the term *malestream* instead of *mainstream* is a reminder of how thoroughly patriarchal attitudes and institutions saturate cultural discourse.
4. See John Stoltenberg, *Refusing to Be a Man* (Portland, Oregon: Breitenbush Books, Inc., 1989).
5. Jane Tompkins, *West of Everything: The Inner Life of Westerns* (Oxford: Oxford University Press, 1992), p. 119.
6. While an extended analysis of just how postmodern theory opens up space for debating the exploitation of animals is beyond the scope of this book, it may be that the concept of personhood, which has clearly been destabilized by postmodern theory, is in addition being enlarged and thus able to encompass animals. Steve Baker notes that "the decentering of the human subject opens up a valuable conceptual space for shifting the animal out from the cultural margins. It does so precisely by destabilizing that familiar clutch of entrenched stereotypes which works to maintain the illusion of human identity, centrality and superiority." Steve Baker, *Picturing the Beast: Animals, Identity and Representation* (Manchester, England: Manchester University Press, 1993), p. 26.
7. Derrick Bell, *Faces at the Bottom of the Well: The Permanence of Racism* (New York: Basic Books, 1992), p. 48n.
8. Sandra Lee Bartky, *Femininity and Domination: Studies in the Phenomenology of Oppression* (New York and London: Routledge, 1990), p. 14.
9. Even though the concept of personhood is extremely problematic from the perspective of feminist philosophy, I use that term in this book because I think that

in a general, less philosophically-based discourse, this is what many animal defenders mean when talking about an animals' beingness.

10. See "'I Just Raped My Wife! What Are You Going To Do About It, Pastor?'—The Church and Sexual Violence" in *Transforming a Rape Culture*, ed. Emilie Buchwald, Pamela Fletcher, Martha Roth (Minneapolis: Milkweed Editions, 1993).

11. The process of associating a person (or for that matter, animals) with "beasts" deserves lexicographical acknowledgment. The term *bestializing* will function as that term in this book.

Epigraph to part 1: Marilyn Frye, *The Politics of Reality* (Trumansburg, New York: The Crossing Press, 1983), pp. 66–67.

Chapter 1: Eating Animals

1. On the cultural production of *meat*, see Nick Fiddes, *Meat: A Natural Symbol* (London and New York: Routledge, 1991).

2. Cora Diamond, "Eating Meat and Eating People," *Philosophy* 53 (1978), p. 469.

3. Stewart Richards, "Forethoughts for Carnivores," *Philosophy* 56 (1981), p. 86.

4. See Carol J. Adams, *The Sexual Politics of Meat: A Feminist-Vegetarian Critical Theory* (New York: Continuum, 1990), p. 64.

5. For a summary of the environmental consequences of eating dead animals, see Alan Thein Durning and Holly B. Brough, "Reforming the Livestock Economy," in Lester R. Brown et al., *State of the World 1992* (New York: W. W. Norton and Co., 1992), pp. 66–82.

6. On discursive control, see Eve Kosofsky Sedgwick, *Epistemology of the Closet* (Berkeley and Los Angeles: University of California Press, 1990).

7. Plutarch, "Of Eating of Flesh," in *Animal Rights and Human Obligations*, ed. Tom Regan and Peter Singer (Englewood Cliffs, NJ: Prentice-Hall, Inc., 1976), p. 111.

8. Lynn Meyer, *Paperback Thriller* (New York: Random House, 1975), pp. 4–5.

9. Cited in Peter Sinclair, "Carrots and Sticks," *Vegetarian Times*, no. 167 (July 1991), p. 68.

10. Willard Van Orman Quine, *Word and Object* (Cambridge: MIT Press, 1960), pp. 99ff. Nancy Tuana pointed out that Quine's explanation of "mass term" was applicable to the cultural construction of animals as edible, and her interpretation of his work has greatly influenced my description.

11. This example is based on an explanation offered by Nancy Tuana.

12. Insight of Nancy Tuana.

13. Wayne Swanson and George Schultz, *Prime Rip* (Englewood Cliffs, NJ: Prentice-Hall, Inc., 1982), p. 24.

14. J. Byrnes, "Raising Pigs by the Calendar at Maplewood Farm," *Hog Farm Management*, September 1976, p. 30, quoted in Jim Mason and Peter Singer, *Animal Factories* (New York: Crown Publishers, 1980), p. 1.

15. "Doublespeak Awards Don't Mince Words," *Dallas Morning News*, November 20, 1988, p. 4a.

16. Colman McCarthy, "Sins of the Flesh," *Washington Post*, March 25, 1990.

17. Thanks to Bill Carl and Tim Morton for discussing the Greek meaning of the term with me. As they both pointed out, the term *sarcophagic* is actually the most

accurate rendering of flesh-eating. Its relationship with the word *sarcophagus* (stone coffin) is a reminder that flesh-eaters literally turn their bodies into graveyards.

18. McCarthy, "Sins of the Flesh."

19. Steven G. Kellman, "Green Freedom for the Cockatoo," *Gettysburg Review* (1991), p. 152.

20. Karen L. T. Iacobbo, "Advertising: Making Risk Acceptable," *Vegetarian Voice*, 1991, p. 9.

21. Bernice Kanner, "The Ways of All Flesh: The New Marketing of Meat," *New York*, November 22, 1982, p. 20.

22. "Scotch and Beef Are Served in a New Shrine to Trousers and $1000 Suits," *New York Times*, 1990. Thanks to Ken Reichley for sending me this clipping.

23. Article on La Madeleine, *Dallas Observer*, June 10, 1993-June 16, 1993, p. 21.

24. Helen Bryant, *Dallas Times-Herald*, n.d.

25. Thanks to Hilary Martinson and Ingrid Newkirk of People for the Ethical Treatment of Animals for sending me a "turkey hooker," and thanks, also, to Patricia Barrera for calling my attention to the image of the can-can and its implications.

26. Paul Langner, "Judge Imposes Gag Order in Rape Suit," *Boston Globe*, November 18, 1990, p. 24.

27. F. K. Plous, Jr. "How to Kill a Chicken," *Reader: Chicago's Free Weekly*, January 18, 1980, p. 24. Thanks to Karen Davis for discovering this metaphor and sending it to me.

28. "Political Art Critics Fed More Raw Meat," *Washington Times*, April 4, 1991.

29. Greg Moyer, "School Daze," *Nutrition Action*, September 1982, p. 7.

30. William Harris, M.D., "Hype Parades as Science" *Ahisma* 31, no. 3 (July/ September 1990), p. 6.

31. Ibid., p. 5.

32. See John Robbins, *Diet for a New America* (Walpole, New Hampshire: Stillpoint Publishing, 1987), and "The *New* Four Food Groups: Summary," Physicians Committee for Responsible Medicine, April 1991.

33. See Marian Burros, "Rethinking Four Food Groups, Doctors Tell U.S.," *New York Times*, April 10, 1991.

34. The reason I wonder whether the PCRM proposal prompted a premature release by the USDA Health and Nutrition Service is because the USDA had printer's proofs of brochures, but had planned to release the graphic later in the spring. See Carole Sugarman and Malcolm Gladwell, "Pyramid Deserted as Symbol of Foods," *Buffalo Evening News* [originally in the *Washington Post*], April 26, 1991, p. A4.

35. *Dallas Times-Herald*, editorial, May 5, 1991.

36. See Adams, *The Sexual Politics of Meat*, p. 80.

37. Karen Davis, "Chickens Reign a la King, Not Peasant Poultry," *Montgomery Journal*, September 17, 1992, p. A3. United Poultry Concerns can be reached at P. O. Box 59367, Potomac, Maryland 20859, 301–948–2406.

Chapter 2: The Arrogant Eye and Animal Experimentation

Epigraph from Susanne Kappeler, *The Pornography of Representation* (Minneapolis: The University of Minnesota Press, 1986), p. 68.

1. Sandra Harding's *The Science Question in Feminism* (Ithaca, NY: Cornell University Press, 1986) summary of the cultural stereotype of science described by

M. W. Rossiter in *Women Scientists in America: Struggles and Strategies to 1940* (Baltimore: Johns Hopkins University Press, 1982), p. 63.

2. Laura Mulvey, "Visual Pleasure and Narrative Cinema," *Screen* 16, no. 3 (1975), p. 11.

3. Kappeler, *The Pornography of Representation,* pp. 52–53.

4. Ibid., p. 154.

5. Ibid., p. 62.

6. Quoted in "Animal Abuse at Gillette Labs Exposed—International Boycott Called," *Animals' Agenda,* December 1986, p. 15.

7. Nicholas Humphrey, "Seeing and Nothingness," *New Scientist,* March 30, 1972, pp. 682–84.

8. Susanne Kappeler, correspondence, October 31, 1988.

9. Humphrey, "Seeing and Nothingness," p. 682. Peter Singer in *Animal Liberation* (New York: New York Review Book, 1975), notes this incident as well (p. 47).

10. Humphrey, "Seeing and Nothingness," p. 683.

11. Kappeler, *The Pornography of Representation,* p. 58.

12. Quoted in Michael D. Ware, "The ALF Strikes: Animal Liberators Come to North America," *Animals' Agenda,* July/August 1984, p. 8.

13. Kappeler, *The Pornography of Representation,* p. 62.

14. The Animal Legal Defense Fund and the Humane Society of the United States have legally challenged this interpretation, and were successful at the federal district court level. However, the USDA appealed this ruling. In May 1994, the US Court of Appeals threw out the judge's ruling. Thanks to Valerie Stanley of the ALDF for this information. The Animal Legal Defense Fund can be reached at 101 North Adams Street, Rockville, Maryland 20850.

15. Andrew N. Rowan, *Of Mice, Models, and Men: A Critical Evaluation of Animal Research* (Albany, NY: State University of New York Press, 1984), p. 2.

16. Singer, *Animal Liberation,* p. 78. This article appeared in 1970 in the *British Journal of Industrial Medicine.*

17. Singer, *Animal Liberation,* p. 42.

18. Kappeler, *The Pornography of Representation,* p. 165.

19. Quotation from *Fortune* magazine in Troy Soos, "Charles River Breeding Labs," *Animals' Agenda,* December 1986, p. 42.

20. Kappeler, *The Pornography of Representation,* p. 61.

21. Rowan, *Of Mice, Models, and Men,* p. 151.

22. Kappeler, *The Pornography of Representation,* p. 54.

23. Catharine MacKinnon, *Toward a Feminist Theory of the State* (Cambridge: Harvard University Press, 1989), p. 138.

24. Coral Lansbury, *The Old Brown Dog: Women, Workers, and Vivisection in Edwardian England* (Madison: University of Wisconsin Press, 1985), p. 99.

25. Ibid., p. 128.

26. Alice Park, *Vegetarian Magazine* 14, no. 5 (1910).

27. Evelyn Fox Keller, *Reflections on Gender and Science* (New Haven: Yale University Press, 1985), p. 79.

28. Soos, "Charles River Breeding Labs."

29. Carolyn Merchant, *The Death of Nature: Women, Ecology, and the Scientific Revolution* (New York: Harper & Row, 1980), p. 159.

30. Norma Benney, "All of One Flesh: The Rights of Animals." In *Reclaim the*

Earth: Women Speak Out for Life on Earth, ed. Léonie Caldecott and Stephanie Leland (London: The Women's Press, 1983), p. 149.

31. Kappeler, *The Pornography of Representation,* p. 104.

32. Harding, *The Science Question in Feminism,* p. 152.

33. See Mary Daly, *Gyn/Ecology: The Metaethics of Radical Feminism* (Boston: Beacon Press, 1978).

34. Kappeler, *The Pornography of Representation,* p. 3.

35. Conversation, summer 1988.

36. Kappeler, *The Pornography of Representation,* p. 6.

37. Zuleyma Tang Halpin, "Scientific Objectivity and the Concept of the 'Other,'" *Women's Studies International Forum* 12, no. 3 (1989), pp. 292–93.

38. For an argument that recognizes important connnections between environmental pollution and pornography, see H. Patricia Hynes, "Pornography and Pollution: An Environmental Analogy," in *Pornography: Women, Violence, and Civil Liberties,* ed. Catherine Itzin (Oxford: Oxford University Press, 1993), pp. 384–97. She argues that "pornography, incest, woman-battering, traffic in women: all this ugly, necrophilic degradation is 'women's nuclear winter.'. . . We who oppose pornography want no less of a change in consciousness about pornography than environmentalists want about the destruction of rainforests" (pp. 386, 395).

Chapter 3: Abortion Rights and Animal Rights

1. I use this title and the juxtaposition that this title provides more as an organizing principle rather than as an adherence to narrow notions of, on the one hand, animal rights instead of animal liberation, and on the other abortion rights instead of reproductive freedom. I hope to devote an entire book to the subject of reproductive freedom and the animal defense movement, but for the time being and for the purpose of juxtaposition in this chapter I will use the terms *abortion rights* and *animal rights* to encapsulate positions regarding women's moral choices regarding pregnancy and activism against animal exploitation.

2. Nat Hentoff, "How Can the Left Be Against Life?" *Village Voice,* July 16, 1985, p. 20.

3. See Dallas Blanchard and Terry Prewitt, *Religious Violence and Abortion* (Gainesville: University Press of Florida, 1993), p. 259.

4. Donna Haraway, "Otherworldly Conversations: Terran Topics, Local Terms," *Science as Culture* 3, part 1, no. 14 (1992), p. 87.

5. Sperling, for instance, sees both animal rights activists and antiabortionists as anxious about the incursions of technology into nature. (See Susan Sperling *Animal Liberators: Research and Morality* [Berkeley: University of California Press].) I think she is wrong. First, antivivisection activism often involves recommending computer models and other advanced uses of technology in place of animal experimentation. Meanwhile, a large number of antiabortionists are in the anomalous position of using technology (i.e., television and radio) in an attempt to turn back the modernizing effects of technology. For this insight see Blanchard and Prewitt, *Religious Violence and Abortion.* Furthermore, abortion predates technological methods.

6. Susanne v. Paczensky, "In a Semantic Fog: How to Confront the Accusation That Abortion Equals Killings," *Women's Studies International Forum* 13, no. 3 (1990), p. 183. Paczensky is, I think, staking out the affirmative definition of pregnancy, a feminist ideal at the moment. Unfortunately, at this time, pregnancy requires

no specific decision to continue once fertilization has occurred. What I value in this definition is that she clearly establishes the primacy of the pregnant woman in making the decision about the fetus. I do not infer from her definition, nor do I imply in my use of it, that the "fetus is just a physical appendage," as Elizabeth Mensch and Alan Freeman state in alluding to my use of Paczensky's definition. See Elizabeth Mensch and Alan Freeman, *The Politics of Virtue: Is Abortion Debatable?* (Durham and London: Duke University Press, 1993), p. 13.

7. Barbara Ehrenreich, "The Woman behind the Fetus," *New York Times,* April 28, 1989.

8. Beverly Wildung Harrison, *Our Right to Choose: Toward a New Ethic of Abortion* (Boston: Beacon Press, 1983), p. 213.

9. Information from Alan Guttmacher Institute. The failure rate for the oral contraceptive is 6 percent; for the condom, 14 percent; for the diaphragm, 16 percent; and for spermicides, 26 percent.

10. Tom Regan, *The Case for Animal Rights* (Berkeley: University of California Press, 1983), p. 319.

11. Both quoted in Dena Kleiman, "Debate on Abortion Focuses on Graphic Film," *Conscience* 6, no. 2 (March/April 1985), p. 11.

12. Charles A. Gardner, "Is an Embryo a Person?" *Nation,* November 13, 1989, p. 559.

13. Rosalind Pollack Petchesky, *Abortion and Woman's Choice: The State, Sexuality, and Reproductive Freedom* (New York and London: Longman, 1984), p. 375.

14. Ibid., p. 347.

15. Ruth Macklin, "Personhood and the Abortion Debate," *Abortion: Moral and Legal Perspectives,* ed. Jay Garfield and Patricia Hennessey (Amherst: University of Massachusetts Press, 1984), pp. 82, 83.

16. On this see Linda Gordon, *Woman's Body, Woman's Right: Birth Control in America* (New York: Penguin Books, 1977).

17. Quoted in Petchesky, *Abortion and Woman's Choice,* p. 29.

18. Harrison, *Our Right to Choose,* pp. 9, 16.

19. Andrea Dworkin, *Right-wing Women* (New York: Perigee Books, 1983).

20. Greta Gaard suggests another reason: that "the unborn fetus is often seen as *male,* as potentially male—thus, men seek to punish women as mothers." Correspondence, August 8, 1990.

21. Note, I am not arguing for population control here, nor encouraging such a position vis-à-vis the Two-Thirds world. As Betsy Hartmann argues, over-population is not the root cause of development problems in the Two-Thirds world; improvements in living standards and the position of women is what is needed, as well as expanded reproductive choices, rather than restrictive ones. See Betsy Hartmann, *Reproductive Rights and Wrongs: The Global Politics of Population Control and Contraceptive Choice* (New York: Harper & Row, 1987).

22. John Cobb, Jr., *Matters of Life and Death* (Louisville: Westminster/John Knox Press, 1991), p. 71.

23. Rosemary Radford Ruether, "Women, Sexuality, Ecology, and the Church," *Conscience* 9, no. 4, (July/August 1990), p. 10.

24. See for instance Sallie McFague, *The Body of God* (Minneapolis: Fortress Press, 1993).

25. I am indebted to the work of Ronnie Zoe Hawkins, especially "Reproductive Choices: The Ecological Dimension."

26. This viewpoint was most notably expressed by Colman MacCarthy in an interview with *Animals' Agenda*, in which he said:

> In 1971, the American Medical Association [AMA]—one of the most regressive lobbies, and one that has opposed most medical reforms over the years—came out for abortion. How'd that happen, I wonder? It happened because there were enormous profits to be made. Two years later, the Supreme Court came out in favor of abortion. Who wrote the decision? Justice Harry Blackmun. Who's Harry Blackmun? Former general counsel for the AMA. Think that's a coincidence? Blackmun's argument in *Roe v. Wade* was uncannily similar to the AMA position. So you have the reactionary doctors in favor of abortion.

Kim Bartlett, "An Interview with Colman McCarthy, On Peace, Justice, and the American Way," *Animals' Agenda*, 8, no. 7 (September/October 1988), p. 9. Many prochoice advocates would agree with McCarthy that *Roe v. Wade* is troubling because of the role granted medical doctors; but they would argue that what this decision should have affirmed was a woman's constitutional right to abortion, rather than the notion of privacy in the relationship between a woman and her doctor.

27. See, for example, "Use of Animals in Biomedical Research: The Challenge and Response," *AMA White Paper*, March 1988.

28. James C. Mohr, *Abortion in America: The Origins and Evolution of National Policy* (New York: Oxford University Press, 1978), p. 262.

29. Ibid., p. 37.

30. Ibid., p. 167.

31. Ibid., pp. 168–69. See also Carroll Smith-Rosenberg, "The Abortion Movement and the AMA, 1850–1880," in *Disorderly Conduct: Visions of Gender in Victorian America* (New York: Oxford University Press, 1985).

32. Kristen Luker, *Abortion and the Politics of Motherhood* (Berkeley: University of California Press, 1973), p. 33.

33. See, for instance, Connie Clement's "The Case for Lay Abortion: Learning from Midwifery," *Healthsharing*, Winter 1983, pp. 9–14. (Many midwives, however, are discomforted by the argument that midwives should perform abortions.)

34. For a discussion of the continuum of violence against women including harassing phone calls and flashers, see Liz Kelly, *Surviving Sexual Violence* (Minneapolis: University of Minnesota Press, 1989).

Chapter 4: On Beastliness and A Politics of Solidarity

Epigraph from Steve Baker, *Picturing the Beast: Animals, Identity and Representation* (Manchester, England: Manchester University Press, 1993), p. 83.

1. Issues such as "work with pregnant teenagers, prenatal care advocacy, activism to reduce the high infant and maternal death rate of Black women; organizing to end hazardous workplaces, racism, sterilization abuse, and violence; AIDS activism, and the expansion of gay and lesbian rights and child care access." See Marlene Gerber Fried, ed. *From Abortion to Reproductive Freedom: Transforming a Movement* (Boston: South End Press, 1990), p. x.

2. The metaphor is Derrick Bell's, who argues that "Black people are the magical

faces at the bottom of society's well." *Faces at the Bottom of the Well: The Permanence of Racism* (New York: Basic Books, 1992).

3. "Whitened center" is Bettina Aptheker's term, cited in Nancie Caraway, *Segregated Sisterhood: Racism and the Politics of American Feminism* (Knoxville: The University of Tennessee Press, 1991), p. 4.

4. See bell hooks, *Feminist Theory: From Margin to Center* (Boston: South End Press, 1984), pp. 54–55.

5. Term used by Caraway, *Segregated Sisterhood*, p. 22.

6. Zuleyma Tang Halpin, "Scientific Objectivity and the Concept of the 'Other,'" *Women's Studies International Forum* 12, no. 3 (1989), p. 286.

7. Caroline Whitbeck, "A Different Reality: Feminist Ontology," in *Women, Knowledge, and Reality: Explorations in Feminist Philosophy*, ed. Ann Garry and Marilyn Pearsall (Boston: Unwin Hyman, 1989), p. 51.

8. Kimberlé Crenshaw, "Race, Reform, and Retrenchment: Transformation and Legitimation in Antidiscrimination Law," *Harvard Law Review* vol. 101, 7 (May 1988), pp. 1372, 1381.

9. Toni Morrison, *Playing in the Dark: Whiteness and the Literary Imagination* (New York: Random House, 1993), p. 71.

10. Delores S. Williams, "African-American Women in Three Contexts of Domestic Violence," *Concilium: Violence Against Women* (London: SCM Press, Maryknoll: Orbis Books, 1994), p. 41, quoting *The Negro: What is His Ethnological Status* (1867), in John David Smith's *Anti-Black Thought, 1863–1925*, Vols. 5 and 6. See also Winthrop D. Jordan, *White Over Black: American Attitudes Toward the Negro: 1550–1812* (Baltimore: Penguin Books, 1969), pp. 228–39.

11. Williams, "African-American Women in Three Contexts of Domestic Violence," p. 41.

12. Halpin, "Scientific Objectivity," pp. 287–88.

13. Hazel V. Carby, *Reconstructing Womanhood: The Emergence of the Afro-American Woman Novelist* (New York: Oxford, 1987), p. 32.

14. Kimberlé Crenshaw, "Whose Story Is It Anyway? Feminist and Antiracist Appropriations of Anita Hill," in *Race-ing Justice, Engendering Power: Essays on Anita Hill, Clarence Thomas, and the Construction of Social Reality*, ed. Toni Morrison (New York: Pantheon Books, 1992), p. 411.

15. Winthrop D. Jordan, *White Over Black: American Attitudes Toward the Negro: 1550–1812* (Baltimore: Penguin Books, 1969), p. 238.

16. See "Black Women and Porn," *WHISPER: Women Hurt in Systems of Prostitution Engaged in Revolt* 7, no. 1 (Spring 1993), p. 10.

17. Crenshaw, "Whose Story Is It Anyway?," p. 413.

18. See Diana E. H. Russell, *Rape in Marriage: Expanded and Revised Edition with a New Introduction* (Bloomington and Indianapolis: Indiana University Press, 1990), pp. 64–65.

19. See also Angela P. Harris, "Race and Essentialism in Feminist Legal Theory," in *Feminist Legal Theory: Readings in Law and Gender*, ed. Katharine T. Bartlett and Rosanne Kennedy (Boulder: Westview Press, 1991), who points out that "The paradigm experience of rape for black women has historically involved the white employer in the kitchen or bedroom" (p. 246).

20. Kimberlé Crenshaw, "Demarginalizing the Intersection of Race and Sex: A Black Feminist Critique of Antidiscrimination Doctrine, Feminist Theory, and Antiracist Politics" in *Feminist Legal Theory: Readings in Law and Gender*, ed. Katharine

T. Bartlett and Rosanne Kennedy (Boulder: Westview Press, 1991), pp. 68–69. See also Paula Giddings, *When and Where I Enter: The Impact of Black Women on Race and Sex in America* (New York: William Morrow, 1984), p. 86.

21. Paul Hoch, *White Hero, Black Beast: Racism, Sexism and the Mask of Masculinity* (London: Pluto Press, 1979), p. 44.

22. Thanks to Mary Hunt, Marie Fortune, and Kathleen Carlin for helping me to think through this dilemma.

23. Joel Kovel, *White Racism: A Psychohistory* (New York: Vintage Books, 1971), p. 67. See also Jordan, *White Over Black*, pp. 154–63, and Cornel West, "Black Sexuality: The Taboo Subject," in *Race Matters* (New York: Vintage Books, 1994), pp. 117–31.

24. George M. Fredrickson, *The Black Image in the White Mind: The Debate on Afro-American Character and Destiny, 1817–1914* (New York: Harper, 1971), p. 276.

25. Jordan, *White Over Black*, pp. 239, 232. Let us not forget, however, that miscegnation was seen as a social taboo in terms of any *public* relationship between two people of different races, but the white male sexual practice of assaulting and raping black women was tolerated by whites, including many white women.

26. Morrison, *Playing in the Dark*, p. 38.

27. Ibid., p. 57.

28. Ibid., p. 38.

29. Thanks to Mary Hunt for helping me pose these questions.

30. This insight was proposed by Andy Smith. Conversation, May 1994.

31. Crenshaw, "Demarginalizing the Intersection of Race and Sex," p. 58.

32. Patricia Hill Collins, *Black Feminist Thought: Knowledge, Consciousness, and the Politics of Empowerment* (Boston: Unwin Hyman, 1990), pp. 222, 225. See also Deborah H. King, "Multiple Jeopardy, Multiple Consciousness: The Context of a Black Feminist Ideology," *Signs: Journal of Women in Culture and Society*, 14, no. 1 (1988), pp. 42–72.

33. bell hooks, *Talking Back: Thinking Feminist, Thinking Black* (Boston: South End Press, 1989), p. 175.

34. Elisabeth Schüssler Fiorenza, *But She Said: Feminist Practices of Biblical Interpretation* (Boston: Beacon Press, 1992), p. 115.

35. See Robert D. Bullard, *Confronting Environmental Racism: Voices from the Grassroots* (Boston: South End Press, 1993).

36. Karen J. Warren, "The Power and the Promise of Ecological Feminism." *Environmental Ethics* 12 (Summer) 1990, p. 132.

37. See María Lugones, "Playfulness, 'World'-Travelling, and Loving Perception," in *Making Face, Making Soul: Haciendo Caras—Creative and Critical Perspectives by Women of Color*, ed., Gloria Anzaldúa (San Francisco: An Aunt Lute Foundation Book), pp. 390–402.

38. Collins, *Black Feminist Thought*, p. 171.

39. "The P. Word," *Bunny Huggers' Gazette*, no. 13 (1992), p. 14.

40. Tom Juravich, "The Ten Worst Jobs Today Are Not the Dirtiest Ones," *Buffalo News*, March 13, 1991.

41. See Jeremy Rifkin, *Beyond Beef: The Rise and Fall of the Cattle Culture* (New York: Dutton, 1992), pp. 125–31, for more information on this.

42. Michael W. Fox, *Farm Animals: Husbandry, Behavior, and Veterinary Practice (Viewpoints of a Critic)* (Baltimore: University Park Press, 1984), p. 41n.

43. Quoted in Jeremy Rifkin, *Beyond Beef,* p. 127.
44. See Elayne Clift, "Advocate Battles for Safety in Mines and Poultry Plants," *New Directions for Women,* May/June 1990, p. 3, and Andrea Lewis, "Looking at the Total Picture: A Conversation with Health Activist Beverly Smith," in *The Black Women's Health Book: Speaking for Ourselves,* ed. Evelyn C. White (Seattle: Seal Press, 1990), p. 175.
45. Lewis, "Looking at the Total Picture," pp. 175–76.
46. Rosemary Radford Ruether, *To Change the World: Christology and Cultural Criticism* (New York: Crossroad, 1981), p. 61.
47. On this, see the Institute for Natural Process, "In Usual and Accustomed Places: Contemporary American Indian Fishing Rights Struggle," in *The State of Native America: Genocide, Colonization, and Resistance,* ed. M. Annette Jaimes (Boston: South End Press, 1992), pp. 217–39.

Epigraphs to part 2: Katie Cannon, cited in Patricia Hill Collins, *Black Feminist Thought: Knowledge, Consciousness, and the Politics of Empowerment* (Boston: Unwin Hyman, 1990), p. 201. Jacqueline Rose, *Sexuality in the Field of Vision* (London: New Left Books, 1986), p. 148.

Chapter 5: Ecofeminism and the Eating of Animals

1. My starting point here is that ecofeminists seek to end the pernicious logic of domination that has resulted in the interconnected subordination of women and nature. The ecofeminist analysis of nature requires a more vocal naming of animals as a part of that subordinated nature. Ecofeminists and environmental theorists generally favor a more biotic way of framing the problem of the oppression of nature than that represented in animal rights theory. The problem is that each time the biotic environmentalist discourse is willing to sacrifice individual animals as edible bodies, it endorses an ideology that is a part of the logic of domination it ostensibly resists, while participating in the human-animal dualism. It also demonstrates the reason that arguments for rights and interests of individual animals have been so insistently raised.
2. Among those interviewed were activists and writers such as Judy Norsigian and Wendy Sanford of the Boston Women's Health Book Collective, Lisa Leghorn, Kate Cloud, Karen Lindsey, Pat Hynes, Mary Sue Henifin, Kathy Maio, Susan Leigh Starr, and many others.
3. Ingrid Newkirk with C. Burnett, "Animal Rights and the Feminist Connection," pp. 67–69; Victoria Moran, "Learning Love at an Early Age: Teaching Children Compassion for Animals," pp. 54–56; Donna Albino, "C.E.A.S.E.: Building Animal Consciousness. An Interview with Jane Lidsky," pp. 64–66; and Alice Walker, "Why Did the Balinese Chicken Cross the Road?" p. 50. In *Woman of Power: A Magazine of Feminism, Spirituality, and Politics* 9 (1988).
4. Norma Benney, "All of One Flesh: The Rights of Animals." In *Reclaim the Earth: Women Speak Out for Life on Earth,* ed. Léonie Caldecott and Stephanie Leland (London: Women's Press, 1983), pp. 141–51.
5. Sally Abbott, "The Origins of God in the Blood of the Lamb," in *Reweaving the World: The Emergence of Ecofeminism,* ed. Irene Diamond and Gloria Feman Orenstein (San Francisco: Sierra Club Books, 1990), p. 36.
6. Marti Kheel, "Ecofeminism and Deep Ecology: Reflections on Identity and

Difference," in *Reweaving the World: The Emergence of Ecofeminism*, ed. Irene Diamond and Gloria Feman Orenstein (San Francisco: Sierra Club Books, 1990), pp. 128–37.

7. See Greta Gaard, ed., *Ecofeminism: Women, Animals, Nature* (Philadelphia: Temple University Press, 1993).

8. See Greta Gaard, "Feminists: Animals, and the Environment: The Transformative Potential of Feminist Theory." Paper presented at the annual convention of the National Women's Studies Association, Towson State University, June 14–18, 1989, Baltimore.

9. Noël Sturgeon, "Editorial Statement," in *Ecofeminist Newsletter* 2, no. 1 (Spring 1991), p. 1.

10. Charlene Spretnak, "Ecofeminism: Our Roots and Flowering," in *Reweaving the World: The Emergence of Ecofeminism*, ed. Irene Diamond and Gloria Feman Orenstein (San Francisco: Sierra Club Books, 1990), pp. 5–6.

11. Sheila Collins, *A Different Heaven and Earth* (Valley Forge: Judson Press, 1974), p. 161.

12. My own *Sexual Politics of Meat: A Feminist-Vegetarian Critical Theory* (New York: Continuum, 1990) began as a paper for Daly's class on feminist ethics and was published in the *Lesbian Reader* the following year. In her book, *The Rape of the Wild: Man's Violence against Animals and the Earth* (London: Women's Press, 1988), Daly's close friend, Andrée Collard, applies Daly's feminist philosophy of biophilia to animals. As early as 1975, Collard was working on the intersection of the oppression of women and oppression of animals.

13. See Karen J. Warren, "Feminism and Ecology: Making Connections" *Environmental Ethics* 9, no. 1 (1987), pp. 3–20.

14. Warren, "Feminism and Ecology," p. 6.

15. See ibid. and Karen J. Warren "The Power and the Promise of Ecological Feminism," *Environmental Ethics* 12 (Summer) 1990, pp. 128–33.

16. This pattern of identification with animals in the early years of the women's liberation movement has been noted by Bleier in discussing research on primates. She summarizes Sarah Blaffer Hardy's recounting of how women primatologists "identified with the female primates they were observing and with their problems, at the same time (in the 1970s) that they began to be aware of and to articulate problems that women confront in their world." Ruth Bleier, ed., *Feminist Approaches to Science* (Elmsford, NY: Pergamon Press), p. 13.

17. Warren's fourth point, that ecological movements must include a feminist perspective, is not as apparent in the 1976 interviews. The movement to defend animals traces its roots to Peter Singer's 1975 text *Animal Liberation;* thus the feminist critique of this movement was not readily apparent in 1976 because the movement itself was in its gestational period. Subsequent feminist writings apply a feminist critique to animal defense while agreeing with the premise that the exploitation of animals must be challenged. (See, for instance, Josephine Donovan, "Animal Rights and Feminist Theory," *Signs: Journal of Women in Culture and Society* 15, no. 2 [1990], pp. 350–75.) The politics of identification is a de facto critique of arguments on behalf of animals based on dominant philosophies, since it does not attempt to establish criteria for rights but speaks to responsibility and relationships. In *The Sexual Politics of Meat,* I use feminist literary criticism as the starting point for developing feminist theory about the exploitation of animals. By choosing this as my methodology, I immediately located my terrain as the study of women's lives,

thoughts, experiences, and writings. This was consistent with my theory that once we place women's lives and experiences as central to our understanding of animal defense, we are starting from a radically different place.

18. Some environmentalists have argued that the complete conversion to vegetarianism will precipitate a population crisis and thus is less ecologically responsible than flesh eating. (See J. Baird Callicott, *In Defense of the Land Ethic: Essays in Environmental Philosophy* [Albany: State University of New York Press, 1989], p. 35.) While Callicott restates and revises many of the positions in this seminal paper to create a more conciliatory dialogue between animal rights and environmentalism (pp. 49–59), I could not find evidence that he renounces this position, which he stated baldly as, "A vegetarian human population is therefore *probably* ecologically catastrophic" (p. 35). This assumes that we are all heterosexual and that women never will have reproductive freedom. (On the sexism of environmentalists regarding overpopulation see Jennifer Sells, "An Eco-feminist Critique of Deep Ecology: A Question of Social Ethics," *Feminist Ethics*, Winter 1989–90, pp. 12–27.)

19. For environmental issues associated with flesh production see Keith Akers, *A Vegetarian Sourcebook: The Nutrition, Ecology, and Ethics of a Natural Foods Diet* (New York: G. P. Putnam's Sons, 1983); John Robbins, *Diet for a New America* (Walpole: Stillpoint, 1987); David Pimental, "Energy and Land Constraints in Food Protein Production," *Science* 190 (1975), pp. 754–61, and "Land Degradation: Effects on Food and Energy Resources," *Science* 194 (1976), pp. 149–55. See a series on this subject in the *Vegetarian Times* by Robin Hur and Dr. David Fields, "Are High-Fat Diets Killing Our Forests?," February 1984, pp. 22–24; "America's Appetite for Meat Is Ruining Our Water," January 1985, pp. 16–18; "How Meat Robs America of Its Energy," April 1985, pp. 24–27; Judy Krizmanic, "Is a Burger Worth It?" *Vegetarian Times* 152 (April 1990), pp. 20–21, and "Why Cutting Out Meat Can Cool Down the Earth," *Vegetarian Times* 152 (April 1990), pp. 18–19; Jeremy Rifkin, *Beyond Beef: The Rise and Fall of the Cattle Culture* (New York: Dutton, 1992); and Alan Thein Durning and Holly B. Brough, "Reforming the Livestock Economy," in *State of the World: A Worldwatch Institute Report on Progress Toward a Sustainable Society* (New York: W. W. Norton & Co.), pp. 66–82.

20. A vegan diet is a vegetarian one that relies on no animal products (including honey, eggs, and dairy products). The vegan diet is becoming increasingly popular because of the intersection of health and ethics: a vegan diet is a low-fat diet because it omits all animal products. Low-fat diets are healthier than high-fat diets for they are less likely to contribute to heart disease or cancer. As I indicated in chapter one, the ethical motivation for veganism arises from the recognition that cows and chickens are exploited in the production of milk and eggs. Researchers have made visible the miserable nature of the lives of these female animals. See, for instance, Jim Mason and Peter Singer *Animal Factories* (New York: Crown Publishers, 1980); C. David Coats, *Old MacDonald's Factory Farm: The Myth of the Traditional Farm and the Shocking Truth about Animal Suffering in Today's Agribusiness* (New York: Continuum, 1989); and Robbins, *Diet for a New America*.

21. Frances Moore Lappé, *Diet for a Small Planet: Tenth Anniversary Edition* (New York: Ballantine Books, 1982), p. 10.

22. Ibid., p. 84.

23. See Hur and Fields, "How Meat Robs America of Its Energy," p. 25.

24. A by-product of livestock production is methane, a greenhouse gas that can trap twenty to thirty times more solar heat than carbon dioxide. Largely because of

their burps, "ruminant animals are the largest producers of methane, accounting for 12 to 15 percent of emissions, according to the E.P.A." Molly O'Neill, "The Cow's Role in Life is Called into Question by a Crowded Planet," *New York Times*, May 6, 1990, section 4, p. 4.

25. Lappé, *Diet for a Small Planet*, p. 66.

26. See chapter 4, p. 82.

27. On this see Marilyn Waring, *If Women Counted: A New Feminist Economics* (San Francisco: Harper & Row, 1988).

28. See Hur and Fields, "America's Appetite for Meat Is Ruining Our Water," p. 17.

29. See Jane E. Brody, "Huge Study Indicts Fat and Meat," *New York Times*, May 8, 1990.

30. Jane Brody, *Jane Brody's Nutrition Book* (New York: W. W. Norton & Co., 1981), p. 71.

31. Jane E. Brody, "Huge Study Indicts Fat and Meat;" "Leaps Forward: Postpatriarchal Eating," *Ms.*, July–August 1990, p. 59; and Nathaniel Mead, "Special Report: 6,500 Chinese Can't Be Wrong," *Vegetarian Times* 158 (October 1990), pp. 15–17.

32. Peter Singer, *Animal Liberation*, 2d ed. (New York: New York Review Book, 1990), p. 216.

33. Coats, *Old MacDonald's Factory Farm*, p. 32.

34. Ibid., p. 34.

35. James Serpell, *In the Company of Animals: A Study of Human-Animal Relationships* (Oxford: Basil Blackwell, 1986), p. 9.

36. Coats, *Old MacDonald's Factory Farm*, p. 34.

37. See ibid., p. 36.

38. Serpell, *In the Company of Animals*, p. 7.

39. Michael W. Fox, *Farm Animals: Husbandry, Behavior, and Veterinary Practice (Viewpoints of a Critic)* (Baltimore: University Park Press, 1984), p. 66. David Fraser reports: "Among confined sows, the pre-farrowing restlessness includes frequent changes of body position, intermittent grunting, grinding the teeth, and biting and rooting at the pen fixtures. Presumably, this activity would take the form of nest-building in a less restrictive environment. However, physical discomfort and thwarting of normal nest-building may make confined animals particularly agitated. Sows farrowing in crates get up and down more often than sows in pens." In his discussion of pregnant, birthing, and nursing sows, the author refers to them as "its" when they are obviously "shes." David Fraser, "The Role of Behavior in Swine Production: A Review of Research," *Applied Animal Ethology* 11 (1983–84), p. 318.

40. Coats, *Old MacDonald's Factory Farm*, p. 39.

41. Serpell, *In the Company of Animals*, p. 8.

42. See David Fraser, "Attraction to Blood as a Factor in Tail-Biting by Pigs," *Applied Animal Behaviour Science* 17 (1987), pp. 61–68.

43. "Aristotle believed that each animal has a telos or purpose to which it is directed, a 'that for the sake of which' it exists. If [William] Hedgepeth [in *The Hog Book*] is right, the telos of a hog is the will to root, to find his food at least three inches underground, and to get his snout into every tractor tire, hole, and crevice within reach. Not forgetting sleeping and investigating and eating and mating and playing, rooting must be one thing for the sake of which God made hogs." Gary Comstock, "Pigs and Piety: A Theocentric Perspective on Food Animals," *Good*

News for Animals? Christian Approaches to Animal Well-Being, ed. Charles Pinches and Jay B. McDaniel (Maryknoll: Orbis Books, 1993), p. 108. On what happens when "flat-deck cages were enriched by the addition of a trough containing sterilized earth," see D. G. M. Wood-Gush and R. G. Beilharz, "The Enrichment of a Bare Environment for Animals in Confined Conditions," *Applied Animal Ethology* 10 (1983), pp. 209–17.

44. Serpell, *In the Company of Animals,* pp. 8–9.

45. See Mason and Singer, *Animal Factories,* p. 8.

46. See A. B. Lawrence, M. C. Appleby, and H. A. Macleod, "Measuring Hunger in the Pig Using Operant Conditioning: The Effect of Food Restriction," *Animal Production* 47 (1988), pp. 131–37.

47. John Elson, "This Little Piggy Ate Roast Beef: Domesticated Porkers Are Becoming the Latest Pet Craze," *Time,* January 22, 1990, p. 54.

48. Julia Ahlers, "Thinking like a Mountain: Toward a Sensible Land Ethic," *Christian Century,* April 25, 1990, p. 433.

49. See, for instance, Bettyann Kevles, "Meat, Morality and Masculinity," *Women's Review of Books,* May 1990, pp. 11–12.

50. See Neal Barnard, "The Evolution of the Human Diet," in *The Power of Your Plate* (Summertown, TN: Book Publishing Co., 1990), pp. 165–75.

51. Sarah Lucia Hoagland, *Lesbian Ethics: Toward New Values* (Palo Alto: Institute for Lesbian Studies, 1988), pp. 17–18.

52. While some might argue that the method of the relational hunt eliminates the *violence* inherent in other forms of flesh eating, I do not see how that term, as it is commonly used today, can be seen to be illegitimately applied in the context in which I use it here. I use *violent* in the sense of the *American Heritage Dictionary*'s definition: "caused by unexpected force or injury rather than by natural causes." Even if the animal acquiesces to her/his death, which I argue we simply do not know, this death is still not a result of natural causes but of external force that requires the use of implements and the intent of which is to cause mortal injury. This is violence, which kills by wounding a being who would otherwise continue to live.

53. I suspect that aspects of ecofeminist theory that derive from the enviromental movement will demonstrate conceptual flaws because of the androcentrism of the enviromental discourse; the relational hunt is one example of this. The critique that follows, therefore, should be seen as targeting the enviromental movement's valorization of the relational hunt. The motivations for the favoring of this method by the largely human male environmental discourse may be very different from those of ecofeminists who adopt this argument. On this see Marti Kheel, "Ecofeminism and Deep Ecology: Reflections on Identity and Difference," in *Reweaving the World: The Emergence of Ecofeminism,* ed. Irene Diamond and Gloria Feman Orenstein (San Francisco: Sierra Club Books, 1990), pp. 128–37.

54. John Skow notes that Ortega y Gasset's defense of hunting is often given by hunters to nonhunters. See John Skow, "Heroes, Bears and True Baloney," *Time,* November 13, 1989, p. 122.

55. José Ortega y Gasset, *Meditations on Hunting,* Howard B. Wescott, trans. (New York: Charles Scribner's Sons, 1985), p. 96.

56. Conversation, February 1994. On the misappropriation of native cultures, see Andy Smith, "For All Those Who Were Indian in a Former Life," in *Ecofeminism and the Sacred,* ed. Carol J. Adams (New York: Continuum, 1993), pp. 168–71.

57. Rayna Green raises the issue of selective interest in Native American cultures,

referring to "American scholars' almost pathological attachment to Indian wars, horsemen of the Plains, and 'End of the Trail' chiefs." Rayna Green, "Review Essay: Native American Women," *Signs: Journal of Women in Culture and Society,* 6, no. 2 (1980), p. 249. Just as the "choice of tribes and topics shows a distinct preference for those that already interest anthropologists rather than for those which might offer contradictions to older ideas" (266), so it seems the interest in hunting reflects the choice of an activity that confirms the right to ontologize animals as edible.

58. Rosemary Radford Ruether, "Men, Women, and Beasts: Relations to Animals in Western Culture," in *Good News for Animals? Christian Approaches to Animal Well-being,* ed. Charles Pinches and Jay B. McDaniel (Maryknoll: Orbis Books, 1993), p. 22.

59. See Peggy Sanday, *Female Power and Male Dominance: On the Origins of Sexual Inequality* (Cambridge and New York: Cambridge University Press, 1981) and Richard E. Leakey and Roger Lewin, *People of the Lake: Mankind and Its Beginnings* (New York: Doubleday, 1978).

60. I believe the argument that "plants have life too" arises from two sources. The first is that corpse eaters fear giving up the eating of animals. The issue of plants is chosen as diversionary. The second is the environmental respect for all of nature and the accompanying concern that human-centeredness will only be extended to certain animals and no transvaluation of values with respect to an environmental ethics will occur. That those who raise the second concern may also themselves experience the first reaction is entirely possible and explains the apparent inconsistency of failing to provide any contextualization.

61. Here I differentiate between the intrinsically renewable resource of plants, which can regenerate themselves, and the extrinsic nature of animals as renewable resources. A dead cow cannot reproduce herself; most plants whose fruits are harvested can. Animals are seen to be renewable resources only because of the manipulation of their reproductive systems and the objectification of their offspring.

62. Sharon Ann Rhoads, *Cooking with Sea Vegetables* (Brookline, MA: Autumn Press, 1978), p. 19, and Alice Walker, "Not Only Will Your Teachers Appear, They Will Cook New Foods for You," *Living by the Word: Selected Writings, 1973–1987* (San Diego: Harcourt Brace Jovanovich, 1988), pp. 134–38.

63. Marlene Anne Bumgarner, *The Book of Whole Grains* (New York: St. Martin's Press, 1976), p. 259.

64. This has been phrased in more traditional ways as "What are our direct responsibilities in terms of pain and suffering to that without a central nervous system?" Jay McDaniel pursues this question of conflicting claims by proposing a metaphoric monarchy (to describe those with complex nervous systems) and democracy ("a system of energy pulsations without a presiding psyche"). [Jay B. McDaniel, *Of Gods and Pelicans: A Theology of Reverence for Life* (Louisville, KY: Westminster/John Knox Press, 1989), pp. 77–78.] Vic Sussman and Peter Singer (*Animal Liberation*) explore it by discussing the fact that plants have not evolved a way to defend themselves or avoid pain. Vic Sussman, *The Vegetarian Alternative: A Guide to a Healthful and Humane Diet* (Emmaus, PA: Rodale Press, 1978), pp. 227–30. For a corresponding analysis, see Daniel A. Dombrowski, *Hartshorne and the Metaphysics of Animal Rights* (Albany, NY: State University of New York Press, 1988): "To sum up, animals are sentient in two senses: (1) They are sentient at a microscopic level in the experiences of each concrete individual, which occur in plants and rocks as well. We shall call this Sentiency 1 (S1). (2) They have sentiency per se, which consists in those

experiences, lapsing in dreamless sleep, that enable the animal as a whole to feel pain, or, at times, to remember or anticipate pain, that is, to suffer. This is Sentiency 2 (S2). In that S1 is sufficient to refute the materialist, but not sufficient to attribute pain or suffering to plants—where S2 is needed—plants can be eaten with equanimity, even if they too have some inherent value." (p. 43)

65. See Evelyn Fox Keller, *A Feeling for the Organism: The Life and Work of Barbara McClintock* (San Francisco: W. H. Freeman and Co., 1983).

66. Using Starhawk's terminology, it could be argued that the killing of animals is power-over, while the process of gathering is power-from-within (Starhawk, *Dreaming the Dark: Magic, Sex and Politics,* [Boston: Beacon Press, 1982]). Or using Marilyn Frye's categories, when one sees animals as consumable one can do so only with an "arrogant eye," but when one sees plants as food one can do so with a "loving eye."

67. See Vanduna Shiva, *Staying Alive: Women, Ecology and Development* (London: Zed Books, 1988), pp. 41–48, and Sanday, *Female Power and Male Dominance.*

68. Catharine A. MacKinnon, *Feminism Unmodified: Discourses on Life and Law* (Cambridge: Harvard University Press, 1987), pp. 57–58.

Chapter 6: The Feminist Traffic in Animals

1. Claudia Card, "Pluralist Lesbian Separatism," in *Lesbian Philosophies and Cultures,* ed. Jeffner Allen (Albany: State University of New York Press, 1990), p. 139.

2. Joan Cocks, *The Oppositional Imagination* (London: Routledge, 1989), p. 223, n. 3.

3. Barbara Noske uses the term *animal industrial complex* in *Humans and Other Animals* (London: Pluto Press, 1989), p. 24.

4. On government coercion through flesh advocacy in the four basic food groups see chapter 1.

5. The NWSA Ecofeminist Task Force recommended to the 1990 National Women's Studies Association meeting that its conferences be vegan. See excerpts from the 1990 NWSA Ecofeminist Task Force Resolution, *Ecofeminist Newsletter* 2, no. 1 (Spring 1991), p. 3.

6. See Carol J. Adams, *The Sexual Politics of Meat* (New York: Continuum, 1990), pp. 80–81.

7. Emma Goldman, "The Traffic in Women," *The Traffic in Women and Other Essays on Feminism* (New York: Times Change Press, 1970); Gayle Rubin, "The Traffic in Women: Notes on the 'Political Economy' of Sex," in *Toward an Anthropology of Women,* ed. Rayna R. Reiter (New York and London: Monthly Review Press, 1975), pp. 157–210. See also Janice Raymond, "The International Traffic in Women," *Reproductive and Genetic Engineering* 2, no. 1 (1989), pp. 51–70.

8. See C. David Coats, *Old MacDonald's Factory Farm: The Myth of the Traditional Farm and the Shocking Truth about Animal Suffering in Today's Agribusiness* (New York: Continuum, 1989); Jim Mason and Peter Singer, *Animal Factories* (New York: Crown Publishers, 1980); John Robbins, *Diet for a New America* (Walpole: Stillpoint, 1987); Jeremy Rifkin, *Beyond Beef: The Rise and Fall of the Cattle Culture* (New York: Dutton, 1992).

9. As Eve Kosofsky Sedgwick observes in *Epistemology of the Closet* (Berkeley and Los Angeles: University of California Press, 1990): "The simple, stubborn fact

or pretense of ignorance ... can sometimes be enough to enforce discursive power" (p. 6).

10. Ellen Goodman, "Debate Rages over Animals: Where Do Ethics End and Human Needs Begin?" *Buffalo News*, December 20, 1989.

11. Nancy Fraser, *Unruly Practices: Power, Discourse, and Gender in Contemporary Social Theory* (Minneapolis: University of Minnesota Press, 1989), p. 168.

12. Ibid., p. 168. While a case could be made that the discourse of animal defense represents a runaway need in accordance with Fraser's analysis of needs, to establish the way in which animal defense follows Fraser's analysis is beyond the scope of this chapter. The following argument uses Fraser's analysis of the way that issues become politicized and then reprivatized, but it will not establish a direct match between her categories and the discourse of animal defense. I wish to thank Nancy Tuana for calling my attention to Fraser's work.

13. Fraser, *Unruly Practices*, p. 168.

14. Nel Noddings, "Comment on Donovan's 'Animal Rights and Feminist Theory'" *Signs* 16, no. 2 (1991), p. 420.

15. Susanna J. Sturgis, "Arsenal of Silencers," *Sojourner: The Women's Forum*, December 1991, p. 5.

16. Elizabeth V. Spelman, "Woman as Body: Ancient and Contemporary Views," *Feminist Studies* 8, no. 1 (1982), pp. 109–31.

17. Noske, *Humans and Other Animals*, p. 157.

18. Nancy C. M. Hartsock, *Money, Sex, and Power: Toward a Feminist Historical Materialism* (Boston: Northeastern University Press, 1983, 1985), p. 302, n. 9.

19. Noske, *Humans and Other Animals*, p. 125.

20. For information on downed animals contact Farm Sanctuary, P.O. Box 150, Watkins Glen, New York 14891, 607–583–2225, or fax 607–583–2041. A video entitled "The Down Side of Livestock Marketing" is available from them for $15.00.

21. Mary Zeiss Stange, "Hunting—an American Tradition," *American Hunter*, January 1991, p. 27.

22. Paulo Freire, *Pedagogy of the Oppressed* (New York: Continuum, 1970, 1993), p. 36.

23. Ibid., p. 26.

24. See Alison M. Jaggar, *Feminist Politics and Human Nature* (Totowa, NJ: Rowman & Littlefield Publisher, 1988), pp. 6–7.

25. See ibid., pp. 6–7.

26. See ibid.

27. See ibid.

28. Beverly Harrison, *Making the Connections: Essays in Feminist Social Ethics*, ed. Carol S. Robb (Boston: Beacon Press, 1985), p. 255.

29. Ellen Bring, "Moving towards Coexistence: An Interview with Alice Walker," *Animals' Agenda* 8 (April 1988), pp. 6–9.

30. Stange, "Hunting," p. 26.

31. Noddings, "Comment," p. 421.

32. Hartsock, *Money, Sex, and Power*, p. 9.

33. Noddings, "Comment," p. 421.

34. Indeed, Nodding's entire response to Donovan is contaminated by this refusal to engage the actual issues. While admitting that the greatest difference between herself and Donovan is their position on the eating of animals, she continually strays from that issue. Diversionary issues such as a discussion of whales and dolphins

(who are rarely eaten by Americans), and her cats' predatory nature (which has no resemblance to the human traffic in animals), have little to do with the social construction of flesh consumption.

35. Luisah Teish, *Jambalaya: The Natural Woman's Book of Personal Charms and Practical Rituals* (San Francisco: Harper & Row, 1985), pp. 92–93.

36. This problem is discussed at length in Adams, *Sexual Politics of Meat*, pp. 63–82.

37. Sally McConnell-Ginet, "Review Article on Language and Sex," *Language* 59, no. 2, (1983), pp. 387–88, quoted in *A Feminist Dictionary*, ed. Cheris Kramarae and Paula A. Treichler (Boston: Pandora, 1985), p. 264.

38. Fraser, *Unruly Practices*, p. 164.

39. Jennie Ruby, Farar Elliot, and Carol Anne Douglas, "NWSA: Troubles Surface at Conference," *off our backs*, August–September 1990, p. 11.

40. Pat Parker, "To a Vegetarian Friend," *Womanslaughter* (Oakland, CA: Diana Press, 1978), p. 14.

41. Alice Walker, *Living by the Word: Selected Writings, 1973–1987* (San Diego: Harcourt Brace Jovanovich, 1987), p. 172.

42. Jaggar, *Feminist Politics and Human Nature*, p. 6.

43. Freire, *Pedagogy of the Oppressed*, p. 73.

44. Goodman, "Debate Rages over Animals."

45. Freire, *Pedagogy of the Oppressed*, p. 32.

46. Ibid., p. 31.

47. Walker, *Living by the Word*, pp. 182–83.

48. Fraser, *Unruly Practices*, p. 181.

49. Summarized in the *Ecofeminist Newsletter*, Spring 1991, p. 3. Thanks to Batya Bauman for her work on this recommendation.

50. See Ibid.

Chapter 7: Reflections on a Stripping Chimpanzee: on the Need to Integrate Feminism, Animal Defense, and Environmentalism

1. Judy Romero, letter to the editor, *Dallas Times Herald*, August 11, 1989.

2. See Kim Bartlett, "Editorial: A Patriarchal World," *Animals' Agenda*, October 1990, p. 2.

3. See Mary Zeiss Stange, "Religious Ethics and Fur," *Fur Age Weekly* 140, no. 2 (1990), n.p.; Sherrie Hicks, "Accessory to Ignorance," *Fur Age Weekly* September 24, 1990; Fred Le Brun, "Warm, Furry Thoughts at Dawn," *Albany Times-Union*, November 12, 1990; responses by Holly Cheever, letter to the editor, *Albany Times-Union*, November 1990, and Canadian Anti-Fur Alliance, Press Release defending "Shame of Fur" ads against charge of sexism, November 30, 1990. Address: 11 River Street, Toronto, Ontario, Canada M5A 4C2.

4. See Stange, "Religious Ethics and Fur"; Germaine Greer, "Home Thoughts: Germaine Greer on the Fallacy of Animal Rights," *Independent*, January 1990; response by Carol J. Adams, "On the Fallacy of Germaine Greer," *Newsletter of the International Association against Painful Experiments on Animals*, Fall 1990, pp. 6–7.

5. An alternative to this rejection of animal defense because of its dependence on rights-based discourse is available. Since the mid-1980s several feminists have

offered non-rights-based arguments on behalf of the other animals. In particular, see Barbara Noske, *Humans and Other Animals* (London: Pluto Press, 1989); Josephine Donovan, "Animal Rights and Feminist Theory" *Signs: Journal of Women in Culture and Society* 15, no. 2 (1990), pp. 350–75; Marti Kheel, "Ecofeminism and Deep Ecology: Reflections on Identity and Difference," in *Reweaving the World: The Emergence of Ecofeminism,* ed. Irene Diamond and Gloria Feman Orenstein (San Francisco: Sierra Club Books, 1990), pp. 128–37; the essays collected in Greta Gaard, ed., *Ecofeminism, Women, Animals, Nature* (Philadelphia: Temple University Press, 1993), and the essays by Deane Curtin ("Toward an Ecological Ethic of Care," pp. 60–74), Roger J. H. King ("Caring about Nature: Feminist Ethics and the Environment," pp. 75–89), and Deborah Slicer ("Your Daughter or Your Dog?," pp. 108–24), in *Hypatia: A Journal of Feminist Philosophy,* special Issue on ecological feminism, 6, no. 1 (1991).

6. See Susan Finsen, "Making Ends Meet: Reconciling Ecoholism and Animal Rights Individualism," *Between the Species: A Journal of Ethics,* 4, no. 1 (1988), pp. 11–20 for an admirable discussion of the points of dissension and her attempt to resolve these points.

7. Besides writings by Kheel, Slicer, Donovan, Gaard cited above, see, for instance, the writings of Andrée Collard, with Joyce Contrucci, *Rape of the Wild: Man's Violence against Animals and the Earth* (London: Women's Press, 1988); Connie Salamone, "The Prevalence of the Natural Law within Women: Women and Animal Rights," in *Reweaving the Web of Life: Feminism and Nonviolence,* ed. Pam McAllister (Philadelphia: New Society Publishers, 1982); Genoveffa Corea, "Dominance and Control: How Our Culture Sees Women, Nature and Animals," *Animals' Agenda,* May/June 1984, p. 37; Karen Davis, "Farm Animals and the Feminine Connection," *Animals' Agenda,* January/February 1988, pp. 38–39; Zoe Weil, "Feminism and Animal Rights," *Labyrinth: The Philadelphia Women's Newspaper,* February 1990; Sally Abbott, "The Origins of God in the Blood of the Lamb," in *Reweaving the World: The Emergence of Ecofeminism,* ed. Irene Diamond and Gloria Feman Orenstein (San Francisco: Sierra Club Books, 1990), pp. 35–40; Norma Benney, "All of One Flesh: The Rights of Animals," in *Reclaim the Earth: Women Speak Out for Life on Earth,* ed. Léonie Caldecott and Stephanie Leland (London: Women's Press, 1983); and Aviva Cantor, "The Club, the Yoke, and the Leash: What We Can Learn from the Way a Culture Treats Animals," *Ms.* magazine, August 1980, pp. 27–29.

8. Corea, "Dominance and Control," p. 37.

9. See Rosemary Radford Ruether, "Men, Women, and Beasts: Relations to Animals in Western Culture," in *Good News for Animals? Christian Approaches to Animal Well-Being,* ed. Charles Pinches and Jay B. McDaniel (Maryknoll: Orbis Books, 1993).

10. Peggy Sanday, *Female Power and Male Dominance: On the Origins of Sexual Inequality* (Cambridge and New York: Cambridge University Press, 1981).

11. See Nancy Jay, "Sacrifice as Remedy for Having Been Born of Woman," in *Immaculate and Powerful: The Female in Sacred Image and Social Reality,* ed. Clarissa W. Atkinson, Constance H. Buchanan, and Margaret R. Miles (Boston: Beacon Press, 1985).

12. Marti Kheel, "Animal Liberation and Environmental Ethics: Can Ecofeminism Bridge the Gap?" Prepared for delivery at the 1988 Annual Meeting of the Western Political Science Association, March 10–12, 1988, p. 14. See the arguments in chapter 5.

13. Admittedly, some environmentalists do not see the issue of domesticated animals as a pressing concern or one that falls under the rubric of environmental concerns. J. Baird Callicott contends that farm animals "have been bred to docility, tractability, stupidity, and dependency. It is literally meaningless to suggest that they be liberated" (J. Baird Callicott, *In Defense of the Land Ethic: Essays in Environmental Philosophy* [Albany: State University of New York Press], 1989). Creating a dichotomy of wild, independent, valued animals and docile, domesticated, unvalued animals enacts at the environmental level the traditional view of men and women, as Davis points out ("Farm Animals and the Feminine Connection," p. 38). One of the strengths of the ecofeminist-animal liberation position evidenced in Davis and Kheel, especially her 1985 response to Callicott, is the analysis that recognizes all animals— "domesticated" and "wild"—as worthy of theoretical concern. See Marti Kheel, "The Liberation of Nature: A Circular Affair," *Environmental Ethics* 7, no. 2 (1985), pp. 135–49. And also Harriet Schleifer, "Images of Death and Life: Food Animal Production and the Vegetarian Option," in *In Defense of Animals*, ed. Peter Singer (New York: Basil Blackwell, 1985), pp. 63–73.

14. Thus, even if some animal rights *philosophy* appears to err by being extensionalist—that is, by arguing that a select group of animals ought to possess the rights that at this time only (some) humans possess—the animal-defense *movement* is much broader in its goals and activism than this, including environmental degradation under its rubric. The change in the subtitle of one of the leading animal-defense magazines the *Animals' Agenda* in the early 1990s indicated this. Formerly called the *Animal Rights Magazine,* it was renamed the *International Magazine of Animal Rights and Ecology.* Also, the British magazine, the *Beast: The Magazine that Bites Back,* a short-lived production that flourished in the early 1980s, carried extensive environmental coverage as well.

15. See, for instance, the writings of Jay B. McDaniel, especially *Of Gods and Pelicans: A Theology of Reverence for Life* (Louisville, KY: Westminster/John Knox Press, 1989).

16. See, for instance, Noske, *Humans and Other Animals.*

17. See, for instance, the essays in Carol J. Adams, ed., *Ecofeminism and the Sacred* (New York: Continuum 1993), and the writings of Karen J. Warren, "Feminism and Ecology: Making Connections," *Environmental Ethics* 9, no. 1 (1987), pp. 3–20, and "The Power and the Promise of Ecological Feminism," *Environmental Ethics* 12 (Summer) 1990, pp. 128–33.

18. See chapter 4.

19. See Warren, "The Power and the Promise of Ecological Feminism," pp. 128–33.

20. See Mary Midgley, *Animals and Why They Matter* (Athens: University of Georgia Press, 1983), pp. 98–111.

21. Wendy Brown, *Manhood and Politics: A Feminist Reading in Political Theory* (Totowa, New Jersey: Rowman & Littlefield, 1988), p. 56.

22. For an interesting discussion of the Wollstonecraft-Taylor controversy and why Singer's use of this in *Animal Liberation* errs, see Mary Ann Elston, "Women and Anti–vivisection in Victorian England, 1870–1900," in *Vivisection in Historical Perspective,* ed. Nicolaas Rupke (London: Croom Helm, 1987), pp. 260–61.

23. Ruth Ginzberg, "Feminism, Rationality, and Logic," *American Philosophical Association Newsletter on Feminism and Philosophy,* 88, no. 2 (March 1989), p. 35.

24. Sandra Harding, "Is Gender a Variable in Conceptions of Rationality? A Sur-

vey of Issues," in *Beyond Domination: New Perspectives on Women and Philosophy*, ed. Carol C. Gould (Totowa, New Jersey: Rowman & Littlefield Publishers, Inc., 1983), p. 43.

25. In 1920, at the behest of a feminist friend active in the campaign for a plumage bill, Virginia Woolf wrote a short essay for the *Woman's Leader*. The political dynamics swirling around that issue are similar to those of the antifur campaign: blaming women for wearing apparel derived from animals. But how is this apparel obtained? Woolf wrote about birds who are robbed of their feathers, "We may fairly suppose then that the birds are killed by men, starved by men, and tortured by men." [Echoing Woolf, feminists in response to the current ad painted on one of its billboards: "*MEN* kill animals. *MEN* make the profits . . . and *MEN* make sexist ads! with friends like Greenpeace, who needs enemies?" See p. 135.] Virginia Woolf, "The Plumage Bill," from the *Woman's Leader*, July 23, 1920, in *The Diary of Virginia Woolf*, vol. 2: 1920–24, ed. Anne Olivier Bell (New York and London: Harcourt Brace Jovanovich, 1978), pp. 337–38.

26. Lorraine Code, "The Impact of Feminism on Epistemology," *American Philosophical Association Newsletter on Feminism and Philosophy*, 88, no. 2 (March 1989), p. 25.

27. See, for instance, Jane Flax, "Political Philosophy and the Patriarchal Unconscious: A Psychoanalytic Perspective on Epistemology and Metaphysics," in *Discovering Reality: Feminist Perspectives on Epistemology, Metaphysics, Methodology, and Philosophy of Science*, ed. S. Harding and M. Hintakka (Dordrecht: Reidel, 1983).

28. For background see Genevieve Lloyd, *The Man of Reason: "Male" and "Female" in Western Philosophy* (Minneapolis: University of Minnesota Press, 1984) and Susan Bordo, *The Flight to Objectivity: Essays on Cartesianism and Culture* (Albany: SUNY Press, 1987).

29. See Tom Regan, *The Case for Animal Rights* (Berkeley and Los Angeles: University of California Press, 1983), and Donovan, "Feminist Theory and Animal Rights," pp. 364–65.

30. See Regan, *The Case for Animal Rights*, p. xii; Peter Singer, *Animal Liberation* 2d ed. (New York: New York Review Book, 1990), pp. ix–x; and Donovan critique, "Feminist Theory and Animal Rights," pp. 350–52.

31. Roberta Kalechofsky, "Descartes' Niece." Paper presented at the Spoleta Festival for the Animals, Raleigh, North Carolina, October 6, 1990. In fact, women have been disproportionately represented in animal-welfare work. The emotional, intellectual, and political reasons that women become involved with fighting on behalf of animals differ in many ways from those of men. Coral Lansbury suggests that women acted on behalf of animals out of sense of identification or shared oppression. See Coral Lansbury, *The Old Brown Dog: Women, Workers, and Vivisection in Edwardian England* (Madison: Wisconsin, 1985) and R. D. French, *Antivivisection and Medical Science in Victorian Society* (Princeton: Princeton University Press, 1975).

32. Beverly Harrison, *Making the Connections: Essays in Feminist Social Ethics*, ed. Carol S. Robb (Boston: Beacon Press, 1985), p. 13.

33. Evelyn Fox Keller, *Reflections on Gender and Science* (New Haven: Yale University Press, 1985); Sandra Harding, *The Science Question in Feminism* (Ithaca: Cornell University Press, 1986); and Carolyn Merchant, *The Death of Nature: Women, Ecology, and the Scientific Revolution* (New York: Harper & Row, 1980).

34. See Lorenne M. G. Clark and Lynda Lange, *The Sexism of Social and Political Theory: Women and Reproduction from Plato to Nietzsche* (Toronto: University of Toronto Press, 1979); Carole Pateman, *The Sexual Contract* (Stanford: Stanford University Press, 1988); and Pateman, *The Disorder of Women: Democracy, Feminism, and Political Theory* (Stanford: Stanford University Press, 1989).

35. See Harrison, *Making the Connections*, pp. 235–36. Chapter 9 engages this insight more fully.

36. See Carol Gilligan, *In a Different Voice* (Cambridge: Harvard University Press, 1982); Sara Ruddick, *Maternal Thinking: Toward a Politics of Peace* (New York: Ballantine Books, 1989), and Catherine Keller, *From a Broken Web: Separation, Sexism, and Self* (Boston: Beacon Press, 1986).

37. See Donovan, "Feminist Theory and Animal Rights," p. 374.

Epigraphs to part 3: Carol Emshwiller, *Carmen Dog* (San Francisco: Mercury House, Inc. 1990), pp. 16, 63. Roberta Kalechofsky, "Introduction," in *Haggadah for the Liberated Lamb*, ed. by Roberta Kalechofsky (Marblehead, MA: Micah Productions, 1988), p. v. For a list of their publications on Jewish vegetarianism and animal issues, write them at Micah Publications, Inc., 255 Humphrey St., Marblehead, MA 01945.

Chapter 8: Bringing Peace Home: a Feminist Philosophical Perspective on the Abuse of Women, Children, and Pet Animals

1. See Karen J. Warren, "Women, Nature, and Technology: An Ecofeminist Philosophical Perspective," *Research in Philosophy and Technology*, special issue "Technology and Feminism," guest ed. Joan Rothschild, vol. 13 (1992), and *Ecofeminism: Multidisciplinary Perspectives* (Bloomington: Indiana University Press, forthcoming).

2. See Elizabeth V. Spelman, "Woman as Body: Ancient and Contemporary Views," *Feminist Studies* 8, no. 1 (1982), pp. 109–31.

3. Just how humans should relate to other animals in any intimate way, that is, the feminist implications of "pet" keeping and whether domestication of animals is consistent with a nonhierarchical feminist theory, is beyond the scope of this book, but see in general Barbara Noske, *Humans and Other Animals: Beyond the Boundaries of Anthropology* (London: Pluto Press, 1989); Yi-Fu Tuan, *Dominance and Affection: The Making of Pets* (New Haven: Yale University Press, 1984); James Serpell, *In the Company of Animals: A Study of Human-Animal Relationships* (Oxford: Basil Blackwell, 1986); and Jim Mason, *An Unnatural Order: Uncovering the Roots of Our Domination of Nature and Each Other* (New York: Simon and Schuster, 1993).

4. Catharine MacKinnon, *Feminism Unmodified: Discourses on Life and Law* (Cambridge: Harvard University Press, 1987), p. 92.

5. See my discussion of her analysis on pp. 101–2.

6. Warren, "Women, Nature, and Technology: An Ecofeminist Philosophical Perspective."

7. Anne L. Ganley, *Court-Mandated Counseling for Men Who Batter: A Three-Day Workshop for Mental Health Professionals* (Washington, DC: Center for Women Policy Studies, 1985), p. 16.

8. Lenore Walker, *Terrifying Love: Why Battered Women Kill and How Society Responds* (New York: Harper & Row, 1989), p. 76.

9. See Jan Berliner Statman, "Life Doesn't Have to Be like This: How to Spot a

Batterer before an Abusive Relationship Begins." In *The Battered Woman's Survival Guide: Breaking the Cycle* (Dallas: Taylor Publishing Co., 1990). Note these are some factors that abusers, especially those who are violent, share in common, but there is no one profile of a batterer.

10. Deborah J. Pope-Lance and Joan Chamberlain Engelsman, *A Guide for Clergy on the Problems of Domestic Violence* (Trenton, NJ: New Jersey Department of Community Affairs Division on Women, 1987), p. 40.

11. Bonnie Burstow, *Radical Feminist Therapy: Working in the Context of Violence* (Newbury Park, CA: Sage, 1992), p. 149. This should not be understood to suggest that the absence of this behavior means that the batterer's actions are not life-threatening. It is very difficult to assess the danger to or predict the safety of battered women because any one incident can result in her death.

12. Reported in the *Dallas Times Herald*, June 15, 1991.

13. Angela Browne, *When Battered Women Kill* (New York: Free Press, 1987), p. 133; see also Walker, *Terrifying Love*, pp. 20–21.

14. Diana E. H. Russell, *Rape in Marriage*, rev. ed. (Bloomington and Indianapolis: Indiana University Press, 1990), p. 296.

15. Ganley, *Court-Mandated Counseling for Men who Batter*, p. 15.

16. Browne, *When Battered Women Kill*, p. 157.

17. Ibid., pp. 153–54.

18. These same acts of battering occur in some lesbian relationships. While human male violence is responsible for most of the damage to women and the other animals in cases of battering, a patriarchal, hierarchical culture will find expressions of this form of violence in some women's same-sex relationships. Where there is an acceptance of a patriarchal value hierarchy, some will wish to establish control (and be on top in terms of the hierarchy) through violence. Claire Renzetti reports that her research regarding lesbian battering revealed that "thirty-eight percent of the respondents who had pets reported that their partners had abused the animals" (Claire M. Renzetti, *Violent Betrayal: Partner Abuse in Lesbian Relationships* [Newbury Park, CA: Sage, 1992], p. 21). These acts of battering, like heterosexual battering, are considered violent and coercive behavior. (See Barbara Hart, "Lesbian Battering: An Examination," in *Naming the Violence: Speaking Out about Lesbian Battering*, ed. Kerry Lobel [Seattle: Seal Press, 1986], p. 188.) The battered lesbian whose partner injures or destroys a pet faces a triple burden: overcoming the invisibility or trivializing of lesbian battering, the invisibility or trivializing of abuse to animals, and overcoming homophobia in seeking help.

19. See Russell, *Rape in Marriage*, p. xii.

20. Lenore Walker, *The Battered Woman* (New York: Harper and Row, 1979), p. 120.

21. Linda "Lovelace" [Linda Marchiano], with Mike McGrady, *Ordeal* (New York: Berkley Books, 1980), pp. 105–13; specifically pp. 113, 112, see also p. 206.

22. Linda "Lovelace" [Linda Marchiano], *Out of Bondage* (Secaucus, NJ: Lyle Stuart Inc., 1986), p. 141, quoting Chip Visci of the Detroit *Free Press*.

23. "Lovelace," *Out of Bondage*, p. 194.

24. See Diana E. H. Russell, *Sexual Exploitation: Rape, Child Sexual Abuse, and Workplace Harassment* (Newbury Park, CA: Sage, 1984), p. 126.

25. Sylvia Fraser, *My Father's House: A Memoir of Incest and of Healing* (New York: Harper and Row, 1987), pp. 11–12.

26. Alice Vachss, *Sex Crimes* (New York: Random House, 1993), p. 46.

27. See Kathleen Coulborn Faller, *Understanding Child Sexual Maltreatment* (Newbury Park, CA: Sage, 1990), p. 196.

28. See Faller, *Understanding Child Sexual Maltreatment*, pp. 56–57.

29. See Frank R. Ascione, "Children Who Are Cruel to Animals: A Review of Research and Implications for Developmental Psychopathology." *Anthrozoos* 6, no. 4 (1993), pp. 226–47.

30. See American Psychiatric Association, *Diagnostic and Statistical Manual of Mental Disorders*, 3rd ed. rev. (Washington, DC: American Psychiatric Association, 1987), p. 53.

31. Kathryn Brohl, *Pockets of Craziness: Examining Suspected Incest* (Lexington, MA: Lexington Books, 1991), p. 24.

32. Ascione, "Children Who Are Cruel to Animals," p. 238–39.

33. See, for instance, Carl A. Raschke, *Painted Black: From Drug Killings to Heavy Metal—the Alarming True Story of How Satanism Is Terrorizing Our Communities* (New York: Harper and Row, 1990), pp. 39–41, 61, and passim.

34. See Pamela S. Hudson, *Ritual Child Abuse: Discovery, Diagnosis, and Treatment* (Saratoga, CA: R & E Publishers, 1991); anonymous, *Ritual Abuse: A Broad Overview* (Baltimore, MD: Survivors of Incest Anonymous, P. O. Box 21817, 1992); Catherine Gould, "Diagnosis and Treatment of Ritually Abused Children," and Walter C. Young, "Recognition and Treatment of Survivors Reporting Ritual Abuse," in *Out of Darkness: Exploring Satanism and Ritual Abuse*, ed. David K. Sakheim and Susan E. Devine (New York: Lexington Books, 1992); and Margaret Smith, *Ritual Abuse: What It Is, Why It Happens, How to Help* (San Francisco: Harper San Francisco, 1993).

35. Elizabeth S. Rose, "Surviving the Unbelievable: A First-Person Account of Cult Ritual Abuse," *Ms*, January/February 1993, p. 44.

36. Donald T. Lunde, *Murder and Madness* (San Francisco: San Francisco Book Co., 1976), p. 53.

37. Quoted in Robert Dvorchak, "Dahmer's Troubled Childhood Offers Clues but No Simple Answers," *Dallas Times Herald*, August 11, 1991.

38. See Robert K. Ressler, Ann W. Burgess, Carol R. Hartman, John E. Douglas, and Arlene McCormack, "Murderers Who Rape and Mutilate," *Journal of Interpersonal Violence* 1, no. 3 (1986), pp. 273–87.

39. Timothy M. Phelps and Helen Winternitz, *Capitol Games: The Inside Story of Clarence Thomas, Anita Hill, and a Supreme Court Nomination* (New York: Harper Perennial, 1993), p. 315.

40. Spelman, "Woman as Body," pp. 120, 127.

41. See ibid., p. 127.

42. See, for instance, Linda LeMoncheck, *Dehumanizing Women: Treating Persons as Sex Objects* (Totowa, NJ: Rowman & Allanheld, 1985), especially pp. 14–21.

43. Kimberlé Crenshaw, "Whose Story Is It Anyway? Feminist and Antiracist Appropriations of Anita Hill," In *Race-ing Justice, En-gendering Power: Essays on Anita Hill, Clarence Thomas, and the Construction of Social Reality*, ed. Toni Morrison (New York: Pantheon Books, 1992), p. 412.

44. Lorene Cary, *Black Ice* (New York: Vintage Books, 1991), p. 156.

45. Patricia Hill Collins, *Black Feminist Thought: Knowledge, Consciousness, and the Politics of Empowerment* (Boston: Unwin Hyman, 1990), pp. 170–71, 172.

46. Sander L. Gilman, "Black Bodies, White Bodies: Toward an Iconography of Female Sexuality in Late Nineteenth-Century Art, Medicine, and Literature," *Critical*

Inquiry 12 (1985), p. 212. bell hooks extends Gilman's analysis in "Selling Hot Pussy," *Black Looks: Race and Representation* (Boston, South End Press, 1992), pp. 61–77.

47. See Alice Mayall and Diana E. H. Russell, "Racism in Pornography," in *Making Violence Sexy*, ed. Diana E. H. Russell (New York: Teachers College, 1992).

48. This discussion of epistemological issues was worked out with the supportive insights and patient prodding of Nancy Tuana.

49. Lorraine Code, *What Can She Know? Feminist Theory and the Construction of Knowledge* (Ithaca: Cornell University Press, 1991), p. 82, quoting Annette Baier, "Cartesian Persons," in *Postures of the Mind: Essays on Mind and Morals* (Minneapolis: University of Minnesota Press, 1985). I concede that the article that introduces the concept of second persons appears to exclude animals from being participants in this process, as Baier distinguishes between human and animal consciousness. Thus, I may be extending the concept beyond the bounds that I suspect Baier, or perhaps even Code, might grant. However, I believe that such extension is legitimate, and question the epistemological assumptions that undergird claims about animals' lack of certain forms of consciousness.

50. Code, *What Can She Know?*, p. 85.

51. Ibid., p. 86.

52. Ibid., p. 121.

53. See Tom Regan, *The Case for Animal Rights* (Berkeley and Los Angeles: University of California Press, 1983) on animals having a biography, and Barbara Noske, *Humans and Other Animals*, on the need for an anthropology of animals.

54. Catharine MacKinnon, *Toward a Feminist Theory of the State* (Cambridge: Harvard University Press, 1989), p. 168.

55. Carole Pateman, *The Sexual Contract* (Stanford: Stanford University Press, 1988).

56. See Karen J. Warren, "Feminism and Ecology: Making Connections," *Environmental Ethics 9*, no. 1 (1987), pp. 3–20 and "The Power and the Promise of Ecological Feminism," *Environmental Ethics* 12 (Summer) 1990, pp. 125–46.

57. Sara Ruddick, "Notes toward a Feminist Peace Politics," in *Gendering War Talk*, ed. Miriam Cooke and Angela Woollacott (Princeton: Princeton University Press, 1993), p. 118.

58. Wendy Brown, *Manhood and Politics: A Feminist Reading in Political Theory* (Totowa, NJ: Rowman & Littlefield, 1988), p. 56.

59. Challenges to the ways by which we draw the line between "human" and "animal" can be found in the writings of Donna Haraway, *Simians, Cyborgs, and Women* (New York: Routledge, 1990) and *Primate Visions: Gender, Race, and Nature in the World of Modern Science* (New York: Routledge, 1989); Lynda Birke, "Science, Feminism, and Animal Natures I: Extending the Boundaries" and "Science, Feminism, and Animal Natures II: Feminist Critiques and the Place of Animals in Science," *Women's Studies International Forum* 14, no. 5 (1991), pp. 443–50, 451–58; Mary Midgley, *Animals and Why They Matter* (Athens: University of Georgia Press, 1983) and *Beast and Man: The Roots of Human Nature* (Ithaca, New York: Cornell University Press, 1978); and Noske, *Humans and Other Animals*, among others.

60. Karen J. Warren, correspondence July 1993.

61. Warren, "Feminism and Ecology," p. 6.

62. See Susan Moller Okin, *Justice, Gender, and the Family* (New York: Basic Books, 1989).

63. See, for instance, Lynne A. Foster, Christine Mann Veale, and Catherine Ingram Fogel, "Factors Present When Battered Women Kill," *Issues in Mental Health Nursing* 10 (1989), pp. 273–84, on the presence of a firearm in the home as one of the factors present in battering relationships that end in homicide.

64. See Richard A. Stordeur and Richard Stille, *Ending Men's Violence against Their Partners: One Road to Peace* (Newbury Park, CA: Sage, 1989).

65. I acknowledge the logistical problem this issue presents, and the concern that women might abandon the animals, not because of cruelty or insensitivity, but because they are overwhelmed with reshaping their own lives and feel that the animals are safer removed from the batterer's presence. Still, I believe it is an important step to make in protecting women and animals. I am indebted to DeLora Frederickson and Pam Wilhoite for their advocacy of this program. For information on setting up such a program, which is currently a project of Feminists for Animal Rights, please send a stamped (fifty-two cent) self-addressed envelope to Feminists for Animal Rights at P. O. Box 16425, Chapel Hill, North Carolina 27516.

66. See Joan Zorza, "Woman-Battering: A Major Cause of Homelessness," *Clearinghouse Review* (special issue, 1991), pp. 421–29.

67. See Maria P. Root, "Persistent, Disordered Eating as a Gender-Specific, Post-Traumatic Stress Response to Sexual Assault," *Psychotherapy* 28, no. 1 (1991), pp. 96–102 and G. Sloan and P. Leichner, "Is There a Relationship between Sexual Abuse or Incest and Eating Disorders?" *Canadian Journal of Psychiatry* 31, no. 7 (1986), pp. 656–60.

68. Judy Krizmanic, "Perfect Obsession: Can Vegetarianism Cover up an Eating Disorder?," *Vegetarian Times*, June 1992, p. 58.

69. Hudson, *Ritual Child Abuse*, p. 32; see also Gould, "Diagnosis and Treatment of Ritually Abused Children," p. 214.

70. See Carol J. Adams, *The Sexual Politics of Meat: A Feminist-Vegetarian Critical Theory* (New York: Continuum, 1990), pp. 159–62.

71. Krizmanic, "Perfect Obsession," p. 59.

72. Vachss, *Sex Crimes*, p. 172.

73. Jay McDaniel, "Green Grace," *Earth Ethics: Evolving Values for an Earth Community* 3, no. 4 (1992), p. 1.

74. See, for instance, Susan Brownmiller, *Against Our Will: Men, Women, and Rape* (New York: Simon and Schuster, 1975), p. 39.

75. Ascione, "Children Who Are Cruel to Animals," p. 232.

76. Lunde, *Murder and Madness*, pp. 53, 56. Jane Caputi challenges Lunde's assertion that this occurs only in rare individuals, she sees it instead as constitutive of "the age of sex crime." Jane Caputi, *The Age of Sex Crime* (Bowling Green, OH: Bowling Green State University Popular Press, 1987).

77. Conversation, September 1993.

78. See Wendy Doniger, "Diary," *London Review of Books*, September 23, 1993, p. 25.

79. See Susanne Kappeler, "Animal Conservationism and Human Conservationism," forthcoming in Carol J. Adams, Josephine Donovan, and Susanne Kappeler, eds., *Animals and Women: Feminist Theoretical Explorations*.

80. David Levinson, *Family Violence in Cross-cultural Perspective* (Newbury Park, CA: Sage, 1989), p. 45, cited in Ascione, "Children Who Are Cruel to Animals."

81. See Cynthia Enloe, *Bananas, Beaches, and Bases: Making Sense of International Politics* (Berkeley: University of California Press, 1989).

82. See Noske, *Humans and Other Animals.*

83. bell hooks, "Feminism and Militarism: A Comment," in *Talking Back* (Boston: South End Press, 1989), p. 97. She in turn is quoting Patty Walton, "The Culture in Our Blood."

Chapter 9: Feeding on Grace: Institutional Violence, Feminist Ethics, and Vegetarianism

1. Kathy and Bob Kellogg, *Raising Pigs Successfully* (Charlotte, VT: Williamson Publishing, 1985), p. 110.

2. Adrienne Rich, *On Lies, Secrets, and Silences* (New York: W. W. Norton and Co., 1979).

3. Kellogg, *Raising Pigs Successfully*, p. 13.

4. Ibid., p. 109.

5. These descriptions of malestream thinking are derived from Lorraine Code, *What Can She Know? Feminist Theory and the Construction of Knowledge* (Ithaca: Cornell University Press, 1991), pp. 150–51.

6. Joan Ullyot, *Women's Running* (Mountain View, California: World Publications, 1976), p. 78.

7. Elisabeth Schüssler Fiorenza, *Bread Not Stone: The Challenge of Feminist Biblical Interpretation* (Boston: Beacon Press, 1984), p. xiii.

8. Cuthbert Simpson and Walter Russell Bowie, *The Interpreter's Bible (Genesis)* (New York and Nashville: Abingdon Press, 1952).

9. Gerhard Von Rad, *Genesis: A Commentary* (Philadelphia: Westminster Press, 1961, 1972), p. 60.

10. James Barr, "Man and Nature—the Ecological Controversy and the Old Testament," *Bulletin of the John Rylands University Library of Manchester*, 1972, p. 22.

11. Quoted in Barr, "Man and Nature," p. 23. Barr adds parenthetically, "a different Hebrew word indeed, but there is no reason to suppose that this makes much difference."

12. Ibid., p. 23.

13. Simpson and Bowie, *The Interpreter's Bible (Genesis)*, p. 486. Cuthbert Simpson's explanation is that verse 29 may have been an addition to P's original narrative, containing the classical conceptualization of the Golden Age—which was seen as vegetarian and peaceful between humans and animals—and so it is more linked to the visions of Isaiah 11:6–8; 65:25; Hosea 2:18. Thus it posits potentiality rather than reality.

14. Barr, "Man and Nature," p. 21. Jean Soler agrees with Barr's conclusion, stating "meat eating is implicitly but unequivocally excluded" and that the reason for this has to do with the way that God and humans are defined in Genesis 1:26 by their relationship to each other. Jean Soler, "The Dietary Prohibitions of the Hebrews," *New York Review of Books*, June 14, 1979, p. 24. See also Rabbi Alfred S. Cohen, "Vegetarianism from a Jewish Perspective," *Journal of Halacha and Contemporary Society* 1, no. 2 (1981), pp. 38–63.

15. Anthony Phillips, *Lower than the Angels: Questions Raised by Genesis 1–11* (Bible Reading Fellowship, 1983), p. 48.

16. Soler, "The Dietary Prohibitions of the Hebrews," p. 24. See also Abraham

Isaac Kook, "Fragments of Light: A View as to the Reasons for the Commandments," in *Abraham Isaac Kook: The Lights of Penitence, The Moral Principles, Lights of Holiness, Essays, Letters, and Poems,* trans. Ben Zion Bokser (New York: Paulist Press).

17. Samuel H. Dresner, *The Jewish Dietary Laws. Their Meaning for Our Time,* revised and expanded edition (New York: Rabbinical Assembly of America, 1982), pp. 21, 26.

18. Ibid., p. 22.

19. Ibid., p. 24.

20. Elizabeth Cady Stanton, *The Woman's Bible: Part One* (Seattle: Coalition Task Force on Women and Religion, 1974 reprint of 1898 edition), p. 91.

21. See Fiorenza, *Bread Not Stone,* p. xv.

22. Elisabeth Schüssler Fiorenza, *In Memory of Her: A Feminist Theological Reconstruction of Christian Origins* (New York: Crossroad, 1984), p. 6.

23. It is here, in the conflict between history and eschatology, for those concerned with Christian feminist ethics, that I would place a Christology of vegetarianism. This Christology is not concerned with whether Jesus was or was not a vegetarian just as feminist theology rejects the relevance that the twelve disciples were men. This is not a quest for historical duplication but for the acquisition of an ability to discern justice-making according to the Christological revelation. With this perspective we would come to see that a piece of flesh turns the miracles of the loaves and fishes on its head. Where Jesus multiplied food to feed the hungry, our current food-producing system reduces food sources and damages the environment at the same time, by producing plant food to feed terminal animals.

A Christology of vegetarianism would argue that just as Jesus challenged historical definitions such as Samaritan, or undercut identities such as the wealthy man, so we are equipped to challenge the historical and individual identity of a corpse eating food habit that fosters environmental and ethical injustice.

24. Beverly Harrison, "Theological Reflection in the Struggle for Liberation," in *Making the Connections: Essays in Feminist Social Ethics,* ed. Carol S. Robb (Boston: Beacon Press, 1985), pp. 235–36.

25. The following quotations about the development of an ethical issue are from Sarah R. Bentley, "For Better or Worse: The Challenge of the Battered Women's Movement to Christian Social Ethics," (Union Theological Seminary doctoral dissertation, 1989), pp. 16–17. Those quotations with both single and double quotation marks are Bentley's references to Gerard Fourez's *Liberation Ethics* (Philadelphia: Temple University Press, 1982), pp. 93, 108–9. Underlined words within the quotation marks contained this emphasis in the original source.

26. See chapter 7, p. 137, where I first refer to this insight. Harrison, *Making the Connections,* p. 13. I believe Harrison's claim is strengthened when coupled with Frye's discussion of the arrogant eye and the loving eye.

27. Alice Walker, "Am I Blue" in *Living by the Word: Selected Writings: 1973–1987* (San Diego: Harcourt Brace Jovanovich, 1988), p. 5.

28. Virginia de Araújo, "The Friend. . . . ," *Sinister Wisdom,* no. 20 (1982), p. 17. See *The Sexual Politics of Meat,* p. 190, where I first invoked this marvelous poem.

Chapter 10: Beastly Theology

Epigraphs: Xenophanes cited in Mary E. Hunt, Comprehensive Examination II, "God-Language: Critique and Construction," Graduate Theological Union, Berkeley,

May 1977. Bernard Rollin, *The Unheeded Cry: Animal Consciousness, Animal Pain, and Science* (Oxford: Oxford University Press, 1989), p. 23.

1. Mary Midgley, *Animals and Why They Matter* (Athens: University of Georgia Press, 1983), p. 125.

2. I develop this idea more fully in chapter 2 of *The Sexual Politics of Meat.*

3. Quoted in Yi-Fu Tuan, *Dominance and Affection: The Making of Pets* (New Haven: Yale University Press, 1984), p. 69. While Lewis inscribes a further dualism upon animals (beasts versus tame animals), I will be using beast to refer to all other-than-human animals.

4. Barbara Noske, *Humans and Other Animals: Beyond the Boundaries of Anthropology* (London: Pluto Press, 1989), p. 77.

5. Conversation, February 28, 1994.

6. This issue is developed more fully in Carol J. Adams and Marjorie Procter-Smith, "Taking Life or 'Taking on Life'?: Table Talk and Animals," in *Ecofeminism and the Sacred*, ed. Carol J. Adams (New York: Continuum, 1993).

7. Bernard Rollin, *Animal Rights and Human Morality* (Buffalo, NY: Prometheus Books, 1981), p. 32.

8. Donald Griffin, "The Problem of Distinguishing Awareness from Responsiveness," in *Self-Awareness in Domesticated Animals: Proceedings of a Workshop Held at Keble College, Oxford*, ed. D. G. M. Wood-Gush, M. Dawkins, R. Ewbank (Hertfordshire, England: The Universities Federation for Animal Welfare), p. 6. Griffin suggests the term "anthropomorphophobia" to convey the "apprehension that one may be accused of uncritical sentimentality if one suggests that any nonhuman animal might experience subjective emotions such as fear, or think consciously in even the simplest terms, such as believing that food is located in a certain place." Donald R. Griffin, "Foreword," *Interpretation and Explanation in the Study of Animal Behavior. Volume 1: Interpretation, Intentionality, and Communication*, ed. Mark Bekoff and Dale Jamieson (Boulder, CO: Westview, 1990,), p. xiii.

9. Catherine Keller, *From a Broken Web: Separation, Sexism, and Self* (Boston: Beacon Press, 1986), p. 9.

10. See Adams, *The Sexual Politics of Meat*, pp. 72–73.

11. Anyone who thinks that this resistance is not keen in the mid-1990s should examine the response by conservative and many mainstream members of the mainline denominations to the "RE-Imagining Conference" held in Minnesota in November 1993. One of the main complaints is that God was referred to as Sophia.

12. Catherine Keller, *From a Broken Web*, pp. 38–39.

13. Sallie McFague, *Models of God* (Minneapolis: Fortress Press, 1987), p. 33.

14. Keith Thomas, *Man and the Natural World: A History of the Modern Sensibility* (New York: Pantheon, 1983), p. 41.

15. Mary Midgley, "The Concept of Beastliness: Philosophy, Ethics, and Animal Behavior," *Philosophy*, 48 (1973), p. 114.

16. Maureen Duffy, "Beasts for Pleasure," in *Animals, Men, and Morals: An Enquiry into the Maltreatment of Non-Humans*, ed. Stanley Godlovitch, Roslind Godlovitch, John Harris (New York: Taplinger, 1972), p. 113.

17. McFague, *Models of God*, p. 3.

18. Milan Kundera, *The Unbearable Lightness of Being*, (New York: Penguin, 1988), p. 286.

19. Genevieve Lloyd, *The Man of Reason: "Male" and "Female" in Western Philosophy* (Minneapolis: University of Minnesota Press, 1984), p. 2.

20. Alison M. Jaggar, "Love and Knowledge: Emotion in Feminist Epistemology," in *Gender/Body/Knowledge: Feminist Reconstructions of Being and Knowing* (New Brunswick: Rutgers University Press, 1989), p. 156. Jaggar is referring to the work of Susan Bordo, *The Flight to Objectivity: Essays on Cartesianism and Culture* (Albany: State University of New York Press, 1987) and Jane Flax, "Political Philosophy and Patriarchal Unconscious: A Psychoanalytic Perspective on Epistemology and Metaphysics," in *Discovering Reality: Feminist Perspectives on Epistemology, Metaphysics, Methodology and Philosophy*, ed. Sandra Harding and Merrill Hintikka (Dordrecht: Reidel, 1983).

21. Barbara Noske, *Humans and Other Animals: Beyond the Boundaries of Anthropology* (London: Pluto Press, 1989), p. 117, see also Stephen Clark, *The Nature of the Beast* (Oxford and New York: Oxford University Press, 1982), pp. 112–15.

22. See Nancy Tuana, *The Less Noble Sex: Scientific, Religious, and Philosophical Conceptions of Woman's Nature* (Bloomington and Indianapolis: Indiana University Press, 1993).

23. Noske, *Humans and Other Animals* (London: Pluto Press, 1989), p. 88.

24. Josephine Donovan, "Animal Rights and Feminist Theory" *Signs: Journal of Women in Culture and Society* 15, no. 2 (1990), p. 353.

25. Jaggar, "Love and Knowledge," p. 161.

26. Ibid., p. 163.

27. Quoted in "Second Strike Against Noted Author in California Test," *New York Times*, February 27, 1994.

28. Cited in Sharon D. Welch, *Communities of Resistance and Solidarity* (Maryknoll, New York: Orbis Books, 1985), p. 9.

29. While many of these examples may appear to arise and apply only to specific cultures, i.e., the animals deemed inedible in the West may not be deemed inedible elsewhere (dogs, for instance), what is universal is that animals are viewed as less valuable than human, and thus can be made into an object for humans' survival or pleasure, so that some kinds of animals—even if they differ within cultures—will fill these roles.

30. Donna Haraway, "Situated Knowledges: The Science Question in Feminism and the Privilege of Partial Perspective," *Feminist Studies* 14, no. 3 (Fall 1988), p. 586.

31. Haraway, "Situated Knowledges," p. 584.

32. Virginia Woolf, *A Room of One's Own*, (New York: Harcourt, Brace, Jovanovich, 1929), p. 48. When Virginia Woolf grants subjectivity to a dog in her biography of Elizabeth Barrett Browning's dog Flush, she seems to get even with the Bishop's denigration of both women writers and animals.

33. As Brigid Brophy suggests in an imagined heavenly conversation between Bernard Shaw and God:

"I suppose," God said, "theology impresses them with the notion that animals have no souls—and hence no ghosts."

. . . "No, what prevents people from, on the whole, seeing animals' ghosts is not theology but bad conscience. If they do see an animal ghost, it will be a dog or a cat, not an animal they are in the habit of eating. . . . [P]eople see ghosts for the same reason that they read ghost stories: as self indulgence. It is not murderers who are haunted. It is the innocent. . . . It is because people truly are guilty of murdering animals that the folk imagination has to contrive not to see the ghosts of the folk diet."

Brigid Brophy, *The Adventures of God in His Search for the Black Girl* (Boston: Little, Brown & Co., 1968), pp. 189–90. Regarding the question of whether animals have souls see Keith Thomas, *Man and the Natural World*, (New York: Pantheon, 1983), pp. 137–42.

34. Lorraine Code, *What Can She Know? Feminist Theory and the Construction of Knowledge* (Ithaca: Cornell University Press, 1991), p. 148.

35. Donovan, "Animal Rights and Feminist Theory," p. 375.

36. This is a paraphrase of a remark by Melinda Vadas as she analyzed Catharine MacKinnon's insights and their applicability to the issue of animal exploitation.

37. These are Catharine MacKinnon's insights, with my addition of species construction to her analysis of gender construction. See Catharine MacKinnon, *Toward a Feminist Theory of State* (Cambridge: Harvard University Press, 1989), p. 237.

38. Ibid., p. 238.

39. Ibid., p. 240.

40. Vicki Hearne, *Adam's Task: Calling Animals by Name* (New York: Alfred A. Knopf, 1986), p. 33.

41. Code, *What Can She Know?*, p. 82, quoting Annette Baier, "Cartesian Persons," in *Postures of the Mind: Essays on Mind and Morals* (Minneapolis: University of Minnesota Press, 1985).

42. Code, *What Can She Know?*, p. 85.

43. Ibid., p. 121.

44. Hearne, *Adam's Task*, p. 59.

45. Sally Carrighar, *Home to the Wilderness: A Personal Journey* (Baltimore: Penguin Books, 1974), p. 304. This is excerpted in Theresa Corrigan and Stephanie Hoppe, eds., *With a Fly's Eye, Whale's Wit, and Woman's Heart* (Pittsburgh: Cleis Press, 1989), pp. 23–24.

46. Brigid Brophy interviewed in Rynn Berry, Jr., *The Vegetarians* (Brookline, MA: Autumn Press, 1979), p. 80.

47. Noske, *Humans and Other Animals*, p. 53.

48. Keller, *From a Broken Web*, p. 2.

Coda

1. "Many people, but especially women, observe that as they get toward middle age they are less attracted to meat, while finding dairy products, fruits and vegetables more appetizing." Barbara Seaman and Gideon Seaman, M.D., *Women and the Crisis in Sex Hormones* (New York: Rawson Associates Publishers, Inc., 1977), p. 372.

2. Mary Daly in cahoots with Jane Caputi, *Websters' First New Intergalactic Wickedary of the English Language* (Boston: Beacon Press, 1987), p. 114. On crones, see also, Jane Caputi, *Gossips, Gorgons, and Crones: The Fates of the Earth* (Santa Fe, New Mexico: Bear & Company Publishing, 1993).

3. Anne Llwellyn Barstow argues that the figures in the millions often cited are too high, she proposes a conservative estimate of two hundred thousand accusations and "a figure of one hundred thousand dead." Anne Llwellyn Barstow, *Witchcraze: A New History of the European Witch Hunts* (San Francisco: Pandora, 1994), p. 23.

4. Barstow reports that "though the majority of alleged witches in New England

were middle-aged, most European victims were older, over fifty." She continues: "One aspect of the witchcraze, undeniably, was an uneasiness with and hostility toward dependent older women. Witch charges may have been used to get rid of indigent elderly women, past childbearing and too enfeebled to do productive work." *Witchcraze,* pp. 27, 29.

5. Keith Thomas, *Religion and the Decline of Magic: Studies in Popular Beliefs in Sixteenth- and Seventeenth-Century England* (Hammondsworth: Penguin University Books, 1973), p. 626, quoting J. R. Ackerly, *My Father and Myself* (1968), p. 174.

6. Benedict de Spinoza, *Ethic* 4, prop. 37, trans. W. Hale White, 4th ed., 1910, p. 209. Quoted in Keith Thomas, *Man and the Natural World: A History of the Modern Sensibility* (New York: Pantheon Books, 1983), p. 298.

7. Louise Armstrong, "Ideal Freedoms, Real Fears," a review of Wendy Kaminer's *A Fearful Freedom: Women's Flight from Equality,* in *The Women's Review of Books* 8, no. 2 (November 1990), p. 9.

8. See, for instance, David Fraser, "The Role of Behavior in Swine Production: A Review of Research," *Applied Animal Ethology* 11 (1983–84), pp. 317–39; and David Fraser, "Attraction to Blood as a Factor in Tail-Biting by Pigs," *Applied Animal Behaviour Science* 17 (1987), pp. 61–68; A. B. Lawrence, M. C. Appleby, and H. A. Macleod, "Measuring Hunger in the Pig Using Operant Conditioning: The Effect of Food Restriction," *Animal Production* 47, pp. 131–37; D. G. M. Wood-Gush and R.G. Beilharz, "The Enrichment of a Bare Environment for Animals in Confined Conditions," *Applied Animal Ethology* 10 (1983), pp. 209–17.

9. bell hooks, *Feminist Theory: From Margin to Center* (Boston: South End Press, 1984), p. x.

10. See Kay Mills, *This Little Light of Mine: The Life of Fannie Lou Hamer* (New York: Penguin Books, 1993), p. 1.

11. For a fuller analysis see Carol Wiley, "Why It's Impossible to be a Vegetarian," *Vegetarian Times,* May 1991.

12. Howard W. Winger, "Book," *Encyclopedia Britannica,* vol. 3 (Chicago: William Benton, 1966), p. 921.

Bibliography

Abbott, Sally. "The Origins of God in the Blood of the Lamb." In *Reweaving the World: The Emergence of Ecofeminism*. Edited by Irene Diamond and Gloria Feman Orenstein. San Francisco: Sierra Club Books, 1990, pp. 35–40.

Achenbach, T. M. *Child Behavior Checklist (for Ages 2–3, for ages 4–16)*. Burlington, VT: Center for Children, Youth, and Families, 1988.

Adams, Carol J. "Anima, Animus, Animal." *Ms. Magazine* (May/June 1991).

———. "Antifur . . . Antiwoman?" *Animals' Voice Magazine* 2, no. 8 (1989).

———. "'Deena'—the World's Only Stripping Chimp." *Animals' Voice Magazine* 3, no. 1 (1990).

———. "'I Just Raped My Wife! What Are You Going to Do about It, Pastor?'—the Church and Sexual Violence." In *Transforming a Rape Culture*. Edited by Emilie Buchwald, Pamela Fletcher, Martha Roth. Minneapolis: Milkweed Editions, 1993.

———. "The Oedible Complex: Feminism and Vegetarianism." In the *Lesbian Reader*. Edited by Gina Covina and Laurel Galana. Oakland, CA: Amazon, 1975.

———. "On the Fallacy of Germaine Greer." *Newsletter of the International Association against Painful Experiments on Animals* (Fall 1990): pp. 6–7.

———. *The Sexual Politics of Meat: A Feminist-Vegetarian Critical Theory*. New York: Continuum, 1990.

———. "Down to Earth." *Ms. Magazine* (May/June 1994).

Adams, Carol J., editor. *Ecofeminism and the Sacred*. New York: Continuum, 1993.

Adams, Carol J., and Marjorie Procter-Smith. "Taking Life or 'Taking on Life': Table Talk and Animals." In *Ecofeminism and the Sacred*. Edited by Carol J. Adams. New York: Continuum, 1993.

Ahlers, Julia. "Thinking like a Mountain: Toward a Sensible Land Ethic." *Christian Century* (April 25, 1990): pp. 433–34.

Akers, Keith. *A Vegetarian Sourcebook: The Nutrition, Ecology, and Ethics of a Natural Foods Diet*. New York: G. P. Putnam's Sons, 1983.

Albino, Donna. "C.E.A.S.E.: Building Animal Consciousness. An Interview with Jane Lidsky." *Woman of Power: A Magazine of Feminism, Spirituality, and Politics. Nature* 9 (1988): pp. 64–66.

Allen, Paula Gunn. *The Sacred Hoop: Recovering the Feminine in American Indian Tradition*. Boston: Beacon, 1986.

American Psychiatric Association. *Diagnostic and Statistical Manual of Mental Disorders.* 3rd ed. rev. Washington, DC: American Psychiatric Association, 1987.

Animal Rights Handbook: Everyday Ways to Save Animal Lives. Venice, CA: Living Planet Press, 1990.

Anonymous. *Ritual Abuse: A Broad Overview.* Baltimore, MD: Survivors of Incest Anonymous, P. O. Box 21817, 1992.

Ascione, Frank R. "Children Who Are Cruel to Animals: A Review of Research and Implications for Developmental Psychopathology." *Anthrozoos* 6, no. 4 (1993): pp. 226–247.

Baier, Annette. "Cartesian Persons." In *Postures of the Mind: Essays on Mind and Morals.* Minneapolis: University of Minnesota Press, 1985.

Baker, Steve. *Picturing the Beast: Animals, Identity and Representation.* Manchester, England: Manchester University Press, 1993.

Barnard, Neal. "The Evolution of the Human Diet." In *The Power of Your Plate.* Summertown, TN: Book Publishing Co., 1990.

Barr, James. "Man and Nature—the Ecological Controversy and the Old Testament." *Bulletin of the John Rylands University Library of Manchester.* (1972): pp. 9–32.

Barstow, Anne Llwellyn. *Witchcraze: A New History of the European Witch Hunts.* San Francisco: Pandora, 1994.

Bartky, Sandra Lee. *Femininity and Domination: Studies in the Phenomenology of Oppression.* New York and London: Routledge, 1990.

Bartlett, Kim. "Editorial: A Patriarchal World." *Animals' Agenda: The Magazine of Animal Rights and Ecology* (October 1990): p. 2.

———. "Support Animal Rights." *On the Issues* (Winter 1990): p. 43.

Bauman, Batya. "Flesh or No Flesh." Letter to *Womanews.* (September 1989).

———. "Ecofeminist Statement." *Vegan Street: Cruelty-Free and Environmentally Safe Products.* Rockville, MD: Vegan Street, 1990.

———. "What Is Loving Animals All About?" *Feminists for Animal Rights Newsletter* 5, no. 3–4 (1990): pp. 1, 12.

Bell, Derrick. *Faces at the Bottom of the Well: The Permanence of Racism.* New York: Basic Books, 1992.

Benney, Norma. "All of One Flesh: The Rights of Animals." In *Reclaim the Earth: Women Speak Out for Life on Earth.* Edited by Léonie Caldecott and Stephanie Leland. London: Women's Press, 1983.

Bentley, Sarah R. *For Better or Worse: The Challenge of the Battered Women's Movement to Christian Social Ethics.* Union Theological Seminary doctoral diseration, 1989.

Benton, Ted. *Natural Relations: Ecology, Animal Rights, and Social Justice.* London and New York: Verso, 1993.

Berry, Rynn Jr. *The Vegetarians.* Brookline, MA: Autumn Press, 1979.

Birke, Lynda. "Science, Feminism, and Animal Natures I: Extending the Boundaries." *Women's Studies International Forum* 14, no. 5 (1991): pp. 443–50.

———. "Science, Feminism, and Animal Natures II: Feminist Critiques and the Place of Animals in Science." *Women's Studies International Forum* 14, no. 5 (1991): pp. 451–58.

———. "'They're Worse than Animals': Animals in Biological Research." In *More than the Parts: Biology and Politics.* Edited by Lynda Birke and Jonathan Silvertown. London: Pluto Press, 1984, pp. 219–35.

Blanchard, Dallas, and Terry Prewitt. *Religious Violence and Abortion.* Gainesville: University Press of Florida, 1993.

Bleier, Ruth. *Science and Gender: A Critique of Biology and Its Theories on Women.* New York: Pergamon Press, 1984.

Bleier, Ruth, ed. *Feminist Approaches to Science.* New York: Pergamon Press, 1986.

Bloodroot Collective. *The Political Palate: A Feminist Vegetarian Cookbook.* Bridgeport, CT: Sanguinaria Publishing, 1980.

———. *The Second Seasonal Political Palate: A Feminist Vegetarian Cookbook.* Bridgeport, CT: Sanguinaria, 1984.

———. *The Perennial Political Palate: The Third Feminist Vegetarian Cookbook.* Bridgeport, CT: Sanguinaria, 1993.

Bordo, Susan. *The Flight to Objectivity: Essays on Cartesianism and Culture.* Albany: State University of New York Press, 1987.

Bring, Ellen. "Moving Towards Coexistence: An Interview with Alice Walker." *Animals' Agenda* 8 (April 1988): pp. 6–9.

Brody, Jane E. *Jane Brody's Nutrition Book.* New York: W. W. Norton & Co., 1981.

———. "Huge Study Indicts Fat and Meat." *New York Times,* May 8, 1990.

Brohl, Kathryn. *Pockets of Craziness: Examining Suspected Incest.* Lexington, MA: Lexington Books, 1991.

Brophy, Brigid. "The Rights of Animals." In Brigid Brophy, *Don't Never Forget: Collected Views and Reviews.* New York: Holt, Rinehart and Winston, 1966, pp. 15–21.

———. "The Way of No Flesh." In *The Genius of Shaw.* Edited by Michael Holroyd. New York: Holt, Rinehart and Winston, 1979.

———. *The Adventures of God in His Search for the Black Girl.* Boston: Little, Brown & Co., 1968.

Brown, Wendy. *Manhood and Politics: A Feminist Reading in Political Theory.* Totowa, NJ: Rowman & Littlefield, 1988.

Browne, Angela. *When Battered Women Kill.* New York: Free Press, 1987.

Brownmiller, Susan. *Against Our Will: Men, Women, and Rape.* New York: Simon and Schuster, 1975.

Bullard, Robert D. *Confronting Environmental Racism: Voices from the Grassroots.* Boston: South End Press, 1993.

Bumgarner, Marlene Anne. *The Book of Whole Grains.* New York: St. Martin's Press, 1976.

Burstow, Bonnie. *Radical Feminist Therapy: Working in the Context of Violence.* Newbury Park, CA: Sage, 1992.

Byrnes, J. "Raising Pigs by the Calendar at Maplewood Farm," *Hog Farm Management* (September 1976).

Callicott, J. Baird. *In Defense of the Land Ethic: Essays in Environmental Philosophy.* Albany, NY: State University of New York Press, 1989.

Canadian Anti-Fur Alliance. Press Release defending "Shame of Fur" ads against charge of sexism. November 30, 1990. Address: 11 River Street, Toronto, Ontario, Canada M5A 4C2.

Canadine, David. "Dangerous Liaisons." Review of *Road to Divorce: England 1530–1987* by Lawrence Stone. *New Republic.* (December 24, 1990).

Cantor, Aviva. "The Club, the Yoke, and the Leash: What We Can Learn from the Way a Culture Treats Animals." *Ms. Magazine* (August 1980): pp. 27–29.

Caputi, Jane. *The Age of Sex Crime.* Bowling Green, OH: Bowling Green State University Popular Press, 1987.

———. *Gossips, Gorgons, and Crones: The Fates of the Earth.* Santa Fe, New Mexico: Bear & Company Publishing, 1993.

Caraway, Nancie. *Segregated Sisterhood: Racism and the Politics of American Feminism.* Knoxville: The University of Tennessee Press, 1991.

Card, Claudia. "Pluralist Lesbian Separatism." In *Lesbian Philosophies and Cultures.* Edited by Jeffner Allen. Albany: State University of New York Press, 1990.

Carby, Hazel V. *Reconstructing Womanhood: The Emergence of the Afro-American Woman Novelist.* New York: Oxford, 1987.

Cary, Lorene. *Black Ice.* New York: Vintage Books, 1991.

Cheever, Holly. Letter to the editor, *Albany Times-Union* (November 1990).

Cheney, Jim. "Eco-Feminism and Deep Ecology." *Environmental Ethics* 9 (1987): pp. 115–45.

Clark, Lorenne M. G. and Lynda Lange. *The Sexism of Social and Political Theory: Women and Reproduction from Plato to Nietzsche.* Toronto: University of Toronto Press, 1979.

Clark, Stephen. *The Nature of the Beast.* Oxford and New York: Oxford University Press, 1982.

Clement, Connie. "The Case for Lay Abortion: Learning from Midwifery." *Healthsharing* (Winter, 1983): pp. 9–14.

Clift, Elayne. "Advocate Battles for Safety in Mines and Poultry Plants," *New Directions for Women* (May/June 1990), p. 3.

Coats, C. David. *Old MacDonald's Factory Farm: The Myth of the Traditional Farm and the Shocking Truth about Animal Suffering in Today's Agribusiness.* New York: Continuum, 1989.

Cobb, John, Jr. *Matters of Life and Death.* Louisville: Westminster/John Knox Press, 1991.

Cocks, Joan. *The Oppositional Imagination.* London: Routledge, 1989.

Code, Lorraine. "The Impact of Feminism on Epistemology." *American Philosophical Association Newsletter on Feminism and Philosophy* 88, no. 2 (March 1989): pp. 25–29.

———. *What Can She Know? Feminist Theory and the Construction of Knowledge.* Ithaca: Cornell University Press, 1991.

Cohen, Alfred S. (Rabbi). "Vegetarianism from a Jewish Perspective." *Journal of Halacha and Contemporary Society* 1, no. 2 (1981): pp. 38–63.

Collard, Andrée, with Joyce Contrucci. *Rape of the Wild: Man's Violence against Animals and the Earth.* London: Women's Press, 1988.

Collins, Patricia Hill. *Black Feminist Thought: Knowledge, Consciousness, and the Politics of Empowerment.* Boston: Unwin Hyman, 1990.

Collins, Sheila. *A Different Heaven and Earth.* Valley Forge: Judson Press, 1974.

Comstock, Gary. "Pigs and Piety: A Theocentric Perspective on Food Animals." *Good News for Animals? Christian Approaches to Animal Well-being.* Edited by Charles Pinches and Jay B. McDaniel. Maryknoll: Orbis Books, 1993.

Corea, Genoveffa (Gena). "Dominance and Control: How Our Culture Sees Women, Nature, and Animals," *Animals' Agenda* (May/June 1984).

———. *The Mother Machine: Reproductive Technologies from Artificial Insemination to Artificial Wombs.* New York: Harper & Row, 1985.

Corrigan, Theresa. "A Woman Is a Horse Is a Dog Is a Rat: An Interview with Ingrid

Newkirk." In *And a Deer's Ear, Eagle's Song and Bear's Grace: Animals and Women*. Edited by Theresa Corrigan and Stephanie Hoppe. Pittsburgh: Cleis Press, 1990.

Crenshaw, Kimberlé. "Demarginalizing the Intersection of Race and Sex: A Black Feminist Critique of Antidiscrimination Doctrine, Feminist Theory, and Antiracist Politics." In *Feminist Legal Theory: Readings in Law and Gender*. Edited by Katharine T. Bartlett and Rosanne Kennedy. Boulder: Westview Press, 1991

———. "Race, Reform, and Retrenchment: Transformation and Legitimation in Antidiscrimination Law." *Harvard Law Review* vol. 101, 7 (May 1988).

———. "Whose Story Is It Anyway? Feminist and Antiracist Appropriations of Anita Hill." In *Race-ing Justice, En-gendering Power: Essays on Anita Hill, Clarence Thomas, and the Construction of Social Reality*. Edited by Toni Morrison. New York: Pantheon Books, 1992, pp. 402–40.

Curtin, Deane. "Toward an Ecological Ethic of Care." *Hypatia: A Journal of Feminist Philosophy*, Special Issue on Ecological Feminism, 6, no. 1 (1991): pp. 60–74.

Daly, Mary. *Gyn/Ecology: The Metaethics of Radical Feminism*. Boston: Beacon Press, 1978.

Daly, Mary in cahoots with Jane Caputi. *Websters' First New Intergalactic Wickedary of the English Language*. Boston: Beacon Press, 1987.

Davies, Katherine. "What Is Ecofeminism?" *Women and Environments* (Spring 1988): pp. 4–6.

Davis, Karen. "Farm Animals and the Feminine Connection." *Animals' Agenda* (January/February 1988): pp. 38–39.

de Araújo, Virginia. "The Friend." *Sinister Wisdom*, no. 20 (1982): p. 17.

de Beauvoir, Simone. *The Second Sex*. Translated and edited by H. M. Parshley. Jonathan Cape, 1953. Hammondsworth, England: Penguin. 1972.

D'Eaubonne, Francoise. *Feminism or Death*. In *New French Feminisms: An Anthology*. Edited by Elaine Marks and Isabelle de Courtivron. New York: Shocken Books, 1981.

Diamond, Cora. "Eating Meat and Eating People," *Philosophy* 53 (1978).

Dombrowski, Daniel A. *Hartshorne and the Metaphysics of Animal Rights*. Albany, NY: State University of New York Press, 1988.

Doniger, Wendy. "Diary." *London Review of Books* (September 23, 1993): p. 25.

Donovan, Josephine. "Animal Rights and Feminist Theory." *Signs: Journal of Women in Culture and Society* 15, no. 2 (1990): pp. 350–75.

———. Response to Nell Noddings. *Signs* 16, no. 2 (1991): pp. 422–25.

Dresner, Samuel, H. *The Jewish Dietary Laws. Their Meaning for Our Time*. Revised and Expanded Edition. New York: Rabbinical Assembly of America, 1982.

Dunayer, Joan. "On Speciesist Language: English Usage Glorifies Humans at the Expense of Other Animals." *On the Issues* (Winter 1990): pp. 30–31.

Durning, Alan Thein, and Holly B. Brough. "Reforming the Livestock Economy." In *State of the World: A Worldwatch Institute Report on Progress Toward a Sustainable Society*. New York: W. W. Norton & Co., pp. 66–82.

Dvorchak, Robert. "Dahmer's Troubled Childhood Offers Clues but No Simple Answers." *Dallas Times Herald*, August 11, 1991.

Dworkin, Andrea. *Right-wing Women*. New York: Perigee Books, 1983.

———. *Pornography: Men Possessing Women*. New York: Perigee Books, 1981.

Ecofeminist Task Force Recommendation—Item #7. Presented to the National Women's Studies Association National Meeting, Akron, OH, June 1990.

Elshtain, Jean Bethke. "Why Worry about the Animals?" *Progressive* (March 1990): pp. 17–23.

Elson, John. "This Little Piggy Ate Roast Beef: Domesticated Porkers Are Becoming the Latest Pet Craze." *Time* (January 22, 1990): p. 54.

Elston, Mary Ann. "Women and Anti–vivisection in Victorian England, 1870–1900." In *Vivisection in Historical Perspective*. Edited by Nicolaas Rupke. London: Croom Helm, 1987.

Enloe, Cynthia. *Bananas, Beaches, and Bases: Making Sense of International Politics*. Berkeley: University of California Press, 1989.

Faller, Kathleen Coulborn. *Understanding Child Sexual Maltreatment*. Newbury Park, CA: Sage. 1990.

Feminists for Animal Rights. "Animal Rights Is a Feminist Issue." Flyer. n.d.

Fiddes, Nick. *Meat: A Natural Symbol*. London and New York: Routledge, 1991.

Finsen, Susan. "Making Ends Meet: Reconciling Ecoholism and Animal Rights Individualism." *Between the Species: A Journal of Ethics* 4, no. 1:11–20.

Flax, Jane. "Political Philosophy and Patriarchal Unconscious: A Psychoanalytic Perspective on Epistemology and Metaphysics." In *Discovering Reality: Feminist Perspectives on Epistemology, Metaphysics, Methodology, and Philosophy*. Edited by Sandra Harding and Merrill Hintikka. Dordrecht: Reidel, 1983.

Forbes, Dana. "Liberating the Killing Fields." *Ms.* 2, no. 4 (1992): pp. 84–85.

Foster, Lynne A., Christine Mann Veale, and Catherine Ingram Fogel. "Factors Present When Battered Women Kill." *Issues in Mental Health Nursing* 10 (1989): 273–84.

Fourez, Gerard. *Liberation Ethics*. Philadelphia: Temple University Press, 1982.

Fox, Michael W. *Agricide: The Hidden Crisis That Affects Us All*. New York: Shocken Books, 1986.

———. *Farm Animals: Husbandry, Behavior, and Veterinary Practice (Viewpoints of a Critic)*. Baltimore: University Park Press, 1984.

Fraser, David. "The Role of Behavior in Swine Production: A Review of Research." *Applied Animal Ethology* 11 (1983–84): pp. 317–39.

———. "Attraction to Blood as a Factor in Tail-Biting by Pigs." *Applied Animal Behaviour Science* 17 (1987): pp. 61–68.

Fraser, Nancy. *Unruly Practices: Power, Discourse, and Gender in Contemporary Social Theory*. Minneapolis: University of Minnesota Press, 1989.

Fraser, Sylvia. *My Father's House: A Memoir of Incest and of Healing*. New York: Harper and Row, 1987.

Frederickson, George M. *The Black Image in the White Mind: The Debate on Afro-American Character and Destiny, 1817–1914*. New York: Harper, 1971.

French, R. D. *Antivivisection and Medical Science in Victorian Society*. Princeton: Princeton University Press, 1975.

Freire, Paulo. *Pedagogy of the Oppressed*. New York: Continuum, 1970, 1993.

Fried, Marlene Gerber, ed. *From Abortion to Reproductive Freedom: Transforming a Movement*. Boston: South End Press, 1990.

Frye, Marilyn. *The Politics of Reality: Essays in Feminist Theory*. Trumansburg, NY: Crossing Press, 1983.

Fund for Animals. "Factory Farming: Misery on the Menu." Animal Agriculture Fact Sheet no. 2. New York, 1990.

Gaard, Greta. "Feminists, Animals, and the Environment: The Transformative Potential of Feminist Theory." Paper presented at the Annual Convention of the National

Women's Studies Association, Towson State University, Baltimore, June 14–18, 1989.

Gaard, Greta, ed. *Ecofeminism, Women, Animals, Nature.* Philadelphia: Temple University Press, 1993.

Ganley, Anne L. *Court-mandated Counseling for Men Who Batter: A Three-Day Workshop for Mental Health Professionals.* Washington, DC: Center for Women Policy Studies, 1985.

Gardner, Charles A. "Is an Embryo a Person?" *The Nation* (November 13, 1989).

Giddings, Paula. *When and Where I Enter: The Impact of Black Women on Race and Sex in America.* New York: William Morrow, 1984.

Gilligan, Carol. *In a Different Voice.* Cambridge: Harvard University Press, 1982.

Gilman, Sander L. "Black Bodies, White Bodies: Toward an Iconography of Female Sexuality in Late Nineteenth-Century Art, Medicine, and Literature." *Critical Inquiry* 12 (1985): pp. 204–42.

Ginzberg, Ruth. "Feminism, Rationality and Logic." *American Philosophical Association Newsletter on Feminism and Philosophy* 88, no. 2 (March 1989): pp. 34–39.

Godlovitch, Stanley, Roslind Godlovitch, and John Harris, eds. *Animals, Men, and Morals: An Enquiry into the Maltreatment of Non-Humans.* New York: Taplinger, 1972.

Goldman, Emma. "The Traffic in Women." *The Traffic in Women and Other Essays on Feminism.* New York: Times Change Press, 1970.

Goodman, Ellen. "Debate Rages over Animals: Where Do Ethics End and Human Needs Begin?" *Buffalo News.* (December 20, 1989).

Goodyear, Carmen. "Man Kind?" *Country Women* (December 7–9, 1977).

Gordon, Linda. *Woman's Body, Woman's Right: Birth Control in America.* New York: Penguin Books, 1977.

Gould, Catherine. "Diagnosis and Treatment of Ritually Abused Children." In *Out of Darkness: Exploring Satanism and Ritual Abuse.* Edited by David K. Sakheim and Susan E. Devine. New York: Lexington Books, 1992.

Green, Rayna. "Review Essay: Native American Women," *Signs: Journal of Women in Culture and Society* 6, no. 2 (1980): pp. 248–67.

Greer, Germaine. "Home Thoughts: Germaine Greer on the Fallacy of Animal Rights." *Independent.* (January 1990).

Griffin, Donald R. "Foreword." In *Interpretation and Explanation in the Study of Animal Behavior. Volume I: Interpretation, Intentionality, and Communication.* Edited by Marc Bekoff and Dale Jamieson. Boulder: Westview Press, 1990.

———. "The Problem of Distinguishing Awareness from Responsiveness." In *Self-Awareness in Domesticated Animals: Proceedings of a Workshop Held at Keble College, Oxford.* Ed. D. G. M. Wood-Gush, M. Dawkins, R. Ewbank. Hertfordshire, England: The Universities Federation for Animal Welfare, 1991.

Griffin, Susan. *Woman and Nature: The Roaring inside Her.* New York: Harper & Row, 1982.

Gruen, Lori. "Gendered Knowledge? Examining Influences on Scientific and Ethological Inquiries." In *Interpretation and Explanation in the Study of Animal Behavior. Volume I: Interpretation, Intentionality, and Communication.* Edited by Marc Bekoff and Dale Jamieson. Boulder: Westview Press, 1990.

———. "Exclusion and Difference: Reflections on 'Women, Nature, and Animals.'" *Feminism and Philosophy Newsletter of the American Philosophical Association* (Spring 1992).

———. "Dismantling Oppression: An Analysis of the Connection between Women and Animals." In *Ecofeminism: Women, Animals, and Nature*. Edited by Greta Gaard. Temple University Press, 1993.

Halpin, Zuleyma Tang. "Scientific Objectivity and the Concept of the 'Other.'" *Women's Studies International Forum* 12, no. 3 (1989): pp. 285–94.

Haraway, Donna. *Primate Visions: Gender, Race, and Nature in the World of Modern Science*. New York: Routledge, 1989.

———. "Otherworldly Conversations: Terran Topics, Local Terms," *Science as Culture* 3, part 1, no. 14 (1992): pp. 64–98.

———. *Simians, Cyborgs, and Women*. New York: Routledge, 1990.

———. "Situated Knowledges: The Science Question in Feminism and the Privilege of Partial Perspective," *Feminist Studies* 14, no. 3 (Fall 1988): pp. 575–99.

Harding, Sandra. "Is Gender a Variable in Conceptions of Rationality? A Survey of Issues." In *Beyond Domination: New Perspectives on Women and Philosophy*. Edited by Carol C. Gould. Totowa, NJ: Rowman & Littlefield Publishers, 1983.

———. *The Science Question in Feminism*. Ithaca: Cornell University Press, 1986.

Harding, Sandra, and Jean F. O'Barr. *Sex and Scientific Inquiry*. Chicago: University of Chicago Press, 1983.

Harris, Angela P. "Race and Essentialism in Feminist Legal Theory." In *Feminist Legal Theory: Readings in Law and Gender*. Edited Katharine T. Bartlett and Rosanne Kennedy. Boulder: Westview Press, 1991.

Harris, William, M.D. "Hype Parades as Science" *Ahisma*. 31, no. 3 (July/September 1990).

Harrison, Beverly. *Making the Connections: Essays in Feminist Social Ethics*. Edited by Carol S. Robb. Boston: Beacon Press, 1985.

———. *Our Right to Choose: Toward a New Ethic of Abortion*. Boston: Beacon Press, 1983.

Hart, Barbara. "Lesbian Battering: An Examination." In *Naming the Violence: Speaking Out about Lesbian Battering*. Edited by Kerry Lobel. Seattle: Seal Press, 1986.

Hartmann, Betsy. *Reproductive Rights and Wrongs: The Global Politics of Population Control and Contraceptive Choice*. New York: Harper & Row, 1987.

Hartsock, Nancy C. M. *Money, Sex, and Power: Toward a Feminist Historical Materialism*. Boston: Northeastern University Press, 1985.

Hawkins, Ronnie Zoe. "Reproductive Choices: The Ecological Dimension." University of Florida, n.d.

Hearne, Vicki. *Adam's Task: Calling Animals by Name*. New York: Alfred A. Knopf, 1986.

Hentoff, Nat. "How Can the Left Be against Life?" *Village Voice* (July 16, 1985): pp. 18, 20.

Hicks, Sherrie. "Accessory to Ignorance," *Fur Age Weekly* (September 24, 1990).

Hoagland, Sarah Lucia. *Lesbian Ethics: Toward New Values*. Palo Alto: Institute for Lesbian Studies, 1988.

Hoch, Paul. *White Hero, Black Beast: Racism, Sexism and the Mask of Masculinity*. London: Pluto Press, 1979.

Hoffman, Merle. "Editorial [On the Connection between Women's Liberation and Animal Liberation]." *On the Issues* 16 (Fall 1990): pp. 2–3, 40–41.

hooks, bell. "Feminism and Militarism: A Comment." In *Talking Back*. Boston: South End Press, 1989.

———. *Feminist Theory: From Margin to Center*. Boston: South End Press, 1984.

———. "Selling Hot Pussy." *Black Looks: Race and Representation*. Boston, South End Press, 1992. pp. 61–77.

———. *Talking Back: Thinking Feminist, Thinking Black*, Boston: South End Press, 1989.

Hoppe, Stephanie, and Theresa Corrigan. "Paper into Flesh into . . ." In *And a Deer's Ear, Eagle's Song, and Bear's Grace: Animals and Women*. Edited by Theresa Corrigan and Stephanie Hoppe. Pittsburgh: Cleis Press, 1990.

Hubbard, Ruth. *The Politics of Women's Biology*. New Brunswick and London: Rutgers University Press, 1990.

Hudson, Pamela S. *Ritual Child Abuse: Discovery, Diagnosis, and Treatment*. Saratoga, CA: R & E Publishers, 1991.

Humphrey, Nicholas. "Seeing and Nothingness." *New Scientist* (March 30, 1972): pp. 682–84.

Hunt, Mary E. *Fierce Tenderness: A Feminist Theology of Friendship*. New York: Crossroad, 1991.

Hur, Robin. "Six Inches from Starvation: How and Why America's Topsoil Is Disappearing." *Vegetarian Times* (March 1985): pp. 45–47.

Hur, Robin, and Dr. David Fields. "America's Appetite for Meat Is Ruining Our Water." *Vegetarian Times* (January 1985): pp. 16–18.

———. "Are High-Fat Diets Killing Our Forests?" *Vegetarian Times* (February, 1984): pp. 22–24.

———. "How Meat Robs America of Its Energy." *Vegetarian Times* (April 1984): pp. 24–27.

Hynes, H. Patricia. "Pornography and Pollution: An Environmental Analogy." In *Pornography: Women, Violence, and Civil Liberties*. Edited by Catherine Itzin. Oxford: Oxford University Press, 1993, pp. 384–97.

Institute for Natural Process. "In Usual and Accustomed Places: Contemporary American Indian Fishing Rights Struggle." In *The State of Native America: Genocide, Colonization, and Resistance*. Edited by M. Annette Jaimes. Boston: South End Press, 1992.

Jay, Nancy. "Sacrifice as Remedy for Having Been Born of Woman." In *Immaculate and Powerful: The Female in Sacred Image and Social Reality*. Edited by Clarissa W. Atkinson, Constance H. Buchanan, and Margaret R. Miles. Boston: Beacon Press, 1985.

Iacobbo, Karen L. T. "Advertising: Making Risk Acceptable." *Vegetarian Voice* (1991).

Jaggar, Alison M. *Feminist Politics and Human Nature*. Totowa, NJ: Rowman & Littlefield Publisher, 1988.

———. "Love and Knowledge: Emotion in Feminist Epistemology." In *Gender/Body/Knowledge: Feminist Reconstructions of Being and Knowing*. New Brunswick: Rutgers University Press, 1989, pp. 145–171.

Jordan, Winthrop D. *White Over Black: American Attitudes Toward the Negro: 1550–1812*. Baltimore: Penguin Books, 1969.

Kalechofsky, Roberta. "Metaphors of Nature: Vivisection and Pornography—The Manichean Machine" and "Dedicated to Descartes' Niece: The Women's Movement and Anti–vivisection in the Nineteenth Century." In *Autobiography of a Revolutionary: Essays on Animal and Human Rights*. Marblehead, MA: Micah Press, 1991.

————. "Descartes' Niece." Paper presented at the Spoleta Festival for the Animals, Raleigh, North Carolina, October 6, 1990.

Kappeler, Susanne. *The Pornography of Representation*. Minneapolis: The University of Minnesota Press, 1986.

————. "Animal Conservationism and Human Conservationism." In *Animals and Women: Feminist Theoretical Explorations*. Edited by Carol J. Adams, Josephine Donovan, and Susanne Kappeler. Forthcoming.

Keller, Catherine. *From a Broken Web: Separation, Sexism, and Self*. Boston: Beacon Press, 1986.

Keller, Evelyn Fox. *A Feeling for the Organism: The Life and Work of Barbara McClintock*. San Francisco: W. H. Freeman and Co, 1983.

————. *Reflections on Gender and Science*. New Haven: Yale University Press, 1985.

Kellert, Stephen. "American Attitudes Toward and Knowledge of Animals: An Update." *International Journal for the Study of Animal Problems* 1, no. 2 (1980): pp. 87–119.

Kellman, Steven G. "Green Freedom for the Cockatoo." *Gettysburg Review* (1991): pp. 145–54.

Kellogg, Kathy and Bob. *Raising Pigs Successfully*. Charlotte, VT: Williamson Publishing, 1985.

Kelly, Liz. *Surviving Sexual Violence*. Minneapolis: University of Minnesota Press, 1989.

Kevles, Bettyann. "Meat, Morality, and Masculinity." *Women's Review of Books* (May 1990): pp. 11–12.

Kheel, Marti. "Animal Liberation and Environmental Ethics: Can Ecofeminism Bridge the Gap?" Prepared for delivery at the 1988 Annual Meeting of the Western Political Science Association, March 10–12, 1988.

————. "Befriending the Beast." *Creation* (September/October 1987): pp. 11–12.

————. "Ecofeminism and Deep Ecology: Reflections on Identity and Difference." In *Reweaving the World: The Emergence of Ecofeminism*. Edited by Irene Diamond and Gloria Feman Orenstein. San Francisco: Sierra Club Books, 1990, pp. 128–37.

————. "Finding a Niche for Animals within the Greens." *Feminists for Animal Rights Newsletter* 5, no. 1–2 (1990): pp. 1, 5–6.

————. "From Healing Herbs to Deadly Drugs: Western Medicine's War against the Natural World." In *Healing the Wounds: The Promise of Ecofeminism*. Edited by Judith Plant. Philadelphia, PA: New Society Publishers, 1989.

————. "If Women and Nature Were Heard." *Feminists for Animal Rights Newsletter* 5, no. 3–4: (1990): pp. 7–8.

————. "The Liberation of Nature: A Circular Affair." *Environmental Ethics* 7, no. 2 (1985): pp. 135–49.

————. Women, Ethics, and Anima(l)s. M.A. thesis. Antioch College, 1986.

King, Roger J. H. "Caring about Nature: Feminist Ethics and the Environment." *Hypatia: A Journal of Feminist Philosophy*, Special Issue on Ecological Feminism, 6, no. 1 (1991): pp. 75–89.

King, Deborah H. "Multiple Jeopardy, Multiple Consciousness: The Context of a Black Feminist Ideology." *Signs: Journal of Women in Culture and Society* 14, no. 1 (1988): pp. 42–72.

King, Ynestra. "Making the World Live: Feminism and the Domination of Nature." In *Women's Spirit Bonding*. Edited by Janet Kalven and Mary I. Buckley. New York: Pilgrim Press, 1984, pp. 56–64.

Kook, Abraham Isaac. "Fragments of Light: A View as to the Reasons for the Commandments." In *Abraham Isaac Kook: The Lights of Penitence, the Moral Principles, Lights of Holiness, Essays, Letters, and Poems.* Trans. Ben Zion Bokser. New York: Paulist Press.

Kovel, Joel. *White Racism: A Psychohistory.* New York: Vintage Books, 1971.

Kramarae, Cheris, and Paula A. Treichler, eds. *A Feminist Dictionary.* Boston: Pandora, 1985.

Krizmanic, Judy. "Is a Burger Worth It?" *Vegetarian Times,* no. 152 (April 1990): pp. 20–21.

———. "Perfect Obsession: Can Vegetarianism Cover up an Eating Disorder?" *Vegetarian Times.* (June 1992): pp. 52–60.

———. "Why Cutting out Meat Can Cool Down the Earth." *Vegetarian Times,* no. 152 (April): pp. 18–19.

Kundera, Milan. *The Unbearable Lightness of Being.* New York: Penguin Books, 1988.

Lansbury, Coral. *The Old Brown Dog: Women, Workers, and Vivisection in Edwardian England.* Madison: University of Wisconsin Press, 1985.

Lappé, Frances Moore. *Diet for a Small Planet: Tenth Anniversary Edition.* New York: Ballantine Books, 1982.

Lawrence, A. B., M. C. Appleby, and H. A. Macleod. "Measuring Hunger in the Pig Using Operant Conditioning: The Effect of Food Restriction," *Animal Production.* 47 (1988): pp. 131–37.

Leakey, Richard E., and Roger Lewin. *People of the Lake: Mankind and Its Beginnings.* New York: Doubleday, 1978.

"Leaps Forward: Postpatriarchal Eating." *Ms. Magazine* (July/August 1990): p. 59.

Le Brun, Fred. "Warm, Furry Thoughts at Dawn." *Albany Times-Union,* November 12, 1990.

LeMoncheck, Linda. *Dehumanizing Women: Treating Persons as Sex Objects.* Totowa, NJ: Rowman & Allanheld, 1985.

Levinson, David. *Family Violence in Cross-cultural Perspective.* Newbury Park, CA: Sage, 1989.

Lewis, Andrea. "Looking at the Total Picture: A Conversation with Health Activist Beverly Smith." In *The Black Women's Health Book: Speaking for Ourselves.* Edited by Evelyn C. White. Seattle: Seal Press, 1990.

Linzey, Andrew. *Christianity and the Rights of Animals.* New York: Crossroad, 1987.

Lloyd, Genevieve. *The Man of Reason: "Male" and "Female" in Western Philosophy.* Minneapolis: University of Minnesota Press, 1984.

Lobel, Kerry. *Naming the Violence: Speaking Out about Lesbian Battering.* Seattle: Seal Press, 1986.

Lorde, Audre. *The Cancer Journals.* Argyle, NY: Spinsters, Ink, 1980.

"Lovelace," Linda [Linda Marchiano]. With Mike McGrady. *Ordeal.* New York: Berkley Books, 1980.

———. *Out of Bondage.* Secaucus, NJ: Lyle Stuart, 1986.

Lugones, María. "Playfulness, 'World'-Travelling, and Loving Perception." In *Making Face, Making Soul: Haciendo Caras—Creative and Critical Perspectives by Women of Color.* Edited by Gloria Anzadúa. San Francisco: An Aunt Lute Foundation Book, 1990.

Luker, Kristen. *Abortion and the Politics of Motherhood.* Berkeley: University of California Press, 1979

Lunde, Donald T. *Murder and Madness.* San Francisco: San Francisco Book Co., 1976.

McCarthy, Colman. "Sins of the Flesh." *Washington Post,* March 1990.

McConnell-Ginet, Sally. "Review Article on Language and Sex." *Language.* 59, no. 2 (1983): pp. 387–88.

McDaniel, Jay. "Green Grace." *Earth Ethics: Evolving Values for An Earth Community.* 3, no. 4 (1992): pp. 1–3, 4.

————. *Of God and Pelicans: A Theology of Reverence for Life.* Louisville: Westminster/John Knox Press, 1989.

McFague, Sallie. *The Body of God.* Minneapolis: Fortress Press, 1993.

————. *Models of God.* Minneapolis: Fortress Press, 1987.

MacKinnon, Catharine A. *Feminism Unmodified: Discourses on Life and Law.* Cambridge: Harvard University Press, 1987.

————. *Toward a Feminist Theory of the State.* Cambridge: Harvard University Press, 1989.

Macklin, Ruth. "Personhoood and the Abortion Debate." *Abortion: Moral and Legal Perspectives.* Edited by Jay Garfield and Patricia Hennessey. Amherst: University of Massachusetts Press, 1984.

Mason, Jim. *An Unnatural Order: Uncovering the Roots of Our Domination of Nature and Each Other.* New York: Simon and Schuster, 1993.

Mason, Jim, and Peter Singer. *Animal Factories.* New York: Crown Publishers, 1980.

Mayall, Alice, and Diana E. H. Russell. "Racism in Pornography." In *Making Violence Sexy.* Edited by Diana E. H. Russell. New York: Teachers College, 1992.

Mead, Nathaniel. "Special Report: 6,500 Chinese Can't Be Wrong." *Vegetarian Times,* no. 158 (October 1990): pp. 15–17.

Mensch, Elizabeth, and Alan Freeman. *The Politics of Virtue: Is Abortion Debatable?* Durham and London: Duke University Press, 1993.

Merchant, Carolyn. *The Death of Nature: Women, Ecology, and the Scientific Revolution.* New York: Harper & Row, 1980.

————. *Ecological Revolutions: Nature, Gender, and Science in New England.* Chapel Hill: University of North Carolina Press, 1989.

Meyer, Lynn. *Paperback Thriller.* New York: Random House, 1975.

Midgley, Mary. *Animals and Why They Matter.* Athens: University of Georgia Press, 1983.

————. *Beast and Man: The Roots of Human Nature.* Ithaca, New York: Cornell University Press, 1978.

————. "The Concept of Beastliness: Philosophy, Ethics and Animal Behavior." *Philosophy* 48 (1973): pp. 111–35.

Mills, Kay. *This Little Light of Mine: The Life of Fannie Lou Hamer.* New York: NAL/Dutton, 1993.

Mohr, James C. *Abortion in America: The Origins and Evolution of National Policy.* New York: Oxford University Press, 1978.

Moran, Victoria. "Learning Love at an Early Age: Teaching Children Compassion for Animals." *Woman of Power: A Magazine of Feminism, Spirituality, and Politics. Nature* 9 (1988): pp. 54–56.

Morrison, Toni. *Playing in the Dark: Whiteness and the Literary Imagination.* New York: Random House, 1993.

Morton, Timothy. *Shelley and the Revolution in Taste: The Body and the Natural World.* Cambridge: Cambridge University Press. Forthcoming.

Mulvey, Laura. "Visual Pleasure and Narrative Cinema." *Screen* 16, no. 3 (1975).

Newkirk, Ingrid, with C. Burnett. "Animal Rights and the Feminist Connection." *Woman of Power: A Magazine of Feminism, Spirituality, and Politics. Nature* 9 (1988): pp. 67–69.

Noddings, Nell. *Caring: A Feminine Approach to Ethics and Moral Education.* Berkeley and Los Angeles, CA: University of California Press, 1984.

———. "Comment on Donovan's 'Animal Rights and Feminist Theory'" *Signs* 16, no. 2 (1991): pp. 418–22.

Noske, Barbara. *Humans and Other Animals: Beyond the Boundaries of Anthropology.* London: Pluto Press, 1989.

O'Brien, Mary. *The Politics of Reproduction.* Boston: Routledge & Kegan Paul, 1981.

O'Neill, Molly. "The Cow's Role in Life is Called into Question By a Crowded Planet." *New York Times* Section 4 (May 6, 1990): pp. 1, 4.

Okin, Susan Moller. *Justice, Gender, and the Family.* New York: Basic Books. 1989.

———. *Women in Western Political Thought.* Princeton: Princeton University Press, 1979.

Ortega y Gasset, José. *Meditations on Hunting.* Howard B. Wescott, trans. New York: Charles Scribner's Sons, 1985.

Paczensky, Susanne v. "In a Semantic Fog: How to Confront the Accusation That Abortion Equals Killing." *Women's Studies International Forum* 13, no. 3 (1990): pages 177–84.

Pateman, Carole. *The Disorder of Women: Democracy, Feminism, and Political Theory.* Stanford: Stanford University Press, 1989.

———. *The Sexual Contract.* Stanford: Stanford University Press. 1988.

Petchesky, Rosalind Pollack. *Abortion and Woman's Choice: The State, Sexuality, and Reproductive Freedom.* New York and London: Longman, 1984.

Phelps, Timothy M., and Helen Winternitz. *Capitol Games: The Inside Story of Clarence Thomas, Anita Hill, and a Supreme Court Nomination.* New York: Harper Perennial, 1993.

Phillips, Anthony. *Lower than the Angels: Questions Raised by Genesis 1–11.* Bible Reading Fellowship, 1983.

Plutarch. "Of Eating of Flesh." In *Animal Rights and Human Obligations.* Edited by Tom Regan and Peter Singer. Englewood Cliffs, NJ: Prentice-Hall, 1976.

Pimental, David. "Energy and Land Constraints in Food Protein Production." *Science.* 190 (1975): pp. 754–61.

———. "Land degradation: Effects on Food and Energy Resources." *Science* 194 (1976): pp. 149–55.

Pimental, David, P. A. Oltenacu, M. C. Nesheim, John Krummel, M. S. Allen, and Sterling Chick. "The Potential for Grass-fed Livestock: Resource Constraints." *Science.* 207 (1980): pp. 843–48.

Pope-Lance, Deborah J., and Joan Chamberlain Engelsman. *A Guide for Clergy on the Problems of Domestic Violence.* Trenton, NJ: New Jersey Department of Community Affairs Division on Women, 1987.

Quine, Willard Van Orman. *Word and Object.* Cambridge: MIT Press, 1960.

Randal, Jonathan, and Nora Boustany. "Children of War in Lebanon." In *Betrayal: A Report on Violence Toward Children in Today's World.* Edited by Caroline Moorehead. New York: Doubleday, 1990, pp. 59–82.

Raschke, Carl A. *Painted Black: From Drug Killings to Heavy Metal—the Alarming*

True Story of How Satanism Is Terrorizing Our Communities. New York: Harper and Row, 1990.

Raymond, Janice. "The International Traffic in Women." *Reproductive and Genetic Engineering* 2, no. 1 (1989): pp. 51–57.

Regan, Tom. *The Case for Animal Rights.* Berkeley and Los Angeles: University of California Press, 1983.

———. "Environmental Ethics and the Ambiguity of the Native Americans' Relationship with Nature." In *All That Dwell Therein: Essays on Animals Rights and Environmental Ethics.* Edited by Tom Regan. Berkeley and Los Angeles: University of California Press, 1982, pp. 206–39.

Renzetti, Claire M. *Violent Betrayal: Partner Abuse in Lesbian Relationships.* Newbury Park, CA: Sage, 1992.

Ressler, Robert K., Ann W. Burgess, Carol R. Hartman, John E. Douglas, and Arlene McCormack. "Murderers Who Rape and Mutilate." *Journal of Interpersonal Violence* 1, no. 3 (1986): pp. 273–87.

Rhoads, Sharon Ann. *Cooking with Sea Vegetables.* Brookline, MA: Autumn Press, 1978.

Rich, Adrienne. *On Lies, Secrets, and Silences.* New York: W. W. Norton and Co., 1979.

Richards, Stewart. "Forethoughts for Carnivores." *Philosophy* 56, 1981.

Rifkin, Jeremy. *Beyond Beef: The Rise and Fall of the Cattle Culture.* New York: Dutton, 1992.

Robbins, John. *Diet for a New America.* Walpole: Stillpoint, 1987.

Rollin, Bernard. *Animal Rights and Human Morality.* Buffalo, NY: Prometheus Books, 1981.

———. *The Unheeded Cry: Animal Consciousness, Animal Pain, and Science.* Oxford: Oxford University Press, 1989.

Root, Maria P. "Persistent, Disordered Eating as a Gender-Specific, Post-Traumatic Stress Response to Sexual Assault." *Psychotherapy.* 28, no. 1 (1991): pp. 96–102.

Rose, Elizabeth S. "Surviving the Unbelievable: A First-Person Account of Cult Ritual Abuse." *Ms. Magazine* (January/February 1993): pp. 40–45.

Rose, Jacqueline. *Sexuality in the Field of Vision.* London: New Left Books, 1986.

Rowan, Andrew N. *Of Mice, Models, and Men: A Critical Evaluation of Animal Research.* Albany, NY: State University of New York Press, 1984.

Rubin, Gayle. "The Traffic in Women: Notes on the 'Political Economy' of Sex." In *Toward an Anthropology of Women.* Edited by Rayna R. Reiter. New York and London: Monthly Review Press, 1975, pp. 157–210.

Ruby, Jennie, Farar Elliot, and Carol Anne Douglas. "NWSA: Troubles Surface at Conference." *off our backs* (August/September 1990).

Ruddick, Sara. *Maternal Thinking: Toward a Politics of Peace.* New York: Ballantine Books, 1990.

———. "Notes toward a Feminist Peace Politics." In *Gendering War Talk.* Edited by Miriam Cooke and Angela Woollacott. Princeton: Princeton University Press, 1993.

———. "Remarks on the Sexual Politics of Reason." In *Women and Moral Theory.* Edited by Eva Feder Kittay and Diana T. Meyers. Totowa, NJ: Rowman & Littlefield, 1987.

Ruether, Rosemary Radford. "Men, Women, and Beasts: Relations to Animals in Western Culture." In *Good News for Animals? Christian Approaches to Animal*

Well-Being. Edited by Charles Pinches and Jay B. McDaniel. Maryknoll: Orbis Books, 1993.

————. *New Woman/New Earth: Sexist Ideologies and Human Liberation*. New York: Seabury, 1975.

————. *Sexism and God Talk: Toward a Feminist Theology*. Boston: Beacon Press, 1983.

————. *To Change the World: Christology and Cultural Criticism*. New York: Crossroad, 1981.

————. "Women, Sexuality, Ecology, and the Church." *Conscience: A Newsjournal of Prochoice Catholic Opinion* 9, no. 4 (1990): pp. 1, 4–11.

Russell, Diana E. H.*Rape in Marriage: Expanded and Revised Edition with a New Introduction*. Bloomington and Indianapolis: Indiana University Press, 1982. Reprinted 1990.

————. *Sexual Exploitation: Rape, Child Sexual Abuse, and Workplace Harassment*. Newbury Park, CA: Sage, 1984.

Salamone, Connie. "Feminist as Rapist in the Modern Male Hunter Culture." *Majority Report* (October 1973).

————. "The Knowing." *Woman of Power: A Magazine of Feminism, Spirituality, and Politics. Nature* 9 (1988): p. 53.

————. "The Prevalence of the Natural Law within Women: Women and Animal Rights." In *Reweaving the Web of Life: Feminism and Nonviolence*. Edited by Pam McAllister. Philadelphia: New Society Publishers, 1982.

Sanday, Peggy. *Female Power and Male Dominance: On the Origins of Sexual Inequality*. Cambridge and New York: Cambridge University Press, 1981.

Scholtmeijer, Marian. *Animal Victims in Modern Fiction: From Sanctity to Sacrifice*. Toronto: University of Toronto Press, 1993.

Schüssler Fiorenza, Elisabeth. *Bread Not Stone: The Challenge of Feminist Biblical Interpretation*. Boston: Beacon Press, 1984.

————. *But She Said: Feminist Practices of Biblical Interpretation*. Boston: Beacon Press, 1992.

————. *In Memory of Her: A Feminist Theological Reconstruction of Christian Origins*. New York: Crossroad, 1984.

Sedgwick, Eve Kosofsky. *Epistemology of the Closet*. Berkeley and Los Angeles: University of California Press, 1990.

Sells, Jennifer. "An Eco-feminist Critique of Deep Ecology: A Question of Social Ethics." *Feminist Ethics*. (Winter 1989–90): pp. 12–27.

Sequoia, Anna. *Sixty-seven Ways to Save the Animals*. New York: HarperCollins, 1990.

Serpell, James. *In the Company of Animals: A Study of Human-Animal Relationships*. Oxford: Basil Blackwell, 1986.

Shiva, Vandana. *Staying Alive: Women, Ecology, and Development*. London: Zed Books, 1988.

Simpson, Cuthbert, and Walter Russell Bowie. *The Interpreter's Bible (Genesis)*. New York and Nashville: Abingdon Press, 1952.

Singer, Peter. *Animal Liberation: Second Edition*. New York: New York Review Book. 1990.

Slicer, Deborah. "Your Daughter or Your Dog?" *Hypatia: A Journal of Feminist Philosophy*, Special Issue on Ecological Feminism, 6, no. 1 (1991): pp. 108–124.

Sloan, G., and P. Leichner. "Is There a Relationship between Sexual Abuse or Incest and Eating Disorders?" *Canadian Journal of Psychiatry.* 31, no. 7 (1986): pp. 656–60.

Smedley, Lauren. "Further than F.A.R.: In Search of a New Name." *Feminists for Animal Rights Newsletter 5*, no. 3–4, pp. 1, 12.

Smith, Margaret. *Ritual Abuse: What It Is, Why It Happens, How To Help.* San Francisco: Harper San Francisco, 1993.

Smith-Rosenberg, Carroll. "The Abortion Movement and the AMA, 1850–1880." In *Disorderly Conduct: Visions of Gender in Victorian America.* New York: Oxford University Press, 1985.

Soler, Jean. "The Dietary Prohibitions of the Hebrews." *New York Review of Books* (June 14, 1979): pp. 24–30.

Spelman, Elizabeth V. "Woman as Body: Ancient and Contemporary Views." *Feminist Studies 8*, no. 1, (1982): pp. 109–31.

Sperling, Susan. *Animal Liberators: Research and Morality.* Berkeley: University of California Press, 1988.

Spiegel, Marjorie. *The Dreaded Comparison: Human and Animal Slavery.* Philadelphia: New Society Publishers, 1988.

Spretnak, Charlene. "Ecofeminism: Our Roots and Flowering." In *Reweaving the World: The Emergence of Ecofeminism.* Edited by Irene Diamond and Gloria Feman Orenstein. San Francisco: Sierra Club Books, 1990.

Stange, Mary Zeiss. "Hunting—An American Tradition." *American Hunter.* January 1991. 26–27.

———. "Religious Ethics and Fur." *Fur Age Weekly* 140, no. 2 (1990): n.p.

Stanton, Elizabeth Cady. *The Woman's Bible: Part One.* Seattle: Coalition Task Force on Women and Religion, 1974. Reprint of 1898 European Publishing Co. edition.

Starhawk. *Dreaming the Dark: Magic, Sex, and Politics.* Boston: Beacon Press, 1982.

Statman, Jan Berliner. "Life Doesn't Have to Be like This: How to Spot a Batterer before an Abusive Relationship Begins." In *The Battered Woman's Survival Guide: Breaking the Cycle.* Dallas: Taylor Publishing Co., 1990.

Stoltenberg, John. *Refusing to be a Man.* Portland, Oregon: Breitenbush Books, 1989.

Stordeur, Richard A. and Richard Stille. *Ending Men's Violence Against Their Partners: One Road to Peace.* Newbury Park, CA: Sage, 1989.

Sturgeon, Noël. "Editorial Statement." *Ecofeminist Newsletter 2*, no. 1 (Spring 1991): p. 1.

Sussman, Vic. *The Vegetarian Alternative: A Guide to a Healthful and Humane Diet.* Emmaus, PA: Rodale Press, 1978.

Swanson, Wayne, and George Schultz. *Prime Rip.* Englewood Cliffs, NJ: Prentice-Hall, 1982.

[Taylor, Thomas.] *A Vindication of the Rights of Brutes.* London: Jeffery, 1792.

Teish, Luisah. *Jambalaya: The Natural Woman's Book of Personal Charms and Practical Rituals.* San Francisco: Harper & Row, 1985.

Thomas, Keith. *Man and the Natural World: A History of the Modern Sensibility.* New York: Pantheon, 1983.

———. *Religion and the Decline of Magic: Studies in Popular Beliefs in Sixteenth- and Seventeenth-Century England.* Hammondsworth: Penguin University Books, 1973.

Tompkins, Jane. *West of Everything: The Inner Life of Westerns.* Oxford: Oxford University Press, 1992.

Tuan, Yi-Fu. *Dominance and Affection: The Making of Pets*. New Haven: Yale University Press, 1984.

Tuana, Nancy. *The Less Noble Sex: Scientific, Religious, and Philosophical Conceptions of Woman's Nature*. Bloomington and Indianapolis: Indiana University Press, 1993.

Ullyot, Joan. *Women's Running*. Mountain View, California: World Publications, 1976.

Vachss, Alice. *Sex Crimes*. New York: Random House, 1993.

Von Rad, Gerhard. *Genesis: A Commentary*. Philadelphia: The Westminster Press, 1972.

Wagner, Sally Roesch. "Animal Liberation." In *With a Fly's Eye, Whale's Wit, and Woman's Heart: Relationships between Animals and Women*. Edited by Theresa Corrigan and Stephanie Hoppe. Pittsburgh: Cleis Press, 1989.

Walker, Alice. "Am I Blue?" *Ms. Magazine* (July 1986), p. 30.

―――. *Living by the Word: Selected Writings, 1973–1987*. San Diego: Harcourt Brace Jovanovich, 1987.

―――. "Why Did the Balinese Chicken Cross the Road?" *Woman of Power: A Magazine of Feminism, Spirituality, and Politics* 9, (1988): p. 50.

Walker, Lenore. *The Battered Woman*. New York: Harper and Row, 1979.

―――. *Terrifying Love: Why Battered Women Kill and How Society Responds*. New York: Harper & Row, 1989.

Waring, Marilyn. *If Women Counted: A New Feminist Economics*. San Francisco: Harper & Row, 1988.

Warren, Karen J. *Ecofeminism: Multidisciplinary Perspectives*. Bloomington: Indiana University Press, forthcoming.

―――. "Feminism and Ecology: Making Connections." *Environmental Ethics* 9, no. 1 (1987): pp. 3–20.

―――. "The Power and the Promise of Ecological Feminism." *Environmental Ethics* 12 (Summer 1990): pp. 125–46.

―――. "Women, Nature, and Technology: An Ecofeminist Philosophical Perspective." *Research in Philosophy and Technology*, special issue "Technology and Feminism," guest ed. Joan Rothschild, vol. 13 (1992).

Welch, Sharon D. *Communities of Resistance and Solidarity*. Maryknoll, New York: Orbis Books, 1985.

Weil, Zoe. "Feminism and Animal Rights." *Labyrinth: The Philadelphia Women's Newspaper* (February 1990).

West, Cornel. "Black Sexuality: The Taboo Subject." In *Race Matters*. New York: Vintage Books, 1994.

Whitbeck, Caroline. "A Different Reality: Feminist Ontology." In *Women, Knowledge, and Reality: Explorations in Feminist Philosophy*. Edited by Ann Garry and Marilyn Pearsall. Boston: Unwin Hyman, 1989, pp. 51–76.

Wiley, Carol. "The Feminist Connection." *Vegetarian Times* no. 161 (1991): pp. 59–65, 80.

―――. "Why It's Impossible to Be a Vegetarian." *Vegetarian Times* (May 1991).

Williams, Delores S. "African-American Women in Three Contexts of Domestic Violence." *Concilium: Violence Against Women*. London: SCM Press, Maryknoll: Orbis Books, 1994.

Wollstonecraft, Mary. *A Vindication of the Rights of Woman*. Edited by Charles W. Hagelman, Jr. New York: W. W. Norton & Co., 1967.

Wood-Gush, D. G. M., and R. G. Beilharz. "The Enrichment of a Bare Environment for Animals in Confined Conditions." *Applied Animal Ethology.* 10 (1983): pp. 209–17.

Woolf, Virginia. "The Plumage Bill." From *The Woman's Leader*, July 23, 1920. In *The Diary of Virginia Woolf.* vol. 2: 1920–24. Edited by Anne Olivier Bell. New York and London: Harcourt Brace Jovanovich, 1978, pp. 337–38.

———. *A Room of One's Own.* New York: Harcourt, 1929.

Young, Walter C. "Recognition and Treatment of Survivors Reporting Ritual Abuse." In *Out of Darkness: Exploring Satanism and Ritual Abuse.* Edited by David K. Sakheim and Susan E. Devine. New York: Lexington Books, 1992.

Zorza, Joan. "Woman-Battering: A Major Cause of Homelessness." *Clearinghouse Review* (special issue, 1991): pp. 421–29.

Copyright Acknowledgments

Index